JOHN CRISPO

with MARION E. RAYCHEBA

REBEL
WITHOUT A PAUSE

MEMOIRS OF A
CANADIAN MAVERICK

Warwick Publishing
Toronto

Rebel Without A Pause: Memoirs of a Canadian Maverick

We acknowledge the financial support of the Government of Canada through the Book Publishing Industry Development Program for our publishing activities.

ISBN: 1-894622-27-8

Published by Warwick Publishing Inc.
161 Frederick Street
Toronto, Ontario M5A 4P3 Canada
www.warwickgp.com

Distributed in Canada by:
The Canadian Book Network
34 Armstrong Avenue
Georgetown, Ontario L7G 4R9

Tel: (905) 873-2119 or
Toll Free (Canada) 1-866-444-4930
Fax: (905) 873-6170 or
Toll Free (Canada) 1-866-444-4931
San: 115-3552
Email: cbn@gtwcanada.com

National Library of Canada Cataloguing in Publication

Crispo, John, 1933-
    Rebel without a pause : memoirs of a Canadian maverick / John Crispo ; with Marion E. Raycheba.
    Includes bibliographical references and index.
    ISBN 1-894622-27-8

    1. Crispo, John, 1933- 2. Economists—Canada—Biography. 3. College professors—Canada—Biography. I. Raycheba, Marion E II. Title.

HB121.C75A3 2002   330'.092   C2002-901373-9

Printed and bound in Canada

To Barbara, my wonderful wife

Contents

Foreword

John Crispo is a loveable rogue who leaves few people cold. Bombastic, candid, funny: he is all of these, and he is never shy to let the world know what he thinks and feels. He and I do not agree on many political issues, but neither of us has allowed this to affect our friendship.

I think of John first and foremost as a teacher—that is how I first came to know him. When I returned to Toronto from studying and working in England to go to law school, our mutual friend Peter Russell suggested that I work for John as his teaching assistant for his undergraduate course on industrial relations. I was sceptical, because even then I recognised that we were hardly of one mind. Peter assured me John wouldn't mind, and neither should I. He was right.

The Crispo lecture is an art form in itself. The lecture hall itself was always full. John understood the difference between writing and talking: his lecturing was always a brilliant music hall performance, peppering information with jokes, teasing, and digressions of all kinds. But behind it all was a serious purpose. He wanted students to be engaged, to think, to get off the sidelines. He didn't mind disagreement or argument; in fact, he relished it. It would be a stretch to say he was respectful in these debates; he was too irreverent and forceful for that. But he cared about his subject and cared about his students. Students got the full Crispo in the lectures. My friend Jim McDonald—now a labour lawyer—and I would give the "other side" in tutorials. The students seem to have survived.

Even John's subject matter showed a rebelliousness for its time. As a graduate student he wanted to understand how unions and industrial relations really worked. As he describes in this book, he would come to part company with the established labour leadership over many issues, particularly free trade. But the fact remains that John Crispo knows a lot about unions and working people, was never "anti-union," and has developed many friendships in the labour movement.

John's anti-establishment views and behaviour have always been a refreshing feature of his personality. No doubt a psychiatrist would have a field day on John's attitudes to authority. He didn't enjoy being Dean of the Management School, and he ruled himself out as a potential university President. He enjoys speaking out too much, likes controversy too much, and hates committee meetings too much. He is certainly a conservative on some issues, but can suddenly do a 180° on others. He hates to be pigeonholed, categorised, or labelled. I call him a dinosaur who knows how to dance.

This book will give the reader the unvarnished Crispo. A number of us have encouraged him in this project, because his story is a good one. He faces life's challenges with honesty, courage, and loyalty to friends. His candour will no doubt offend some. His opinions will outrage others. Across a political and philosophical divide, I salute him.

The Honourable Bob Rae, Former Premier of Ontario
and now Partner, Goodmans LLP
Fall 2001

Preface

Trying to recall, review, and, ultimately, judge the worth of one's professional accomplishments is difficult. If variety is the spice of life, then the answer to the fundamental questions—what have I accomplished and of what value have my accomplishments been—are self-evident because I've enjoyed a rich range of experiences and exposures.

But if one looks at the questions from other points of view, then the answers aren't as obvious.

It has been my good fortune to live in a free and democratic society, and it has been my privilege to both challenge and support the hierarchy of basic values and institutions that underpins it.

The first basic value is actually a collection of values often referred to as fundamental western values and enunciated in such documents as the Canadian Charter of Rights and Freedoms and the American Bill of Rights. The example I always cite first is freedom of speech because this basic right has been so important to me. Other examples are freedom of association, the right to strike, freedom of contract, and freedom of property.

The second basic value is liberal democracy, the third is free enterprise or capitalism, the fourth is free collective bargaining, and the fifth is free trade unionism.

In my view, a market-based economic system is the only one compatible with any true form of liberal democracy and, furthermore, a prerequisite for liberal democracy to develop. Theory, history, and reality all support my view. I also believe that the very survival of capitalism depends on the existence of collective bargaining and trade unions.

Stated bluntly, no free society can be sustained as such without free trade unions and a free labour movement. The critical nature of their role is best illustrated by the example of Lech Walesa and the Solidarity movement that destroyed the Communist government in Poland. The spirit of the Solidarity movement eventually spread across the entire Eastern Bloc, toppling one government after another.

One of the many gifts that a free and open society brings is the right to choose how to live. I have chosen to be something of a loner, if not a maverick, all my working life. Might have I accomplished more in both quantity and quality if I had worked more often and more closely with others? John Evans certainly thought I would. When he was President of the University of Toronto and I was Dean of the Faculty of Management Studies, he urged me to rethink my decision to resign. His considered opinion was that I could accomplish much more if I worked within the Establishment rather than outside it.

I am not objective, nor have I been anything but subjective and opinionated. I have, however, been detached in the sense that I have never had to answer to anyone or any institution for what I have said or written. I find it hard to imagine anyone who has enjoyed more freedom of expression than I've had. Have I made the most of this gift? Have I been as well-informed and well-researched as I have been opinionated?

As for the process of assessment, that is something else again. Although I have essentially held only one job throughout my working life, I have engaged in many related activities, complicating the assessment process. Does a chronological approach make the most sense, or will a thematic view be better, more interesting, and more effective?

I ended up striking a middle course, which is amusing in a way because I've always been a person of extremes. But telling a story, especially when the story is a memoir, demands a means to identify, follow, and connect threads that wander through a life.

I approached the memoir thematically, but I tried within each chapter to give some sense of the time frame, time line, and how I developed my thinking and positions on major public policy issues of the day. Given that this is a memoir of a professional life, I began with my career as an academic, some early lessons, and the perspective I have now that I've retired from the University of Toronto.

The other chapters deal with important influences and interest groups in my life and my relationships in these circles, beginning with the labour movement and going on to corporate Canada and my life as a capitalist, including my work in consulting, media, politics, and government. In the last two chapters I deal with my career as a public speaker, and I address the public policy issue very high on my current critical list, euthanasia.

Throughout the memoir, you will find references to my feelings about things I did and said, but it's in the Epilogue that I actually attempt to answer the "was it worth it question" in a deliberate way.

Thank you for reading this memoir. I hope that you will find it interesting and illuminating.

Acknowledgements

It obviously takes a fair amount of arrogance, egotism, and gall to write a book about oneself. Some would argue that I have more than my share of all of these characteristics, qualities, or faults—call them what you will—and I will not try to dispute that possibility. I think one must have a good deal of self-confidence—that's a much more attractive and becoming way of putting it—if one is going to accomplish anything worthwhile, at least in terms of one's work.

I began this project because I wanted to answer a fundamental question about my professional life: was it worth it? My focus is my professional life, although, of course, aspects of my personal life couldn't help but intrude now and again.

This memoir is based very largely on personal recollections. Where possible, I've documented and dated. I've checked with other individuals and my files to verify. There are occasions when I simply couldn't date precisely, for which I apologize and ask for your understanding.

I am grateful to many people who made a difference to my life, beginning with all those who helped and encouraged me and, just as important, all those who played a part in denying me admission to the Establishment. Without them, my career might have taken a very different course.

I am especially grateful to a number of individuals for helping me bring this project to fruition.

First and foremost, I thank my literary agent Salman A. Nensi for his loyalty and perseverance. His encouragement and enthusiasm made this book possible.

I also owe a major debt of gratitude to Tracey Rynard, who was an undergraduate student when she wandered into my office one day and said she would like to volunteer to help out on any project I might be working on. She, more than anyone else, prompted me to get on with this project. She was also a great help and inspiration.

Thirdly, I am greatly indebted to Marion E. Raycheba, who reshaped the entire manuscript. It was she who suggested bringing in other voices and who interviewed many people who have been part of my life. She humanized the text and gave it more life.

I also wish to thank my friends, associates, colleagues, and others who provided quotes at my request and interviews when Marion called. Their views make an interesting counterpoint. I'd particularly like to thank John Crosbie—Brother John, as I like to call him—who so generously contributed a delightful letter as well as consenting to an interview.

I also wish to give special thanks to Joe Sulpizi, President & C.E.O, The Brand Factory Advertising & Design. Joe, who is my business associate and friend, heads a group of very creative and innovative marketing strategists. When Joe appointed me Vice-President of Business Development right after I retired from the University of Toronto, he changed my life and helped make this book possible by contributing to the launch party.

As well, I extend my thanks to Nick Pitt, Vice-President and Publisher, Warwick Publishing Inc., for his support and advice and to Patti McCabe for her assistance with promoting this book.

In addition, I wish to express my warm appreciation to the Joseph L. Rotman School of Management, University of Toronto, particularly to Roger L. Martin, Dean, and Steve Arenburg, Executive Director, Advancement, for their generaosity in offering the facilities and services for the launch of this book and for using the occasion to announce the creation of the John Crispo Forum on Public Policy.

And finally I wish to thank Bob Rae for writing the Foreword. It was a typically kind and generous gesture and one I appreciate so very much.

For the Record

Academic Highlights

1955:	Charles Stephen MacInnes Scholarship in Commerce and Finance
1956:	Elected a Fellow and Treasurer of Trinity College
1956:	Bachelor of Commerce and Finance, Trinity College, University of Toronto
1956-1957:	Fellow, Westinghouse Fellowship in Industrial Relations
1957-1958:	Fellow, The Ford Foundation Pre-doctoral Fellowship in Business Administration
1958-1959:	Fellow, The Scanlon Plan
1959-1960:	Canada Council Pre-doctoral Fellowship
1960:	Ph.D., Industrial Economics, Massachusetts Institute of Technology
1960-1961:	Assistant Professor, Huron College, University of Western Ontario
1961-1964:	Assistant Professor, School of Business, University of Toronto
1964:	Associate Professor, School of Business, University of Toronto
1965-1996:	Professor, Faculty of Management Studies, University of Toronto
1965-1975:	Founding Director, Centre for Industrial Relations, University of Toronto
1970:	Canada Council Research Grant
1970-1971:	Acting Dean, School of Business, University of Toronto
1971-1975:	Dean, Faculty of Management Studies, University of Toronto
1976:	Visiting Professor, London Graduate School of Business Studies
1976-1977:	Canada Council Research Grant

1977:	Visiting Scholar, International Institute for Labour Studies, Geneva
1981-1982:	Chevron Visiting Professor of Management Studies, Simon Fraser University
1996-present	Professor Emeritus, The Joseph L. Rotman School of Management, University of Toronto

Other Professional Highlights

1961-1962:	Director of Research, Royal Commission on Labour-Management Relations in the Construction Industry
1962-1963:	Director of Research, Select Committee on Manpower Training
1964-1966:	Chairman, Domtar Labour-Management Committee, and Chairman, Domtar Labour-Management Sub-Committee on Human Adjustment to Industrial Conversion
1966-1967:	Director of Research, Canadian Construction Association Centennial Labour Relations Project
1967-1969:	Member, Prime Minister's Task Force on Labour Relations
1967-1970:	Chairman, Ontario Union-Management Council
1970 and onwards:	Research Consultant at various times to Economic Council of Canada, Prices and Incomes Commission, Department of Consumer and Corporate Affairs, Anti-Inflation Board, Department of Labour, Trade Negotiations Office, and others
1991-1994:	Member, Board of Directors, Canadian Broadcasting Corporation
1995-present:	Chair of the Board of Directors and Member of the Board of Directors of several private and public enterprises

Introduction:
The Making of a Rebel

Many times during my life I have been asked what led to my frequent rebelliousness and periodic defiance. I have never known the true reason, but I've thought about it enough to think I have something of a handle on it now.

Two important people in my life probably had a much more profound influence on me than I realized at the time. One was my father and the other was a great professor I had during my second year as an undergraduate at the University of Toronto.

My father Francis Herbert Crispo was a very proud man and a very good provider. But he was also very strong-willed without being a harsh disciplinarian. He just ruled the roost with a very firm hand.

For whatever reason, I began to take him on whenever I could. One incident still stands out in my mind, and it is important because later it became a link to my professor friend. I was on my way with my family to my grandmother's cottage at Eastbourne, Lake Simcoe, on a warm, sunny Saturday. We were delayed by road repairs. I thought it unfair that so many men should be toiling away on that delightful weekend when we were off to the lake. My father told me that people in general were destined for various stations in life and that everyone found their own level. In other words, these workmen didn't deserve anything better. I accepted his explanation, but I still didn't think it was very fair.

Later, I learned how anti-union my father was. This was partly due to strikes which had disrupted his business—he was a manufacturer's agent—but I think deep down it had more to do with something fundamental about his philosophy of life. In any event, as a university student, I ended up in a course in labour economics—it was really more about labour relations—taught by Professor Lorne Morgan, a left-wing radical of sorts who had really got under the skin of the Establishment. He did this most forcefully after World War II, when he wrote a pamphlet entitled *Homo the Sap* in which he took the position that the only thing that ended the Depression was the war and that the only thing that would ensure the viability of capitalism would be a permanent state of war.

In his labour relations class, Lorne taught us about unions and the labour movement, thereby providing me with ample ammunition to use in arguments with my father. I think I sometimes almost drove him crazy. After my father died, my mother remarried, and I challenged my stepfather Clifford Sifton in a similar way, leaving him as distraught as I had left my father. In fact, Clifford used to become quite agitated when I shook up his dinner parties with statements he found outrageous. One on occasion, he shouted "Nonsense!" and nearly broke some china when he pounded the table to reinforce his feelings. Both my father and my stepfather were wont to wonder where I would end up. My guess is that both would be mightily surprised about how things worked out for me.

Meanwhile, as an undergraduate, I was in great awe of Lorne, who persuaded me to go to graduate school and helped get me enrolled at M.I.T. with a scholarship by giving me a great letter of recommendation. At M.I.T. I learned more and more about industrial relations, a subject I taught throughout my academic career.

I have only two regrets with respect to my father and Lorne. I never really made up with my father before he died a painful death due to cancer. And I didn't keep in touch with Lorne, who was never made a full professor at the University of Toronto because, I believe, of his heretical views, even though he sent more students on to graduate school than the rest of his departmental colleagues combined.

Chapter 1

A Bull in the Academic Shop

Since graduating from the Massachusetts Institute of Technology (M.I.T.) with a doctorate in Industrial Economics in 1960, academia has been the core of my professional life.

Sometimes, I'm still astonished that I got over the Ph.D. hurdle. I was a pretty good undergraduate student, but I was always hopeless in mathematics and any subject requiring quantitative work. Luckily, the hieroglyphic crowd, who worshipped econometrics, didn't take complete control of M.I.T. until I'd escaped with my doctorate in hand. Even so, I was already out of step with my peers. When writing my final macro and micro economic examination, I kept trying to answer the questions in words, while they relied on brief mathematical formulae. To this day, I'm convinced I would never have made it if Paul Samuelson and Robert Solow, two of M.I.T.'s leading economic professors and subsequently Nobel Laureates in Economics, hadn't come by to see how we were doing. After assessing the situation and kibitzing with me, they announced that I would be granted twice the time allowed other candidates because of what they termed my "quantitative handicap." I'm convinced their decision was based on sheer fear. In response to a loaded question, I told them that if I failed, they would have to return to Toronto with me to explain my disgrace.

Whatever did the trick, it worked, and armed with my prestigious Ph.D. from the hallowed halls of M.I.T., I returned to Toronto confident that I would land a faculty job at the University of Toronto with ease. Instead, I got my first insight into what it meant to be Canadian, at least at that time. Vincent Bladen, then Dean of Arts and Science and later father of the Auto Pact, told me I couldn't be hired until I had served an apprenticeship in the West, by which he meant a university in British Columbia or the Prairies. Only after I had spent some time among the colonials would I be permitted to join the crème de la crème in Upper Canada.

One day in the early 1960s, I got a call from John asking to visit. At the time, I was Professor of Economics and Head of the Department of Economics and Political Science at the University of Saskatchewan in Saskatoon. If I had never met him again, he would have stayed in my mind.

At lunch with me and some colleagues, he announced that he had two ambitions. First, he said, he was going to become a really good labour economist. He wanted to research, teach, and write books; that was his academic passion. And the second, I asked? "I want to have an impact on public policy outside the classroom," he answered. "I'm going to talk, argue, make speeches, and make people get up and think."

I thought him a very brash young man, telling me how he was going to shape public policy. But I was also impressed. He was very focussed, so determined, at such a young age. Some people think of John as a gadabout. But I don't see him that way. He knew from a very early stage of his career what he wanted to do, and he went out and did it. In spades.

Ed Safarian, Professor Emeritus, Faculty of Management,
The Joseph L. Rotman School of Management, University of Toronto

---

GO WEST, YOUNG MAN

Going west would have been great, if only for the quality of the skiing. Mind you, I hadn't discovered my passion for that sport yet, and, in any case, I didn't get that far. Instead, I spent a rewarding year at Huron College at the University of Western Ontario in London. One year later, when the University of Toronto decided it needed someone in industrial relations with my kind of background, I claimed I had served my required term in the West, albeit not as far west as Vincent Bladen intended. I was hired, and I stayed until 1996, when I took early retirement.

I enjoyed my year at Huron College even though it was the hardest year I ever put in as far as teaching is concerned. At Huron, you had to teach something about everything, and I found myself preparing for two courses (out of the three I was assigned) for the first time. I learned a lot, not the least of which was the distinct possibility that the less you know about a subject, the better you may be able to teach it.

One of my courses was on comparative political systems, about which I knew almost nothing. I told my students that they couldn't ask me anything on any given day beyond the currently assigned chapter— I was, literally, preparing material only one chapter ahead of them. That led to my first experience with student activism, a phenomenon still so new no one had a name for it. Some of the students in the class complained to the Dean that I wasn't fit to teach the course. I survived this complaint, probably because there was no one to replace me, and I worked very hard on my lecture presentations. Ironically, my students in this course topped the University in the final examinations, while my students in industrial relations—my chosen field—barely held their own with an average performance.

Huron College also gave me my first insight into the power of the media. When my comparative political systems students topped the University-wide finals, I insisted on raising their mid-term grades accordingly. Clearly, I had graded them much harder than my colleagues in the other colleges had graded their students. Mine had proved they were the best and, in my view, deserved the mid-term boost. The University authorities refused to go along until I threatened to call a press conference to expose their inequitable treatment of my students. Mind you, by then I knew I was moving to the University of Toronto, something which undoubtedly strengthened my resolve to fight for my students' rights. They'd complained about their mid-term results, and I had promised to do better by them if they proved themselves on the final, which they so effectively did.

When John was preparing for early retirement, the University of Toronto was encouraging it and making up very generous retirement plans. One plan had a provision that John missed by a very small margin of time. John said the Vice-President of Human Resources was rather pleased to inform him that he didn't qualify, and John swore he would fight.

It was characteristic of John that he not only got a lawyer and legal resources but also engaged a public relations firm. He made an appointment with the President, not the Vice-President of Human Resources, and told him that he was going to fight with a maximum of publicity, whereupon U of T decided to give him the deal.

This emphasis on the public relations aspect is a key to John's life and certainly to his work. He's very clever and very good at it. But he always saw and still does see life as a battle between opposing interests.

Ernest Sirluck, Ph.D., Professor, Dean, and Vice-President, Retired, University of Toronto, and President, Retired, University of Manitoba

---

Huron College was then an Anglican college more famous for its parties than its academic standards, and it showed. Once, the brother of Jim Elder, one of Canada's most famous Olympic and international riders, turned up on a horse outside my classroom window to explain why he wouldn't be attending class that day. I can't remember whether I passed him, but if I didn't I should have for his gall alone.

Another time I was sitting in my office when I heard what sounded like a drill coming through the cement block wall which separated me from my neighbour, a psychologist whose name I have long forgotten. I went next door to see what was happening and there he was drilling a large hole through our mutual wall. When I asked him what he was up to, he explained that it was to protect him from what we would today term charges of sexual harassment. I knew what he meant because the women students, coeds we then called them, weren't shy about offering intimate benefits in exchange for a passing grade. The psychologist claimed he was drilling for our mutual protection. Either one of us could pound on the wall if we needed a witness that we weren't up to anything unethical.

PUBLISH OR PERISH

When I started my career at the University of Toronto, I received a joint appointment I retained throughout my career in what were then called the School of Business and the Department of Political Economy. Thanks to the vibrant economy and demographics, it was the beginning of a golden age of academia in Canada. I've often said that if you could be propped up against a wall in a classroom and you could grunt, you would get a position. But, to be fair, you couldn't keep it unless you beat the system.

Surviving and thriving in any institution requires playing the game. In a university, the game was (and still is) publish or perish. How well or poorly you taught hardly mattered.

I started with a severe handicap because Ontario Hydro exercised its right to veto the publication of my Ph.D. thesis, *Collective Bargaining in the Public Service, A Study of Union-Management Relations in Ontario Hydro and TVA (Tennessee Valley Authority)*. I'd granted veto rights at the outset in return for the unlimited access I was granted to both sides in the Ontario Hydro union-management relationship. It was a wonderful learning experience, but the Vice-President of Personnel didn't like what I had to say about some of Ontario Hydro's industrial relations' policies and practices, so I never did get to publish my thesis. Since this is how most academics kickstart their publishing careers, it was a body blow.

I got the details from an Ontario Hydro insider who reported on the Vice-President's reaction. Apparently, he (the Vice-President) thought my thesis was generally poor, union-oriented, and critical of Ontario Hydro. He said it would be "the last time I will be caught off base" and compared it to another time when he'd allowed access to a student from McGill and "there was hell to pay." He was also surprised at the number and level of contacts I'd made within Ontario Hydro. Still, he wasn't overly concerned because he figured doctoral theses are usually condemned to a life in the reference library where the only people to shake off the dust are other students. (I admit to wondering why, if this was the case, he felt compelled to exercise his veto power.) My informant also told me that the Vice-President intended to write to me indicating his feelings, but he never did.

Fortunately, however, a number of other publishing opportunities came my way fairly quickly. The first major one resulted from an assignment I was given by the Canadian-American Committee, now the North American Committee. It led to a monograph entitled *The Role of International Unionism in Canada* (1967), which in turn spawned a book entitled *International Unionism: A Study in Canadian-American Relations* (1967). My findings had a significant impact on the Code of Ethics later adopted by the Canadian Labour Congress (CLC) to guide the conduct of international, that is, American or, at best, bi-national, unions in Canada.

The only reason I got two respectable publications out of this intense study was due to some small "p" politics in the Canadian-American Committee. Some of the things I had to say didn't please the American union officials. Wisely or unwisely, I agreed to publish a more selective monograph than I would otherwise have written. Fortunately, however, this left me with the opportunity to publish a much more comprehensive book on the subject. In my humble judgement, my book is still the best on the topic, but there have been very few other volumes written, so it's an easy judgement to make.

Anyway, here I was, for the second time at a very early stage in my career, with high-level, connected sponsors in a position to put significant roadblocks in my way. I learned quickly how precious academic freedom is and how easily it can be compromised by commitments and obligations assumed in order to gain necessary access. I think these experiences help explain why I spent the latter half of my academic career pursuing my own research interests without either entrée or support from those who might want to stifle my findings for one reason or another.

For every roadblock, though, there is the possibility of a door opening elsewhere. I think I had already learned the compromise lesson when Lester Pearson named me as one of four academic members on what became known as the Prime Minister's Task Force on Labour Relations. (I'll discuss this in greater depth in another chapter.) The Task Force experience resulted in the report titled *Canadian Industrial Relations: The Report of the Task Force on Labour Relations* (1968), which served as an excellent textbook for many years to come. Pride of common authorship still leads me to believe that it is the best compendium of sensible public policies in industrial relations in this country. I don't know of any other more comprehensive guide to such a policies' framework published since.

Thanks to these and other publications, I secured tenure and promotions to Associate and then Full Professor early, some would say prematurely. I could probably have quit publishing then, but I didn't, although I did shift the emphasis in my publishing markedly. I continued to publish some strictly academic works, such as *Industrial Democracy in Western Europe: A North American Perspective* (1978), much of which I drafted on an ocean liner, returning from Western Europe where I spent a year studying industrial relations by interviewing labour, management, and government representatives in leading countries. But I began to concentrate on more policy oriented works, such as *Free Trade: The Real Story* (1988), which I edited, *Making Canada Work: Competing in the Global Economy* (1992), and lots of op-ed articles, especially in the *The Globe and Mail* and *The Toronto Star*. Later, I became a bi-weekly columnist for *The Toronto Sun*, proving I can produce copy for the full range of editorial opinion, at least in Toronto.

This publishing record, as well as my performance as a teacher, ensured me reasonable salary increases through most of my years as an academic. Occasionally, however, I had some significant differences with my deans, especially after I served in that position myself. I had a couple of real battles with one of my favourite successors, Dean Doug Tigert, because we had a fundamental difference of opinion about the role of the professor at a university.

Doug's view was that professors should focus on basic research and scholarship even though he was a very active and highly successful consultant himself. He pointed at what he interpreted as my weaknesses, criticizing me for being a popularizer rather than an originator of ideas and for not failing enough second year students. I responded by rejecting outright his latter assertion and pointing out my strengths, which I felt he had totally ignored. Here is an excerpt from my letter:

"Now what about my strengths? While many of my strong points may somehow seem non-academic to you, it obviously depends on how you define academic. I don't have to tell you that I am in great demand both on the media and on the speaking circuit. I am probably as well known across this country as anyone in the University. Certainly I am far better known than anyone else on our Faculty.

"You may well belittle some of my forums That's not hard to do. They range from the Green Bean Producers Association to a chain of 50 rock and roll stations. But they also include *The Globe and Mail* and *The Financial Post*, the Canadian and Empire Clubs, and any number of important business associations. Although I address myself to a wide range of topics in these various forums, virtually all of them are germane either to our Faculty or to the Department of Political Economy, if not to both.

"Within the last year I have also given addresses or talks—I won't dignify them by terming them lectures—at Universities such as Calgary and Regina in Canada, as well as the Free University of Berlin and the London Business School abroad.

"Indicative of my reputation beyond our Faculty and University is the fact that I have just been asked by Simon Fraser University to serve as their first Chevron Visiting Professor of Management. Outside Canada it is not without note that both the Swedish and the Japanese Governments have recently seen fit to invite me at their expense to spend some time in their countries becoming more familiar with their general socio-economic-political systems.

"Returning to our own Faculty and University, I always do a good job in our Executive Development Programs and I am thought of very highly in the Department of Political Economy. The latter continues to award me average salary increases despite the fact I am one of their highest paid faculty members.

"I think you have an unduly narrow interpretation of what a faculty member can and should contribute to our Faculty. Few of us are able to do everything well. There has to be some specialization. I am very good at what I do well and not bad in other areas."

I ended the letter by saying that I believed he had done me a serious injustice, but that I would not let it interfere with our cordial relations. I kept that promise.

As I recall, Doug did treat me a little better in the merit increase department after this exchange, but it may have had more to do with my regaling business audiences about his maltreatment of me than a change in his opinion. Anyway, I'm glad to report that our friendship survived these and other battles.

I first met John when I joined the University of Toronto in 1970. I came up from the University of Chicago as a young Associate Professor at the Faculty of Management Studies and gradually worked my way up to Dean.

My first memory of John is that he seemed to be fairly active on radio and television as a commentator, sometimes on political issues, especially during elections, and sometimes in his field. He was eclectic. Nothing was sacrosanct; everything was fair game.

We didn't have a lot of academic interests in common because our fields were very different, but we became friends. He wasn't a classic academic; he had too many irons in the fire. But he was always a very supportive member of the faculty, and he made life exciting.

Douglas J. Tigert, Professor of Retail Marketing, Retired,
Babson College, Babson Park, Maine, U.S.A.

STICKS & STONES

Early in my academic career, when I was flying high in terms of traditional scholarly research, I received a number of offers to move elsewhere. The most enticing and intriguing was from Frances Bairstow of McGill University, and it was to become the Director of McGill's Centre for Industrial Relations. Later, I wished I had accepted the offer, if only because it would have forced me to learn French, the lack of which became a major handicap later as I became more and more involved in Canada's continuing constitutional debates. If I had been able to participate *en français*, I'm sure I would have been more effective in putting across my point of view on Quebec to Quebeckers.

Instead, I did what so many other academics do when they get an offer from another reputable university; I parlayed it into a much better deal where I was. Not only was I granted a full professorship, but I was also named the Founding Director of the University of Toronto's new Centre for Industrial Relations. It was financed from a combination of funds from the University, grants, and gifts, and it was supported by distinguished advisors, including Bora Laskin, later Chief Justice of the Supreme Court of Canada.

For years, the Centre ran conferences, provided an information service, and encouraged and facilitated research. To be honest, it also gave me a fantastic front for many of my non-university activities. But I take comfort from the fact that I got a lot of name recognition for the Centre, and that helped set the stage for it to go on to bigger and better things as a degree granting department under the more scholarly leadership of the directors who followed me.

My only concern about the Centre after I left the directorship in 1975 was that it became too academic. In my view, the Centre neglected the non-academic but complementary and important activities that preoccupied me. I believe it could have continued to have much more influence if more engaged in the on-going industrial relations issues of the day by holding regular public forums on them.

In 1964 or so, John and Art Kruger, who was with the Department of Political Science, recommended me for a position at the University of Toronto. I was very interested, but an extremely important part of my decision was the founding of the Centre for Industrial Relations. I felt the University needed such an institutional base, and I wouldn't have come to U of T unless it was part of the picture as it was at Princeton where I did my doctorate. My understanding is that John was offered a position at McGill and he went to the President of U of T and said he would take the McGill appointment unless U of T created the Centre for Industrial Relations. The President agreed and $50,000 was allocated. It was enough to get the Centre up and running.

When I arrived, I went to Scarborough College. I was the first economist at the College and the 10th faculty member. In 1975 I succeeded John as Director of the Centre.

Back in 1964 and 1965, John and Art consulted with me regarding the Centre. We worked very closely on what research would be done, who would do it, the whole direction of the Centre, even what to call it. I remember John preparing for meetings with the Centre's Advisory Board and asking, "What are we going to tell them?" because of course they were interested in our research activities.

During the early years of the Centre, John's personality dominated. He was very dynamic and took a public thrust and role for the Centre. He chaired lots of conferences and brought in important people and got good media coverage. I remember one conference in 1966. After it, there was an editorial in a local newspaper that pronounced, "Give the Centre the resources it needs to solve the problems of Canada."

John had a very high profile and loved it. The sharpest memory I have of him in those days is his public thrust and profile in the media.

The Late Noah Meltz, Ph.D.,
Professor Emeritus, Department of Economics, University of Toronto, and Professor of
Economics, School of Business Administration, Netanya Academic College, Jerusalem

---

In the meantime, I had an opportunity to go for a bigger and better position in academic administration as the first Dean of the renamed Faculty of Management at the University of Toronto. I was not the first choice for this job. That choice was a very able Canadian refugee in the U.S.A. who had made the mistake of becoming an American citizen, thereby rendering him unacceptable to our then weak-kneed, small "l" liberal president, Claude Bissell, who was afraid to appoint him because we were going through one of those spasms of anti-Americanism which periodically sweep through Canada when it's experiencing one of its unwarranted inferiority complexes. This was a sad decision for the Faculty, the University, and, ultimately, for me, although again it may have done more good than harm to my overall career.

I got the job virtually by default, not even having applied for it. I quickly learned that the job was not for me and ended up serving only three years (the usual term was seven years) during which I termed myself in successive years, Dean-Designate, Dean, and then Dean-Resignate. I didn't do a bad job, but my heart and soul were not in it and I suspect my colleagues were as pleased as I was when I stepped down. In some ways, however, some of my successors made them realize I was not all that bad. Our faculty ended up with a series of deans, none of whom was reappointed, although most of them at least served their full sentence—"term" is the word usually used—which I failed to do. I simply couldn't because I felt so constrained by the job.

As Dean, I did have one marked success. We were called a School of Business, but my colleagues and I felt that we would have more status both on and off campus if we became a Faculty. Making the change was one of the conditions I insisted upon before I became Dean. I would probably have been better off if I'd concentrated on improving funding instead. I think that the university administration went along with the name change in lieu of dealing with the much more fundamental issue of the inadequate funding which plagues the Faculty to this day. At least, we did become the Faculty of Management for a time. For reasons I cannot begin to understand, my colleagues recently decided being a School rather than Faculty would give us more prestige. So, we're a School again. Such are the games academics play.

My best memory of John and the University is the big mistake they both made when they made him Dean. He's very bright, but he's not temperamentally suited to that kind of job. He isn't diplomatic. He didn't finish his term. Usually, they run seven years; he served about three and towards the end was signing his letters "Dean Resignate."

An example of why he wasn't suited is how he handled merit pay. Merit pay was in a pot to be distributed by the Dean. The Dean had discretion about how to divide and distribute it. The lowest amount one could get was zero. John wrote letters to some faculty members saying that he was giving them zero only because the rules didn't permit him to go lower and he would reduce their salaries if he could because they were lousy teachers, weren't publishing, or were publishing garbage in journals no one respected. That was his style. But in a university, you are elected Dean by your colleagues who have tenure and you will rejoin them when your term is up.

Arthur M. Kruger, Professor Emeritus,
Department of Economics, University of Toronto

It took another opportunity, though, to make me realize that I didn't want to be an academic administrator of any kind. While I was Dean of our Faculty, the presidency of York University opened up, and I was deemed a suitable candidate. How the search committee at York could have even contemplated me is one thing, but how I could have considered it is even more confounding, at least to me.

My faulty reasoning went something like this. I desperately wanted a better public platform from which to articulate my public policy views, and I already knew there was no place for me in party politics because of the party discipline I so abhor and yet understand is necessary in our parliamentary form of government. Failing a political platform, I thought, what could be better than being a university president?

Luckily, I saw the fault lines before it was too late. In the first place, you have to play so many petty little political games to become and remain a university president that it's doubtful you will retain, let alone develop, anything very useful to say about the broader issues confronting society. Secondly, even if you do, it is unlikely you will be able to express them without offending one or more of a university's many constituencies, estates, or stakeholders, all terms used for the various vested interests involved. To serve effectively as a university president, you have to become a contradiction in terms—a small "p" politician and a potential big "p" Politician. Either way, you are a virtual eunuch.

I'm not sure when this all dawned on me, but it must have been just after Bora Laskin, former Dean of Law and later Chief Justice of Canada, who chaired the York search committee, invited me for an interview with the committee, one of the first of such committees to be composed of representatives of almost all the university's stakeholders.

The evening began with my (now former) wife telling me as I went out the door to be myself because I wasn't meant to be a university president. It ended with Bora—who enjoyed every minute of it—asking me why I hadn't told him earlier that I did not really want to be a university president. The truth is, I don't think I really knew myself until that evening.

Between my wife's admonition and Bora's question, I managed to offend all of the stakeholders represented on the search committee. One of the faculty members on the committee asked me what I would do if negotiations with the faculty association broke down and the faculty refused to hand in grades by way of protest. That led to quite an exchange with me trying to get the committee to accept two propositions, both of which they found hard to comprehend. The first was the assumption that the administration under my direction had offered all it could consistent with its revenues and the other needs of the university. The committee members had difficulty understanding that assumption, but it was nothing compared with their inability to accept as fact that a concerted refusal to hand in grades would amount to a strike. Bora, an expert in labour law, confirmed this second assumption.

After trying to clarify these two points, I told them that if they instigated a collective refusal to hand in their grades, that is, strike, I would announce that anyone not meeting the normal deadline for handing in grades would be removed from the payroll the next day. One of the faculty members complained, "You'd split us!", which I felt was quite a profound insight for him. I acknowledged that and added they would be wise not to confront me if I were president unless they really had a very legitimate case, one stronger than mine.

This exchange ended any support I might have had among the faculty members on the search committee. It quickly became a consensus as I took on the other stakeholders in turn.

The student representatives dismissed me when I told them I would never give them parity—a popular cause among student leaders at that time—on any issues or matters pertaining to the academic integrity of the university. I did tell them I would consider parity in other areas and I would also consider student representation on tenure committees to make sure effective teaching was given more weight in those decisions. (Actually, I profoundly agreed with such representation, and I regret that it has never been accepted by the vast majority of my faculty colleagues.) But once I had rejected parity as a general rule, I was dead meat as far as the student representatives were concerned.

Members of the Board of Governors on the search committee, with the possible exception of Bora himself, were offended by my suggestion that they were little more than a reflection of the white male business establishment. Bill Mahoney, then Canadian director of the steelworkers union, was their token labour member. I've forgotten if there were any token women members and, if there were, who they were.

In the end I'm not sure any of the members of the search committee would have accepted me, with the possible exception of Bora, who might have gone along with my appointment just to see what would happen.

Not long after this experience, I gave up all my administrative responsibilities and returned to the trenches—teaching and research— where I remained until I retired. Being free to speak was just too important to me to compromise it by assuming any academically related administrative responsibilities. I made only one exception. Later, I served briefly as speaker of a Faculty Council in the Faculty of Management. My job was essentially to ensure that every point of view was aired including, very often, my own. That role was much more to my taste.

ACADEMIC LIFE

As I settled into my life as a university professor, I gradually came to appreciate why it was so great to be an academic. First and foremost is the opportunity to be oneself and to enjoy complete freedom of expression and thought. It wasn't until I began the research for this memoir that I realized how early I was warned about how much trouble I could get into if I insisted on being my outspoken self, especially in writing.

In late October 1961, I received a letter from an M.I.T. lecturer I greatly liked and respected. Fred Lesieur was a former president of a steelworkers union local but was never made a professor because, although he had more knowledge and insight than virtually all of his colleagues combined, he didn't have the right union card—a Ph.D.—to make the grade at M.I.T. I'd asked Fred to comment on an article I proposed to publish, and he responded by warning me about the dangers of being too direct when putting my thoughts in writing.

"Depending on where your interests lie in regard to work out in the field, along with your position as Professor at the University, I would be very careful if I were you concerning statements that can be attributed to you concerning either management or labour. I don't know of any union that likes to have the broad implication of feather-bedding attributed to them. Nor for that matter do I know of any management, no matter how poorly the plant may be run, that likes to admit to inefficient management. No, John, I am not trying to say that these problems have to be hidden under the table. What I am trying to say is, in an oral address which will not go into print these things can be said; however, if the talk is printed and then circulated, it is much better to find another way of saying the same thing. Usually when I am going to make a speech for any organization, I always raise the question prior to the speech as to whether they want it written, because of printed publication, or do they want me to speak off the cuff. If the speech is going to be printed, I generally write one, being very careful on how I say things, and then in the address deviate from the written text. As for yourself, I don't think you would want to hurt your chances in arbitration or consultation because of some pamphlet that you had written in the beginning of your career that might alienate you from either management or labor."

I didn't take Fred's advice nor that of many others over the years who tried to get me to tone down my message and/or my style. I always took the view that tenure was there to protect me even when I was outspoken, as long as I had done the research to back up my point of view. Mind you, some would argue that I was sometimes more than outspoken—some critics used the term "outrageous"—and that I did not always back up my position with as thorough research as I might have. There might be a kernel of truth in both of these observations.

Another wonderful thing about academia is the constant exposure to young people. Actually, they didn't seem that young when I started teaching, but I surely realized the difference the first year no student told me it was hard to call me "professor" or "sir" because I seemed so young myself.

As the age gap between me and my students widened, my guess is that they noticed it more than I did. Indeed, I'm convinced teaching young people helps you yourself to remain and stay younger than you really are.

I took to teaching like a duck to water and I kept teaching throughout my academic career. I have always loved it. According to the formal evaluations and other comments I received, few of my students were ambivalent. Some called me arrogant and high minded and were unhappy with my tough grading standards. But most loved me and all liked the mixture of academic theory and real world experience I brought to the classroom.

I got to know John when I was doing my M.B.A. at the University of Toronto. I took a course in Industrial Relations specifically because he was teaching it. He could have been teaching knitting or dressing for success; it wouldn't have mattered. I wanted to leave the university thinking and processing differently than when I arrived. So, I specifically sought out professors who would help me do that. I thought John would be the best of them, and he was.

Each class was an event. I was anxious to go and I didn't want to leave. I loved to sit and listen to him. Of course, John's entertaining, but more than that he talks about how business, politics, government, and unions all work together. I left with more insight than from any other course.

John has a different perspective. You're getting some guy who's right in the middle of it, not some whacked out academic. He has his finger on the pulse, and he's kind enough to share it.

Stephen Dulong, C.E.0., Transcard Canada Inc., Toronto

University teaching is also wonderful because your work allows a form of flex time. Obviously, you have to turn up for your classes and your office hours—I even made the latter flexible—but other than that and some administrative and committee work, it is up to you when and where and even how hard and long you choose to work. If you are at all energetic, you can fulfil your academic responsibilities while taking on a lot of outside activities.

It's easy to get carried away with these activities. When I was serving on the Prime Minster's Task Force on Labour Relations, for example, I was spending roughly half my time on its work.

I believe my outside activities are the reason then President Claude Bissell asked me to chair a Task Force on Outside Income and Related Activities, which were becoming very contentious issues both within and beyond the University. It took a long time and a lot of political manoeuvring to get a consensus out of this Task Force, but we finally managed to agree on some pretty sensible rules in the end. Mind you, we had to wait until one especially cantankerous individual went on sabbatical leave.

Still known as "the Crispo rules," they make it clear that a professor's first and foremost obligation is to the university, with all that entails in terms of teaching, research, and so on. Having fulfilled that overriding responsibility, the rules make it clear that a professor may earn outside income by engaging in related activities as long as they

don't give rise to conflicts of interest. All such activities must be reported annually in writing to the professor's superior, and any involving
major time commitments must be approved in writing in advance.

Another wonderful feature about being an academic is the sabbatical leave. Professors are usually entitled to one every seven years or so at
about 70 to 80 per cent of normal pay. Sabbaticals are meant for research
and recharging intellectual batteries, although they are sometimes used
for other purposes. During my entire 35-year academic career, I took
only two sabbaticals. I believe I needed only two because I was so ener-
gized by the mixture of academic and outside activities I was able to
maintain.

Still another great advantage of being an academic is the intellectual stimulation one receives from one's colleagues or at least from those
you learn to respect. For me, the individuals I learned from most were
a cross-section of faculty drawn from all over the University. We
lunched together regularly at the Faculty Club.

This faculty table apparently has a history going back to the 1930s.
In my time, it brought together a disparate collection of such bright,
eclectic, and interesting characters that I rarely came away without
learning something new. Virtually every time I attended I also found
some of my views challenged, if not corrected.

Gradually, however, the group took on more and more of a right
wing cast. We lost the likes of Mel Watkins and Abe Rotstein, both of
whom I missed greatly as I was going through my more right-wing
period. Eventually, the closest thing to a left winger we were left with
was Peter Russell, a good friend and colleague who is one of the last
remaining sincere small "l" liberals in existence.

The group at this table assumed more and more importance in my
life as I took on more media and speaking engagements. There were
countless times when I tried out my ideas at that table and learned to
qualify or temper them before it was too late. I seldom if ever gave the
group involved public credit for their help in keeping me on the straight
and narrow, or at least on the straighter and narrower, and I'm not sure
they would have welcomed the acknowledgement, at least in public.

But let me say here and now that I owe these colleagues and friends more than I can ever put into words.

John and I had crossed paths for years, but we didn't actually get to know each other until we were both on faculty at U of T. We became very good friends and colleagues.

We've been having lunch at The Trough for years. The Trough is one of those very good institutions every university should have. It's the equivalent of the High Table at Oxford or Cambridge, the place where faculty meet for meals and use as a forum for discussion across disciplines.

There was only one rule at The Trough. No subject was taboo, including university affairs. All university presidents eventually make a visit or two to the equivalent of The Trough and get grilled in as lively a way as you can imagine.

John would come back from his speaking and consulting engagements with war stories about "the ball point pen people" or whatever. He would have humour and he would have a point, with the point usually stuck into the people he'd been addressing.

I have always admired his fiercely independent spirit. He is not taken in by anyone. He speaks his mind freely. He is fully engaged in the affairs of his country. He spoke for many good causes, for example, free trade and the CBC. He always had something to say that's pretty interesting. I don't always agree with him, but I always find him interesting.

Peter Russell, O.C., Professor Emeritus,
Department of Political Science, University of Toronto

TENURE TRACKS

The upside of tenure is academic freedom, which has been so important to me throughout my academic career. The opportunity to and right to speak and write without fear or favour is the greatest privilege I could ever have enjoyed. Tenure has provided me with just that, and I should, therefore, have nothing but good to say about it.

But that wouldn't be fair. I believe in tenure in its original form as a means of assuring academic freedom. I also know that it can be abused when it is used as a shield to protect the incompetent.

The last of my many pronouncements on this subject appeared in 1996 in *The Toronto Star*. (I was a weekly columnist for the newspaper for a relatively short period of time. I lost the position in part because, as the publisher told me, I was too reasonable as a right winger to be their token right winger.) I wrote in response to an unwarranted editorial ("Questioning tenure") by that newspaper on the subject. My 1996 article, titled "Tenure vital to academic freedom," argued that *The Star*'s reference to tenure as "really nothing more than a glorified system of featherbedding" was a gross exaggeration.

The Star's editorial argued that "a majority of professors defend tenure on the grounds that it protects their academic freedom. This is self-serving rhetoric. All kinds of systems are already in place to protect those freedoms."

I argued that tenure has been absolutely vital to the free-wheeling approach I took as an academic. I said I wouldn't have felt anything like as free to aggravate, alienate, and annoy almost every major interest group in the country, including my own university administration and faculty association, if I had not had tenure. I went on to discuss the legitimate and illegitimate sides of tenure.

"This brings me to the heart of the matter, in terms of what is legitimate and what is illegitimate about tenure. To begin with, tenure should be seen as a very special privilege and not an absolute right.

"I still believe that tenure is indispensable to ensure academic freedom for university faculty members. Too many vested interests outside and inside the university would like to silence those with dissenting or unpopular points of view.

"A university that is worthy of the name should have on its faculty individuals who reflect a range of opinions on the major issues confronting our society. Particularly when it comes to a liberal arts education, students should be stimulated by varying points of view so that they can intelligently make up their own minds where they stand on contentious subjects.

"What is illegitimate about tenure is that it has become so pervasive and powerful a force that it is hard to remove a tenured faculty member from a university staff for any reason.

"Tenure is necessary for academic freedom but should only prevail as long as one is performing effectively in an appropriate combination of research, scholarship, teaching and related activities. If faculty members are not carrying out their responsibilities effectively, tenure should not protect them.

"Many, if not most, of my colleagues would argue that this is already the case, but university dismissal rates for incompetence are so low as to make their position indefensible. If academics want to preserve tenure as a legitimate means for protecting their academic freedom, they must not allow it to continue to be used quite illegitimately as a means to protect incompetence.

"If the government's panel on future directions for post-secondary education chooses to take on the issue of tenure—which I think it should—I hope and trust that it will recognize this vital difference. If it does so, it might come up with a sensible set of recommendations on tenure rather than an ill-informed and sweeping denunciation of the concept."

Before I leave the subject of tenure, I should reveal that one of my successors as Dean, Doug Tigert, gave up his tenure when he became Dean and challenged me to do likewise. This was my answer to him and those who supported him. (It was published in the University of Toronto's *University Bulletin*.)

"If Doug really wants to know whether I would be willing to give up my tenure the answer is a combination of a qualified yes and an adamant no. Yes, I would give up my tenure in so far as it serves as a shield behind which to protect any incompetence I may exhibit. Indeed, this distorted and unwarranted use of tenure has been my main complaint about it all along.

"I would ask three things of Doug or anyone else who wants me to surrender that aspect of my tenure. I want some reasonable standards against which my performance will be judged, the right to grieve against any adverse interpretation and, in the event of discharge, an equitable severance pay arrangement similar to that available in most other large institutions.

"But if Doug is asking me to give up my tenure in its legitimate original form—that is, to protect my academic freedom—I hope and trust he will by now have surmised my answer. I have made a career of attacking individuals and institutions of all kinds on a wide array of issues. I have not spared my colleagues nor this University. (Let alone Doug himself.)

"If Doug and the powers that be in this institution can come up with the appropriate distinction between the two forms of tenure I have delineated—and I think this is feasible—I will be glad to be the first to renounce that form of tenure which none of us should ever have had in the first place.

"Having said this, however, let me make it clear that I will fight to my last breath any attack on my tenure or anyone else's to the extent that it serves the appropriate and compelling purpose of upholding one's right to speak one's mind freely."

WAR GAMES

Another feature about Canadian universities that's disturbed me for a long time is the way they are governed. I became very involved in this issue when the University of Toronto was virtually capitulating to student radicals during their most active period. In 1970, I was still an administrator, and I got myself elected to what was called the University-Wide Committee. It was established to review the issue of university governance and especially the advisability of creating a unicameral governing body. My position in favour of the multicameral governing model remains unchanged.

My main concern was that the University was heading down a dangerous path, one that would put the very survival of its community of scholars in serious jeopardy. I described the central question as the nature and composition of the governing structure and stated that it must meet three basic tests if it is to prove effective. The tests were internal acceptability, external credibility and confidence, and operational or administrative feasibility.

In my view, both the Commission on University Governance (CUG) and others involved in the debate were giving too much weight to internal acceptability at the expense of the other criteria. Internal consensus is important, but it will always be elusive, given the fluid character of the academic mind and the constantly shifting composition of the many groups and individuals that make up a modern university.

I also felt that the criterion of external credibility is just as indispensable in the long run to the welfare of a university. A university is a public trust. It depends on public support and confidence not only for its financial well-being but also ultimately to maintain academic freedom. Downgrading the importance of the public understanding is a perilous undertaking.

Equally essential is effective operation and administration. If a university develops an unmanageable system of government, it won't matter a bit if it is done in the name of participatory democracy. The result will still be to win the battle and lose the war.

My proposal was a governing structure that could meet a reasonable combination of the three tests. I didn't start from the proposition that just because the current form of multicameralism wasn't working effectively at the University of Toronto, it was obsolete or useless. Nor did I assume that a unicameral system was the only alternative. I was convinced that a radical revision of the current, multicameral system would be the most effective system.

In my memo, I went into considerable detail describing how I would approach this radical revision. My plan involved renaming and reconstituting the Board of Governors as the Board of Trustees to reflect the characteristic of the university as a public trust. It also involved revamping and rejuvenating the Senate and establishing a Joint Executive Committee with responsibility for integrating financial and academic decision-making.

I ended by reminding everyone that no responsible government will turn over millions of taxpayers' dollars to an institution with a governing structure dominated by those who derive their livelihood or other direct benefits from it. "If we are so naive as to proceed on that assumption," I wrote, "we will invite even more direct and invidious forms of public intervention than now confront us."

I had some support, but not enough. The University persuaded the Government of Ontario to legislate a unicameral governing council to preside over its affairs. At first, it was unworkable, but gradually it began to operate more usefully as it effectively split itself into the three components I had proposed. I guess you could say I lost the battle but won the war....

I met John for the very first time in the Summer of 1989 when I arrived at the University of Toronto. We actually met at a Dean's Retreat at the lunch table. He told me about his book writing on free trade, the GST, and other issues. I admire John's willingness to argue for his positions. It explains why he is so respected at C.D. Howe. He attended all the Round Tables and was often the first to raise his hand. He's very good at putting across his point of view.

This reflects his personality—be engaged, be informed, hear all points of view. He sees how things are done—as a balance of considerations and how important it is to understand all the considerations. He's actually a sensitive person. Many don't appreciate that because of his wild statements. He really does try to understand and listen to others.

John's also very practical. In the Spring of 1993 or 1994, when I was Associate Dean of the Faculty, we were discussing a strategic plan. The Dean wanted to drop the M.B.A. Accounting Program. Politically, it was difficult. We had a bargaining session that lasted from 8:00 a.m. to midnight. John took an active role. His humour really helped. The interesting thing about John is he takes very strong views from principle, but he will turn to the practical to accomplish the job at hand.

Jack Mintz, President & C.E.O., C.D. Howe Institute, Toronto

STUDENT POWER

The student power steamroller really got going in the late 1960s and early 1970s when a small band of activists, militants, or radicals—call them what you will—galvanized enough students in universities around the world to create considerable turmoil on campus and off. Today, the concept of student power seems almost quaint as students seem much more concerned about their grades and career prospects than larger social issues. But then it was a kettle boiling over and splashing everyone within reach.

I found myself in the thick of the debate not only in my classrooms but also in the university at large. For me, it crashed into my classroom on the opening day of my large industrial relations class. (At its peak, this class had more than 700 students.) I've forgotten what year it happened, but I will never forget that particular incident. I didn't actually get to teach that day because a largish number of malcontents came in to warn my students that, if I recall their words accurately, I was a "lackey of the U.S. imperialistic war-mongering military industrial complex."

The next year I was warned the malcontents would be back. I took the initiative by opening with what I presented as an emergency announcement from the President's office. For some reason this silenced the disrupters long enough for me to proclaim that the President wanted me to warn them that I was everything they'd accused me of the year before—I believe I embellished on their accusations to a fair extent—but that I had to teach the course because no one else was available. This strategy worked so well that I kept using it years after it was necessary.

Eventually, I refined my self-proclaimed confession by condemning myself with facts: I was born with a silver spoon in my mouth. I had attended Upper Canada College, Trinity College, and then M.I.T. I had a wife and two daughters, lived in Forest Hill Village, spent the weekends at my farm in the country, and belonged to Devil's Glen Ski Club. For the first few years I used this confessional tactic, some students would boo. Gradually, they grew almost indifferent and finally, in my later years, they didn't quite cheer but did begin to ask how they could get there, too. What a transition in student attitudes to witness!

Outside my classroom I got deeply involved in the student power question. One result was a lengthy analysis published in *The Globe Magazine* in 1969. Under the title "Whipsaw," I explained my intense interest in the issue.

My interest in student power stemmed from several points of view—as a teacher, as a professor, as a student of labour-management relations, and as a citizen.

As a teacher committed to a career in a university, I was concerned because of the implications for the future of higher education. I felt the impact of student activism could be positive. Even when a minority of students attempt to convert the classroom into a venue for espousing political doctrines, the result can be heightened enthusiasm and participation, an experience that may be exhilarating or discouraging, depending on one's circumstances and point of view.

As a professor committed to the integrity of the institution, I was concerned that a small number of individuals might jeopardize the ability or will of the university to fulfil its responsibilities. In my view, any university has four overlapping purposes: to serve as a centre for transmitting knowledge and to prepare students for life in the broadest sense; to provide scholars with the academic freedom and resources they need to push back the frontiers of knowledge; to provide a haven for individuals willing to engage in critical analysis and constructive dissent; and to extend the university's services to the community and to participate in the concerns and life of the community.

As a student of union-management relations, I was fascinated by the parallels between student power, when it takes more structured forms beyond the classroom, and industrial relations in the broader context. Like labour unions, student administrative councils exist within a hierarchy of federations at the provincial and federal levels. Both unions and councils are financed by dues paid by members, with some of the funds used to pay elected officers to take leaves of absence from studies (in councils) or from paid employment (in unions). Student activists were quick to adopt the unions' approach to collective bargaining and to use conflict and confrontation, in the form of sit-ins, strikes, and other tactics of industrial warfare. Strategically, they would extract one concession here and another elsewhere. Then they would insist on every concession everywhere. I call this the whipsaw strategy of building precedents.

As a citizen, I was mindful of the ramifications for society at large by the increasingly pervasive challenge posed by vigorous minority dissent. I believe that due process and the rule of law must be protected and nourished both in universities and in society at large.

While the radicals or extremists were small in number, they were very successful in dominating the organs of student government. The aim of these bright, vigorous, intense, idealistic, and articulate students was to reform not only the university as a university, but also through it society at large. My concern was that they were also highly intolerant of views contrary to their own and had a disturbing tendency to believe that the end always justified the means.

Even at the height of student power, however, the vast majority of the student body was, on balance, uncommitted and inactive or absolutely opposed to the activists. They wanted a university education or professional qualifications, they concentrated their efforts on their personal objectives, and they didn't want anything to get between them and graduation. Turning a blind eye to everything but one's personal concerns, however, isn't any healthier for a society than turning the world upside down without first developing a broad consensus and balanced vision.

My position, in essence, was that the campus ferment presented tremendous potential for both creative, constructive progress and negative, destructive reaction. The challenge confronting universities was to ensure an environment that encouraged the former and inhibited the latter. Universities must anticipate, or at least be responsive to, the legitimate concerns of the student body. Taking the initiative, dealing with each issue on its merits rather than on its ideological colorings, giving thorough airings, providing effective leadership, and promoting legitimate reforms are the most effective means of avoiding the turmoil that can accompany vigorous dissent.

Unfortunately, the nature of the academic is to rise to challenges too late, thereby forfeiting control. That's what happened at the University of Toronto in 1972. Things got pretty ugly over issues such as securing general undergraduate access to the graduate student library. Although I agreed that there was some merit in the students' demands, I was also concerned about the graduate library's ability to maintain the integrity of its collections. So, I was one of those who led the fight to try to stop the University from capitulating in the face of mass student occupations. I submitted two possible resolutions to the special, public meeting of the University's then Senate. One, which captured the essence of my position, was not well received by anyone, colleagues or students. In fact, I was royally booed.

Fortunately, student power became less and less of an issue during the

1970s, but it could emerge again at any time. If it does, my concerns—and my opposition to making concessions under duress—will be the same.

My relationship with John has been primarily at the Long Table at the University of Toronto's Faculty Club. I lunched there once a week, and our schedules often coincided. I still lunch there once a week on Mondays. I also knew John a little while I was Dean, but not well. I came to know him at lunch.

John's very aggressive and he has, until the last year or two, tended to simplify issues. He saw them as right and wrong, rather than as complicated with merit on both sides. My impression is that recently he's begun to see matters are often graded and multi-facetted, but this view came to him very late in life and he's not accustomed to it. You're either right or wrong or on one side or the other.

I don't mean John's a fool. He's not simple-minded, but he has a simplistic view of things. There's an element of sophisticated innocence, which may seem like a contradiction in terms. For me, innocence implies ignorance of complications. With John, it's not ignorance; it's ignoring a complication. He's not unaware, but he chooses to regard complications as irrelevant.

Lately, I've seen a broadening of his view. He seems to have a less assured, more tentative view of existence. He can relapse to his old views with great vehemence but less conviction. I think he's come to regard his day at the Long Table as a kind of reprieve because a variety of interests and points of view are available and he feels less embattled.

Ernest Sirluck, Ph.D., Professor, Dean, and Vice-President, Retired, University of Toronto, and President, Retired, University of Manitoba

---

MONEY MATTERS

More recently, the issue that drew a lot of my attention was financing universities in general and university students in particular. I believe very strongly in the use of income-based vouchers to finance students. It's an idea that is opposed by virtually every faction in North American universities—administrators, faculty, and even students, if one judges by their leaders.

In 1999, in columns for *The Toronto Star* and *The Saturday Sun*, I discussed two fundamental changes I thought needed to be explored if anyone really wants to make a difference to higher education.

The first is relatively simple and straightforward. Based on 35 years of teaching at the University of Toronto, I have come to the conclusion that it's a big mistake to take students directly from high school. Most are too immature to benefit. I call them lost souls because they don't quite know why they are there or why they've chosen the courses in which they find themselves. A transitional year of travel, paid employment, volunteer work, or even just frittering would give them time to grow up and find the personal motivation they need to get the most from post-secondary studies.

I'd also like to see all levels of government introduce youth work programs, particularly on the environmental front. If it were up to me, I'd pay the students a modest living allowance or stipend, together with a voucher to cover the cost of the first year of post-secondary education. I'm convinced that this would make a tremendous difference in the lives of the young people in the broadest sense as well as in terms of the value they would get from subsequent post-secondary education.

The second change I propose is to remove all direct government funding, except for research grants, from colleges and universities, thus turning them into private institutions. Instead of funding based on enrolment numbers, it should come indirectly in the form of income-based vouchers to the most qualified students. Of course, there would be some administrative hurdles. The value of the voucher, for example, would have to accommodate the differing costs of various types of higher education. Another issue is dealing with living costs for students who choose to, or must, leave home to attend university.

Income-based vouchers would ensure that two of the most important prerequisites of a sound educational system are met. On the one hand, they would ensure equality of access and opportunity. On the other, they would ensure choice and competition.

The benefits would be tremendous, both for individuals and for society as a whole. All academically qualified students would be able to get a post-secondary education. No academically qualified student would be barred by lack of money or face a life after graduation burdened with debt as a result of student loans. But the greatest benefit would flow to society at large. Colleges and universities turned into private enterprises, with bottom lines and the risk of going out of business, would have to learn to operate more efficiently, creatively, and productively. They would have to become much more conscious of their potential and current students as clients and treat them as customers who deserve the best of service. As the system now stands, too many professors view students—especially undergraduates—as necessary evils and nuisances who must be suffered in order to generate the money and time required to do their own research. After all, publish or perish still reigns supreme in universities.

Taken together, the transition year and the income-based voucher could have many positive effects. Some institutions might go out of business. Some could thrive by specializing as first-rate undergraduate liberal arts teaching institutions. Few could afford the luxury of professors who were not performing as effectively in the classroom as in peer-juried journals.

The precedent for a transition period already exists. Most M.B.A. programs in Canada, for example, already require entrants to have at least two years of full-time work experience as well as an undergraduate degree. It makes a world of difference. Students seasoned with some real world experience are far more likely to be mature, motivated, and willing and able to share important lessons of life with their classmates. They also place greater demands on faculty, forcing professors to be relevant and up-to-date. Everyone benefits.

I've known John since 1969 or 1970 but I was a lowly M.B.A. student and then a doctoral candidate. I knew him by reputation only, although I sat in on a couple of his lectures. He was certainly the most articulate person I've ever heard. But I didn't take any of his courses and really had very little to do with him.

My first real contact was in 1990 when I came back to U of T to teach. We crossed paths in the halls, etc., but the real event that's stuck in my memory came in 1996 or 1997. John called and said he wanted to ask me a big favour. He wanted me to give a guest lecture on financial markets to his first year commerce students. I got the impression that I didn't have a choice, but I was thrilled anyway and curious, given his reputation. I thought he'd be a real tough cookie, and I wondered how this would work with first year commerce students. They are either totally brash or totally sensitive.

Anyway, John gave me a big build-up and I lectured and of course I tried to cover too much. He invited me back the next year, but he made it clear that the previous year had not been a huge success. I'd tried to cover too much, the level was too high, and I needed to have more on organizations and structure. The second time I came much closer to the mark.

I wasn't surprised by his directness with me. That's the way things are supposed to happen with colleagues. But I was surprised by his relationship with his students. It showed me a different side of him. It was a great revelation for me. They loved him. He had an incredible rapport with them, which was surprising given the large size of the class. He was very specific, somewhat paternalistic (not a bad quality in my view with first year commerce students), very direct, and at the same time very, very supportive. I was surprised by his patience with them. He had a very, very strong relationship with these young students.

Eric Kirzner, Professor of Finance,
The Joseph L. Rotman School of Management, University of Toronto

AT THE PRECIPICE

I'm a lucky man. I enjoyed a career during the golden age of academia. I also think I retired at just about the right time because I believe universities are going to find themselves on the defensive as information technology advances. In fact, I think higher education as we now know it may become obsolete sooner rather than later. Will Internet-based learning replace the bricks and mortar of traditional classroom and libraries? I don't know. But I believe that students can already use the Internet to connect with top authorities on any subject in the world and use tools like chat rooms to participate in small group seminars.

I agree with Neil Seeman's article about on-line learning in the March 23, 2000, issue of *National Post* ("Ivy league faces obsolescence; Internet-based universities can offer an education that's cheaper and more convenient"). Seeman pointed out that virtual schools are already part of the educational picture in Canada and that on-line learning, dis tance learning, or e-learning is being embraced for the promise it offers to economically disadvantaged groups, such as the geographically isolated, youth, minorities, and single mothers.

According to Seeman, the chief opponents of on-line learning are the architects of the intellectual and entrepreneurial elite business schools. For example, in a recent interview with the *Financial Post*, Jim Fisher, at my own school, explained why business schools resist on-line learning:

"The real basis of our programs, especially in the executive M.B.A. program, is that the class should learn from each other. And although theoretically they can do that online, we believe it is more difficult. We do use the Net and electronic technology for support, but, in the end, getting people together and learning from each other is very important."

Seeman went on to discuss what Fisher described as the pride and glory of the modern M.B.A. curriculum, the so-called case study method. In a typical case study session, students read from a short memorandum of facts based on a real-life business scenario. Their task is to devise a winning strategy by consensus after formulating agreed upon goals.

The case study is generally followed by a debriefing moderated by the professor or by a visiting expert in the field. But, as Seeman pointed out, every business school is not Harvard and the standards at most, including many of the better-known Ivy League schools, are relatively low. He noted that admissions criteria at the top 10 per cent of business schools in North America are roughly on par with the middle tier of law schools and many other professional degree programs. Thus, an intellectually charged case study session at Harvard, where the typical student can draw on five or more years of work experience to contribute to a spirited class discussion, bears little resemblance to what Seeman described as the languid atmosphere seen at the less demanding schools.

Rather than seeing on-line learning as a way to provide intellectual riches for all students, said Seeman, many university administrators see it as a threat that cheapens their school's brand name. Actually, their fear is well-founded because, if done properly, on-line learning can provide faster learning at lower costs and with more accountability. Still, their attitude betrays an anti-competitive animus, which is strange considering business schools are allegedly in the business of teaching how to compete effectively.

When asked by Seeman what his biggest fear of on-line learning was, Arthur Levine, the President of Columbia University's Teachers College, answered: "I think in the next few years we're going to see some firms begin to hire well-known faculty [from] our most prestigious campuses and offer an all-star degree over the Internet. So they'll take the best faculty from Columbia, Oxford and Tokyo University and offer a program at lower cost than we can."

Prof. Levine's nightmare is already rapidly unfolding south of the border. Seeman reported that the University of Phoenix, a world leader in on-line learning, with more than 60 campuses world-wide, plans to reach 200,000 students virtually within the next decade. Jones International, a for-profit on-line university based in Englewood, Colorado, recently won full-degree accreditation. My alma mater, M.I.T., has put virtually its entire curriculum on line.

But on-line learning, said Seeman, has a steeper hill to climb in Canada, where for-profit initiatives are legal only insofar as they subsidize a "purely academic" endeavour. For-profit undertakings, such as corporate-sponsored e-learning programs, are viewed as antithetical to the perceived integrity of higher education.

What this means for Canadian universities, especially the business schools, Seeman said, is that they should start worrying more about impending obsolescence than merely diminished prestige. He offered these statistics to buttress his position. According to Market Data Retrieval, a Dun & Bradstreet educational research company, in 1999, the number of American colleges offering on-line degrees doubled. In early 2000, Michael Saylor, the chief executive of Microstrategy, told a group of Washington based philanthropists that he will donate a $100-million (U.S.) to create a nonprofit, tuition-free, on-line university to offer an "Ivy League" education to anyone. Educators and business leaders were predicting on-line learning would make up 15 per cent of the total education market in 2001, including courses covering the spectrum from arts and crafts to business, health, sports, and technology.

Some things may be lost with on-line learning, such as the cama-raderie of the school and the intensity of student-teacher relationships. But Peter Carr, Associate Director of M.B.A. and I.T. management pro-grams at Athabasca University, told Seeman that even these intangibles can be captured. Athabasca, which has been in the distance-learning business for 30 years, has cornered about 25 per cent of the M.B.A. mar-ket in Canada. Carr says that on-line discussions are often pursued longer and in more depth than in traditional classrooms.

Other benefits of on-line learning for students include increased access to higher education (particularly for the non-traditional student); flexible scheduling of personal time; convenience; individual attention by the instructor; less travel time; and more time to think about ques-tions posed by the instructor. Benefits for the institution include attract-ing more students without having to build and maintain expensive facil-ities and signalling to the public that the institution is indeed techno-logically progressive.

Seeman concluded that while he doesn't necessarily agree with Peter Drucker, who predicted (to *Fortune* magazine in 1999) that the tradi-tional campus would be dead within 30 years, he does believe that we no longer have to rely entirely on the traditional campus to meet our edu-cational needs. I believe that our universities will be the better for it.

John Crispo has provided me with a mentorship for my research and teaching. I've been described as opinionated as a lecturer. I'm modelling myself on him. I have delusions of being a junior Crispo. I think academics should have opinions. A university should be a debate of ideas and all should speak candidly.

John is irreplaceable, provocative, a mentor, an educator. He cares for students and very deeply for his craft, the practice of teaching.

Modelling on John is a competitive advantage. I won the teaching award at Schulich in 1998 in my first year as a teacher. This award is given by stu-dents. I learned to teach by modelling after John, and, lo and behold, I got the teaching award. Also, whenever John leaves my class, it's a challenge to fill his shoes, so I have him as a guest lecturer right before they evaluate me, so they're hyped and they give me good marks.

Richard Leblanc, C.M.C., B.Sc., M.B.A., LLB, J.D., LLM, Ph.D. (Candidate),
Corporate Governance Program, Schulich School of Business, York University, Toronto

Chapter 2

Just Another Working Stiff

Many people have this vision of academics as perched in ivory towers where they laze about, untouched by the need to work very hard and unmarked by the vicissitudes of real life. To them I say long before I became a tenured professor, I learned something about working for a living the hard way down in the trenches. I also learned about customer service, drudgery, bribery and corruption, the use of influence, and the power of peer pressure. I continued the pattern of diving into the trenches during my academic career, beginning with deep involvement in the labour movement both directly and indirectly.

SUMMER SERVICE

I started my working life in summer jobs. For me, that meant working in hotels catering to the tourist trade. I began as a busboy at Bigwin Inn in Haliburton, Ontario, then moved on to the Banff Springs Hotel in Banff, Alberta, first as a caddy and later as a bellhop.

I still remember two incidents that occurred at Bigwin. The first was frightening: A fellow busboy accused me of stealing his money and drew a knife on me. Luckily, we were in our shared dormitory, and our work mates intervened quickly and headed off further trouble. The second was amusing: All the busboys were mustered to serve at a very formal dinner. Each of us shouldered a tray with a pile of 20 dinners. As we marched into the dining room, I slipped on something and sent my plates flying in all directions. No one got hurt or even hit by flying food, but that didn't stop Frank Leslie, the eccentric stockbroker cum inn owner, from rising up in wrath at the head table and shouting, "You're

55

fired!" My disgrace, however, turned out to be the highlight of an otherwise exceedingly dull evening, and the next day the convention organizers intervened on my behalf and had my job restored.

Getting hired by the Banff Springs Hotel was a coup. Banff was a mecca for university students looking for summer work. The pay wasn't all that great, but the tips could be very good and the parties were great.

I started as a lowly caddy but soon got a chance to move up in the pecking order by using good, old-fashioned bribery and corruption. I bribed the caddy master, Don Hughes, who was also a student and is still a good friend, to let me be the first to caddy for a V.I.P. Mr. Little (I've forgotten his first name) was then President of the Anglo-Canadian Pulp and Paper Company. He was a very prestigious guest, he had a reputation as an extremely generous tipper, and he was staying at the hotel with his family for a whole month. Don had ruled that we had to take turns caddying for Mr. Little. I paid Don five dollars (a lot of money at the time) in order to be the first to caddy for Mr. Little. My plan was to use my golfing skills, honed over many years at our family cottage at Lake Simcoe, to demonstrate the value of a topnotch caddy who really knew the game.

It worked. Mr. Little insisted that I caddy for him for the rest of his stay. By the third day, I was playing golf with him, and I never took a day off until he left. Don lent a hand by rigging the starting system to ensure that Little and his guests never had to wait to tee off. I made a small fortune in shared winnings and tips, including a final tip of $300 just before he left.

On his last day at the hotel, Mr. Little asked if there was anything else he could do for me. I jumped at the opportunity. Would he use his influence to have my friend Don and me promoted to bellhop the following summer? The very next day Don and I were summoned to the hotel manager's office and told to go to the hotel tailor to be measured for bellhop uniforms to wear the next season.

Being a bellhop at the Banff Springs Hotel was fabulous. We were pretty near the top of the food chain, and we learned to make money every which way. We were also pioneers in the underground economy.

We never reported any of our tips as income for tax purposes. The result was that I netted as much during those summers as I did during my first year as a full-time professor.

They were golden days. Don and I climbed, hiked, and wrecked canoes together. We made money, and we had fun. We got to see the celebrities of the day up close and personal. In fact, I escorted Marilyn Monroe to her room when she came to Banff to film *The River of No Return* with Robert Mitchum. I remember thinking how much more beautiful she was in person than she was on screen. (To this day, Don claims that he's the one who escorted Marilyn, something I dismiss as a figment of his imagination and wishful thinking born out of extreme jealousy. I concede, however, that Don was Robert Mitchum's night-time bootlegger.)

I met John in the summer of 1952 at the Banff Springs Hotel when I was his caddy master and where I introduced him to the finer points of golf.

The following summer, we returned to the hotel as bellhops. I took him mountain climbing (to Mt. Temple, which at 11,636 feet is the third highest mountain in the Rockies). He was so dangerous that I refused to rope-up with him and he had to rescue himself when he slid down a couloir.

I tried to get him dates (500 University girls at Banff) but he insisted on wearing his U.C.C. sweater—which left the girls obviously disinterested. I did manage, however, to get him one date with a Little daughter on condition that I date her sister at the same time.

We reunited in the 1980s and I exposed him to the adventures of floatplane flying in the coastal mountains of B.C.

Later that decade I taught him the "big boy" method of skiing at Whistler, with some success. I failed, however, to educate him in how to shovel snow. John's method is to sit by the fireplace asking when he'll be able to go skiing again.

Then followed a series of enlightenments under my tutelage: entrepreneurship, high finance, pharmaceutical investing, prospecting for gold, and fishing. Finally, in the summer of 1999, I took him camping in the high plateau of the Chilcotin where I saved him from a noisy flap John was convinced was a grizzly clawing at the tent in the middle of the night. This camping trip required that John grasp quickly bad weather flying in the mountains and low-level map reading down the Fraser River. He seemed more interested in taking photographs than keeping watch for hydro wires.

Sharing all these adventures made me think I had some positive influence on John—but I never convinced him to stop running with a "bad crowd" made up of economists, politicians, senators, and other purveyors of untruths. Now, as his memories are fading, I keep them for him, for example, I was Marilyn Monroe's bellhop and confidante at Banff Springs and recorded the experiences with daily writings in my diary. And that's likely to be the only truth printed in this memoir.

Donald W. Hughes, Long-time Friend and North Vancouver Dermatologist

But those golden days also had a sharp edge. My bellhop job taught me how important work rules are and how creative workers often are (or have to be) in the face of them.

We had a lot of rules. One was that bellhops must not tell each other how much they'd made on a particular shift. The stated reason was to keep peace in the ranks. Don and I confided in each other anyway, but to my knowledge all the other bellhops obeyed.

Other rules governed bellhop relations between shifts. The purpose was to prevent one shift from stealing a check-in or check-out from another during shift changes. For example, one rule was that no shift could take guests' baggage up to their rooms until they actually checked in. Don and I paid the front desk staff to let us know if bellhops on the other shift ever pulled a fast one on ours. Sure enough, one day bellhops on the day shift took 60 guests' bags up to their rooms just before the four o'clock shift change and before the guests signed in. They planned to sneak back after the guests had arrived to collect their ill-gotten tips, but Don and I got the room numbers—for a price—and made the rounds first. We didn't share the proceeds with anyone else, not even the other bellhops on our own shift. I thought we'd get killed for this stunt, but we didn't. Maybe it was because nobody could prove anything.

Bellhopping also taught me other important lessons. One was that when you work for tips, you can easily go money mad. You can find yourself driving someone crazy by not leaving the room until you get that tip. I found myself doing that even when the guest was part of a block tour and I was getting a share of the block tip.

You can also find yourself chasing any possibility to make an extra buck. I recall one very dull evening when the Alberta Oilmen's

Convention had taken over the hotel. There was a huge banquet at which the group was giving out all sorts of cups and prizes for various tournaments the Oilmen had run. I spotted an opportunity. When I suggested to the President it would look good to have a bellhop hand him the awards as they were being announced, he agreed. After I did my duty, I insinuated myself into the milling crowd of award-winners who then started tipping me. I was raking it in by the fistful until the President spotted me taking the loot. He came over and asked me how much I'd collected. I had no choice but to count it in front of him. The total was about $70. He congratulated me on my enterprise, handed me another $10, and told me, more or less politely, to get lost. I did.

WORKING WITH CLASS

These jobs were a warm-up for the summer jobs in factories I sought deliberately while I was doing my undergraduate work at the University of Toronto in order to better understand the so-called working class. Of course, I never did learn much about the mentality and perspective of plant workers because, unlike them, I knew I'd be going back to school after Labour Day. But these jobs still taught me a lot. They brought me my first contacts with the labour movement, and they brought me face-to-face with the reality of the drudgery that makes up so much of work in the everyday world. What I found tough to tolerate for just a few weeks was what many people were sentenced to virtually for life.

My most vivid memories are from my summer job in the mid-1950s assembling electric fans in an American Standard plant in Toronto, where workers were represented by the United Steelworkers of America. Many of the workers in the plant were still paid on piecework with the standards based on old-fashioned time and motion studies. The Company apparently felt the standard was too low on one of the jobs I was filling in on and tried to prove it by demonstrating how much faster a summer employee could do the work involved. Everybody except me seemed to know that I was going to be the guinea pig for the time study expert, and I was warned not to beat the existing standard if I wanted to continue to enjoy working there.

When the time study engineers arrived to monitor my performance, I could feel at least a dozen pair of eyes of fellow workers closing in on me. I took the hint and did not beat the standard, which I could have quite easily. Thereafter, I was welcomed by my full-time brothers (there were no sisters) as a most acceptable summer replacement worker.

A couple of years later, in 1956, when I was a graduate student at M.I.T. and the recipient of the Westinghouse Fellowship in Industrial Relations, I had the great good fortune of landing a job working on the issue of automation for what was then the Canadian section of the United Automobile Workers (UAW). The job was at the UAW's Ontario headquarters in Windsor, but I spent a fair amount of time at the Union's head office at Solidarity House in Detroit. It was in Detroit that I saw the Union's president, Walter Reuther, in action several times and came to realize why he was, and remains, the top labour leader ever produced by the American labour movement. His performances at press conferences alone put him in a league by himself.

Walter's idealism ended up making a great difference to me financially because he was a very parsimonious person and took only a modest salary. By tradition, no one else in the Union could earn more than he did, so the only way the UAW could find and keep the calibre of professional staff it needed was to pay very generous expense allowances. Because I was on the road constantly, I was pocketing what to me was a small fortune in the form of established *per diems*. My graduate student spending habits couldn't even begin to eat up my traveling allowance fast enough, and I decided I should return what I didn't use. I will never forget trying to take back money I was not spending. I still recall a wonderful little old lady in Solidarity House's accounting department. She got up, closed her office door, and told me in a shocked tone that I must pocket the money and keep quiet or I would never have another staffer talking to me even if I was lucky enough to keep the job. I took her advice and counsel reluctantly and banked the extra money.

Another challenge arose because I was driving a Volkswagen "Bug." It was my first car and all I could afford as a graduate student struggling to get by on an adequate but hardly generous scholarship. (Just a year

later, in 1957, I was awarded the Ford Foundation Pre-doctoral
Fellowship in Business Administration. Luckily, I hadn't received it
first and used the funds to buy my "Bug." That would have been utterly unforgivable.) Anyway, as a foreign-produced car, the Volkswagen
was not popular with Canadian autoworkers. I was reluctant to use it on
Union business, especially when I was heading to the educational centre
of the Canadian section in Port Elgin to give a progress report on my
work to rank-and-file delegates. But George Burt, who was then the
Canadian Director of the UAW, told me not to worry. He suggested,
however, that I take the precaution of parking in an isolated spot on the
way into the Centre. Unfortunately, I was spotted doing it, and when I
got up to speak, a member of the Council rose on a point of personal
privilege. He challenged me with conduct unbecoming a union member for driving such an infidel product. I thought this was going to end
my union career on the spot, but George saved me. He asserted that as
a struggling graduate student I could not afford to drive an American
car because of the greed of the Big Three auto makers, whose profi-
teering put all of their products beyond my reach. The delegates were
so moved by George's speech that they actually applauded. I became
quite famous (on infamous) in the Union's executive ranks for driving a
hated "Bug."

It was as a Fellow of the Scanlon Plan (1958-1959), however, that I
began to appreciate the potential for harmony between organized
labour and management. The Plan, which was then based at M.I.T.,
motivates an entire workforce, including workers and managers, by
linking them to a common bonus plan based on reducing labour costs as
a share of the total costs of production.

The Plan's premise is that workers know far more about what is
going on in any enterprise than its managers do. Whether organized or
not, workers determine by their co-operation just how efficient, innovative, and productive any operation is going to be. Managers who want
workers to realize their full potential *and* realize the full potential of the
facility within which they work must enlist the co-operation of workers. To facilitate this, joint production committees are established in

each department and at the company-wide level. The idea is that labour and management working together will achieve the common objective of more gains for everyone. Both workers and managers receive a group bonus over and above their normal rates of pay if they manage to lower labour costs as a proportion of the total costs of production on both a monthly and annual basis.

My year as a Scanlon Fellow exposed me to the most positive industrial relations experiences between organized labour and management that I have ever witnessed.

I was assigned to work with the LaPointe Tool and Dye Company, which had a total staff of about 2,500 workers and supplied very refined and sophisticated products to the highly competitive auto industry, and the United Steelworkers of America, which represented the blue collar, and later the white collar, workers at LaPointe. I spent many hours at LaPointe, attended scores of departmental and plant-wide production committee meetings, and witnessed enough encouraging labour-management interactions and relationships to fill a book. I'll give just one example, however.

Before the Scanlon Plan was introduced at LaPointe, co-operation among engineers, draftsmen, and tool-and-dye workers was non-existent. In fact, it was often the reverse. Sometimes, the engineers would design something the draftsmen and later the tool-and-dye workers knew wouldn't work, but they'd go along just to prove the engineers (they called them "the iron ring boys," referring to the pinkie rings engineers are given when they graduate) didn't really know as much as they thought they did.

After the Scanlon Plan was introduced, this changed because all benefitted if they improved results. Wasted labour reduced bonuses. They learned to pool their skills and work together rather than trying to show each other up. They also expressed more satisfaction with their jobs.

Despite its obvious advantages and benefits, the Plan never took root in industry or commerce. The fault almost invariably lies with management. For the Plan to work, there must be a great deal of transparency and a competent and confident management. Pretty well everything is on the table in a Scanlon Plan operation. Management doesn't yield its authority, but it has to live with openness and be prepared to explain its decisions to workers. In my experience, few modern-day managers can live with this kind of challenge. Also, I doubt there are any managers today willing to accept the same bonus system as the workers who report to them.

Whenever I think of John Crispo, I am reminded of that expression—frequently wrong, but never in doubt. John's vehemence and passion highlighted some ideas that were not universally accepted in labour and management circles. But to give him credit, he never had difficulty attracting an audience. In fact, having John Crispo on the program guaranteed an audience. People enjoyed his humour, his perceptiveness about the Canadian labour relations scene, and his "far out" observations, even while they cringed when he pointed out their foibles and prejudices, particularly of the special interest groups and politicians.

One of my responsibilities at McGill University was to organize national conferences on labour relations subjects. John was a frequent speaker at these conferences because I knew everyone would attend these sessions. There was bound to be someone in the audience who would take John on in spirited argument. This made for lively sessions. What impressed me most about John was that he enjoyed the parry and thrust of his opponents more than the remarks of those who agreed with him. To his credit, John never took criticism or opposition personally. He enjoyed the argument.

I've known John for more than 30 years. In all that time, I never stopped regretting and deploring the fact, even to him, that because of his writing and speaking brilliance, he succumbed to media blandishments and spread himself into other areas—family planning, media policy, etc., which distracted him and took him away from the world of industrial relations. This was a great loss to Canadian industrial relations, as in the United States is Harvard professor John Dunlop, now into his eighties. It would have been a great thing for Canada, for industrial relations scholars, and for John. Industrial relations is a dynamic and exciting field of study. It is a rare thing indeed when students can say they "enjoyed" attending lectures. John had the ability to engage and inspire students. I hope he continues.

Frances Bairstow, Arbitrator and Mediator, Former Director,
Industrial Relations Centre, McGill University, Montreal

FROM THE SUBLIME...

My next opportunity to study labour and management relations close up came during my field work for my doctoral thesis. I spent a long and intensive period (from 1958 to 1960) studying the relationship between Ontario Hydro, then called the Commission, and Local 1000, otherwise known as the Ontario Hydro Employees Union (OHEU), of what was then the National Union of Public Service Employees (NUPSE). NUPSE subsequently merged with the National Union of Public Employees (NUPE) to form what is now the Canadian Union of Public Employees (CUPE). I sat in all the major contract and grievance meetings between the parties as well as most of the Union's strategy meetings. Management was never nearly as open with me about its strategies although some of their officials did keep me quite well informed about them.

Local 1000 had a well-educated membership and was very democratic and quite sophisticated in its approach to everything, and Union officials were very generous and patient with me. I quickly became know as "Can I have a copy Crispo" because, of course, I wanted everything I could get on paper so that I could document my thesis in an appropriate academic fashion.

Ontario Hydro's management was far less candid, which no doubt helps to explain why I developed more sympathy for the Union's positions than those of management. The main reason, however, was that the corporation was in the process of shifting from a fairly paternalistic approach towards its employees to a more hard-nosed, business-oriented one.

At the time, I don't think I fully appreciated the reason for the shift. The agreed policy was to keep employee wages and benefits within the upper quartile of the leading industry in the province. As a result, Ontario Hydro workers were always extremely well paid. To this day, the corporation's workers are well treated, making them very costly, very loyal, and a challenge for successive managers as the company faces more bottom line competitive pressures and now almost total privatization.

In any event, my study of Ontario Hydro turned out to be a great learning opportunity and set the stage for even more meaningful work to follow. One of the most enlightening and insightful was my work for Carl Goldenberg (later Senator Goldenberg) as Director of Research for the Ontario Royal Commission on Labour–Management Relations in the Construction Industry. I'll get into more detail in Chapter 4. For now, I'd like to focus on some personal experiences.

The Goldenberg Commission was set up in 1961 by the Ontario government to recommend how to correct the widespread exploitation of New Canadians (then referred to as immigrant labour) in the construction industry in and around Toronto. Recent arrivals from Italy in particular were being employed at very low wage levels and were also expected to pay kickbacks to their bosses. As well, they were victims of a shakedown similar to the one featured in *On the Waterfront*, one of Marlon Brando's most famous movies.

Early every work-day morning, small contractors would drive their pick-up trucks by certain locations around Toronto, but especially near St. Clair and Lansdowne Avenues, where the Italian-Canadian population was then concentrated. Their mission was to find the most desperate workers willing to bid the lowest wage on the spot for a day's work.

Conditions for these workers were particularly poor in residential construction, so some of the unions with solid bases in the commercial, industrial, and heavy construction sectors tried to reach out to help them.

Charley Irwin and Bruno Zanini were two key but maverick union officials during this period. They found themselves in a lot of trouble with the law for their efforts, which involved considerable violence. At one point there were so many law enforcement officials trying to serve subpoenas on them that Charlie and Bruno, together with some of their beefier brothers, commandeered one floor of the then fairly run-down King Edward Hotel in Toronto to use as a secure headquarters.

Carl Goldenberg told me to arrange an interview with these characters as soon as possible to get their side of the story. This was in the early research stage when we were preparing for the planned public hearings. With advance clearance, I headed down to the King Eddie to meet with Charlie and Bruno in their defensive lair. After being searched in case I was carrying a subpoena, I was escorted to the single elevator allowed to disgorge passengers on to their floor. I was taken to a large room, where Charlie, Bruno, and about 10 of their heavies were gathered in a kind of semi-circle to greet me. I was downright scared, but my mouth, which has often saved me, worked better than I had any right to expect. I greeted Charlie, Bruno, and the others boldly, and we settled down for a good bull session. Nevertheless, I admit I was relieved at the time to leave in one piece.

Around the same time, I was also interviewing all sorts of union officials on both sides of the Canadian and American border on the role of international unions between the two countries. One of the most memorable was with Jimmy Hoffa, Sr., when he was President of the Teamsters Union. When I met him in Washington, D.C., Hoffa had completely forgotten why I was coming. When I reminded him, he, like so many of his American counterparts in other international unions, began to rant and rave about those demanding Canadians who always wanted what he thought was special treatment, including more than their share of floor time at the Union's international conventions. The highlight, however, was when Jimmy (which he invited me to call him) took me on a tour of the Teamsters' building, which stands in a very commanding position overlooking the U.S. Congress. The tour culminated in a visit to the boardroom, which was very impressive by any standard. I deliberately avoided noticing what I could tell he wanted me to see, two flags, one American and the other Canadian, behind the imposing chair in which he sat to preside over the Union's Board meetings. Finally, he gave up and told me the two flags were the same size, symbolizing how well the Teamsters thought of and treated their Canadian members.

Before I leave the Teamsters, I want to acknowledge my long association and friendship with Senator Ed Lawson. Some people find both our friendship and Ed himself difficult to understand because Ed served on the International Executive Board of the Teamsters under several presidents who ended up in jail for corruption, fraud, taking kickbacks, and sundry other illegal activities.

Our association started when Ed was Canadian Director of the

Teamsters. As a Teamster, he was an enigma to me because he was so gentlemanly, small in stature, well spoken, and a teetotaler, everything the average Teamster was not. Ed lived very well, as did most officers of the Teamsters because they were paid for every Union position they held.

Ed and I enjoyed many occasions, including flying in the Canadian Teamsters' private jet. The Teamsters' aircraft was the only union-owned jet in Canada until it was sold when the Teamsters for a Democratic Union won control of the Union.

Over the years, I addressed several Teamster conferences and conventions, and I was always amazed by how little power the rank and file delegates had. At best, they were educational affairs. Often, the only contentious issue was where to hold the next gathering. Fortunately, I got to address the Teamsters at some of their more exotic locales.

Although I felt that the Teamsters were not democratic, I never saw any signs of corruption in the Canadian section of the Union. Still, it always bothered me that Ed served on the Board under so many corrupt presidents. It's still hard for me to believe that he could have been completely unaware of all the shady dealings going on around him.

Ed was certainly a different kind of union leader. As I recall, at one time he was a member of both the Capilano and the Vancouver Golf and Country Clubs, had a Chief Justice of British Columbia as a favourite golfing partner, was on the Board of Directors of the B.C. Lions, and sat on a Royal Commission looking into provincial liquor distribution, to which he had been appointed by W.A.C. (Wacky) Bennett, then Premier of the province. He was also well known as a very witty speaker at charity fund-raisers.

To me, the most intriguing story is how Ed became a Senator. He was named to the Senate by Pierre Elliott Trudeau. When Trudeau called, Ed was so surprised he thought it was one of his friends playing the kind of practical joke that Ed himself liked to play. He told the caller to prove he was who he claimed to be by speaking French. Trudeau did, and that satisfied Ed.

Trudeau asked Ed to be a Senator for the most cynical of reasons. Three of Trudeau's closest advisors, Jim Coutts, Keith Davey, and Michael

Pitfield, the "Liberal Mafia" as I liked to call them, had told Trudeau he had to name a labour leader to the Senate so that it would look a little less like a corporate board of directors. Trudeau balked because he was unwilling to name any labour leader affiliated with the Canadian Labour Congress (CLC), which was then vehemently opposing Trudeau's wage and price controls. Luckily, the Teamsters were not then members of the CLC—I can't remember whether the Teamsters had been kicked out or had just withdrawn—with the result that Ed was about the only prominent labour leader in the country who could be deemed acceptable to Trudeau.

Ed told Trudeau that he (Ed) couldn't attend the Senate regularly because of his union business commitments. Trudeau wanted Ed anyway because Trudeau didn't have much regard for either the labour movement or the Senate. To be fair to Ed, he sits as an Independent rather than a Liberal, and he was as delinquent as he promised to be until his union responsibilities ended. From the first, however, he knew how to make use of his new title in Canadian as well as foreign restaurants.

John is a great performer on a platform. That's where we met 25 or 30 years ago. We were on the same panel, and John gave a great presentation. As usual, he never used 10 words when 1,000 would do. He was very assertive and very abrasive, but somehow the audience didn't object.

They never did. I remember the two of us being on a panel during the Trudeau wage and price control era. Someone from the CLC couldn't make it, so I was invited instead, which was unusual because the Teamsters were considered the illegitimate child of labour. Anyway, John attacked the scandalous contractors and had the all-labour audience applauding thunderously. Then, after the applause died down, he attacked labour as being totally unreasonable and greedy. Then I got up and I was booed. I had to remind the audience that, unlike John, I was on their side, but it didn't seem to count.

Whatever the subject, John always gave the impression that he totally believed in his position and was passionate about it. He'd ignite the audience. He might be totally wrong, but he seemed convinced he was right.

The first time we met, I remember thinking, "This man's very bright and he has a sense of humour." We quickly became friends. He's easy to know and easy to work with in the old style. After a vigorous debate, we'd go out for a drink or lunch.

John is passionate, humourous, and I think to some degree frustrated that he was not able to achieve more. He has had an outstanding career by any measure, but I think by his own appraisal he believes he was capable of more.

Senator Edward Lawson

John Fryer was another labour leader I got to know well fairly early on in my career. He played a prominent role in the British Columbia Government Employees Union (BCGEU) and went on to become President of CUPE. He was well and more formally educated than most union leaders, and we found ourselves on the same side of many issues confronting the labour movement.

John and I also enjoyed getting each other into trouble. Once it was during the process of the British Columbia Government Employees Association becoming a union, something Wacky Bennett was resisting strongly. John invited me to deliver the keynote address at the banquet during the Association's annual convention. I tore a few strips off the B.C. government for not recognizing reality and took a few swipes at Bennett along the way. Because I'd arrived late, I didn't know two cabinet ministers were at the head table, and I so provoked them, they got up and walked out. Otherwise, I got a great reception and the Association did become a union.

CLOSE CALLS & BATTLES ROYAL

Shortly after I finished my work with the Goldenberg Commission, I was appointed to the Prime Minister's Task Force on Labour Relations. It was the highlight of my many field experiences in industrial relations. I have Bus Woods to thank for the opportunity.

Prime Minister Lester B. Pearson named Bus Woods, who was Dean of Arts and Science at McGill University, to head the Task Force. Bus immediately arranged to have me named as the second member. Shortly thereafter, we were joined by Fred Carruthers of the University of Western Ontario's Law School and Gerard Dion of Laval University's

Industrial Relations Department. Originally, the Government had planned to name some labour, management, and government members as well but took our advice not to do so. Our view was that with them on board we would inevitably be forced to produce a split report with dissents all over the place.

The Government was reluctant, however, to leave four academics totally on their own and so set up two advisory committees. One committee was composed of an equal number of senior labour and management representatives drawn from across the country. The other was made up of Deputy Ministers of Labour, also from across the country. We Commission members met with both committees regularly and discussed virtually everything with them, including our recommendations as we developed them.

The Task Force was set up after a rash of labour disputes and strikes and some very high wage settlements. For several years, Canada had led the world in time lost due to industrial disputes as a percentage of all time worked as measured by the Geneva-based International Labour Organization (ILO). There was a widespread feeling that our industrial relations system was not functioning as well as it should and that it was time to look for a better way. The Task Force's job was to find this better way.

John Crispo may be the only person I know who's written more books than he's read. Seriously, I used to look forward to debating John and his intelligent, quick wit. Of course, once I began to get the better of him on a regular basis, the challenge was gone!

Nancy Riche, Secretary-Treasurer,
Canadian Labour Congress

We spent two years studying every conceivable aspect of industrial relations, not only in this country, but in most other leading Western industrialized countries as well. Aside from commissioning dozens of studies of Canadian and foreign industrial relations experiences, we interviewed leading representatives of government, labour, and management in Canada and abroad.

The Task Force's mandate gave me contacts that have stood me in good stead for many years. What made these contacts even more interesting and useful to me was my (self-appointed) role as the Task Force's gadfly. I argued forcefully with just about everyone we met and in the process discovered what they were really thinking. Sometimes these arguments got quite heated, which usually meant the next time I came across the individual involved, we simply continued where we'd left off.

When the time came to write the Task Force's report, Bus Woods was so busy contending with student activists that I ended up drafting it. Fred Carruthers edited and toned it down, and Gerard Dion worked on the French translation. Fortunately, we had few disagreements among ourselves and ended up with a unanimous report. But, as expected, we had some rough sessions with the two advisory committees, which were split all over the place on what we were planning and eventually recommended.

I am proud of the work of this Task Force to this day. I believe our report was and remains the most comprehensive and sensible public policy document ever produced in Canada on the subject of industrial relations. Unfortunately, by the time we submitted our report Pierre Elliott Trudeau was Prime Minister. He wasn't terribly interested in industrial relations and was still very much under the spell of Bryce Mackasey, then Minister of Labour, and the labour movement, which Mackasey was courting. Bryce didn't like our report because he believed, wrongly in my view, that our recommendations on dispute settlement would lessen his scope for personal involvement in high profile labour disputes, an involvement he relished.

The labour movement was most upset about our call for a comprehensive bill of rights for union members and for state intervention to enforce those rights if unions did not introduce effective procedural safeguards on their own. Fortunately for them, Trudeau had recently coined his phrase about the state having no business in the bedrooms of the nation. The labour movement imaginatively recast it into something like the state having no business in the union bedrooms of the nation. Trudeau found this approach very appealing and, despite his much acclaimed (but also much undeserved) reputation for being a civil libertarian, refused to ensure union members any rights as such.

Our report had little immediate impact except in B.C. where the provincial labour relations act was amended to reflect many of our recommendations. Later, many of these same recommendations were reflected in legislative changes at both the federal and provincial levels. Nonetheless, it is still a source of frustration to me that we worked so long and hard, produced such a useful report, and had so few of our findings and recommendations implemented either because the politicians did not have the nerve or because they were just using us as a diversionary exercise in the first place.

Despite this frustration, the Task Force experience gave me a big boost. As well as making influential international contacts, it also set me up for a series of joint studies of labour and management relations in different industries. The first was a study for the then Railway Association of Canada and the Railway Labour Executives Association of Canada. Like the subsequent studies, this one provided me with an increasingly intimate knowledge of industrial relations. With each study, I found myself quickly becoming an expert on the relationships between the parties.

Actually, it wasn't difficult to do. I used the industrial relations systems approach for interviews with the key labour, management, and, often government individuals involved. The industrial relations systems approach focuses on the environment in which the parties interact, on the parties themselves, on their interaction mechanisms, and on the substantive results. It's a very convenient framework within which to organize all the facts and opinions the interviewer can gather. Best of all, it allows the interviewer to grasp and understand what is going on in the industrial relations setting of a plant, firm, or industry, or even a country, very quickly.

During this same period, I was also honoured to become Chairman of the Domtar (Dominion Tar and Chemical Company) Joint Labour-Management Co-operation Committee. The Committee evolved from a series of meetings between Wilf Hall, then President of Domtar, and Bill Dodge, then Executive Vice-President of the CLC. Between them, they persuaded a very recalcitrant group of company and union executives to join them for an annual retreat in the Laurentians to try to improve their overall working relationships.

Of all the useful lessons I learned from this intriguing experience, two stand out. One relates to the advantage one enjoys when presiding if one has control over the microphones and, therefore, control over whose remarks are going to be heard (and in this case also translated) first. When I chaired these sometimes very contentious meetings, I had Wilf on one side and Bill on the other. More often than I care to admit, we didn't recognize participants in the order they indicated by raising their hands. Instead, we recognized by whom we thought on both sides were going to make the most constructive comments. I'm sure this approach helped us keep things on the rails several times.

The other lesson was how easy it is to take advantage of ill-informed and naïve reporters and editorial writers. We were under growing pressure from the union representatives at our retreats because they in turn were under mounting pressure from union members to demonstrate they weren't just being co-opted at these sessions. To help ease the pressure, Domtar agreed to a joint statement reflecting the Company's underlying philosophy. The statement asserted that while Domtar's ultimate objective was to maximize the shareholders' return on their investment, the Company wanted first to pay its employees fair wages and salaries, take care of the environment, and serve its customers well. Bland as it was, when Wilf and Bill released the statement at a press conference in Montreal, it was greeted as a tremendous breakthrough by reporters and editorial writers alike.

A few years later Domtar's new management, which was brought in to deal with a serious bottom line problem, junked the statement along with just about everything the Co-operation Committee had achieved or been working on. I guess you could call this lesson number three: what happens when reality rubs up against philosophy in the corporate world.

In 1960, I began attending CLC and Ontario Federation of Labour (OFL) conventions regularly and a few other provincial federation of labour conventions from time to time. These gatherings provided a lot of amusement as well as insights.

I first met John in 1974 or 1975 when I went to the CLC as Executive Vice-President. I met him at conventions and when he came to see Joe Morris. John was always in the wings. How he got there I don't know, but he was always around.

John has an extraordinary intellect and he's very persistent. He needed to be aware and up to date. He had a way of knowing whether he was welcome or not, but he kept asking questions regardless because that's the only way you find out things. That's why some people felt he was a pain in the ass. They felt he was trying to interfere because he was always leaping ahead and anxious to move things forward. That's his style.

The greatest thing about John is that he's one fine teacher. I'm really happy he's a teacher because students need that kind of person. He puts his cards on the table and says, "I may not always agree with you, but we're going to talk." I think young people like that kind of challenge. I'm totally sure he was trying to move his students' minds ahead. You could see he wanted them to get off their butts and look to the future. He used to say, "You gotta move on, Shirl." I used to say, "You're going to be a teacher 'til you go underground and then you'll teach everyone there, too."

John has charisma, but he doesn't let it loose too often. He holds it in reserve. He's a bit shy. He has a little suit of armour on and he won't let his guard down with many people. One interesting thing was his human side came out when we talked about international affairs and human rights. You could read it in his eyes.

Tell John if he disagrees with anything I say, he should go jump in the lake. I'll save him only when he apologizes.

Shirley G.E. Carr, O.C., O.O., President Emeritus,
Canadian Labour Congress

I recall one convention of the B.C. Federation of Labour, when Homer Stevens, head of the British Columbia Deep Sea Fishermen's Union and self-proclaimed Communist, was holding forth on some subject which bore absolutely no relationship to the matter being debated. Big Jack Munro of the then International Woodworkers of America was chairing, and he asked Homer to bring himself back to the subject at hand. Homer brought down the house when he said he would be glad to do so if someone could remind him what that subject was.

Another time, at an OFL convention, there was a resolution on the floor calling for the nationalization of all land in Ontario. One brave delegate had the nerve to ask whether that included the land on which his house was situated. David Archer, who was President of the OFL at the time, quickly huddled with John Eleen, who was Director of Research. How, David asked John, had this resolution ever got on the floor and what was he to tell the inquiring delegate? David and John decided to say that, yes, the land did include that on which the delegate's house was situated but that the land would be leased back to him at a very attractive rate. The resolution was passed with very few votes against, even though all who were really following the issue must have known it would command very little real support either at that convention or anywhere else inside or outside the labour movement.

Over the years, I also witnessed many serious debates about weighty issues, and I couldn't help getting involved. I always had press credentials, which allowed me access to the floor but no voice or vote. Behind the scenes, however, I often became a kind of participant-observer, lobbying for or against a wide variety of major issues. I know I had an effect several times. For me, the one that really counted was developing and instituting a code of behaviour for international labour unions. I also think I had a major influence in the CLC's expulsion of the SIU.

Occasionally I used a very public way to try to influence developments at CLC conventions by writing about them in advance. In March 1978, for example, I published an article in a Toronto newspaper about the contentious issues confronting the CLC convention to be held the following week in Quebec City and how the way in which the issues were resolved would affect the incoming president, Dennis McDermott, who was succeeding Joe Morris.

Two of the key issues involved a Manifesto adopted almost unanimously at a previous convention and the question of Quebec's right to self-determination. A third issue related to how the conventions themselves were managed.

The Manifesto stated that organized labour must have more meaningful input into forming national policy and that it must be achieved through tripartite consultation. In return, unions were expected to show some restraint in their collective bargaining activities. Largely because of this expectation, the Manifesto was subsequently rejected by the major provincial federations of labour, many of the large national and international affiliates of the CLC, and the New Democratic Party, organized labour's political ally. My recommendation was to ignore it or neutralize the Manifesto by adopting resolutions dealing separately with each of the areas it covered.

As to the Quebec question, the Quebec Federation of Labour would be pressing the CLC to endorse Quebec's right to self-determination at this convention and other parties, such as CUPE, the United Steelworkers, and the UAW, would be bound to support it. My position was that, as an important national institution, the CLC had to take a tolerant stand on the issue, support the Quebec Federation of Labour's position, and be prepared to deal with the consequences.

As for managing the conventions, I applauded the democratic philosophy, which permitted rank and file union members to constitute a majority of delegates, but I was concerned about how cumbersome the conventions had become. The result, I said, was that although they looked democratic, they were not in fact democratic. I proposed several measures, including a modified block voting system, to deal with the problem.

The last major battle in which I sided with labour was against Trudeau's infamous wage and price controls. Trudeau imposed these controls only six months after he defeated Robert Stanfield by condemning him for proposing essentially the same thing. Trudeau was another of my heroes until he brought in wage and price controls, saddled Canada with an unworkable Charter of Rights, and multiplied the national debt by a staggering amount. From now on, when it comes to heroes, I'm sticking with Winston Churchill.

But back to wage and price controls. I opposed the controls publicly and widely in speeches and in writing, warning of the dangerous territory into which I felt Trudeau's policies were taking the country. One of my concerns was what was likely to happen when the controls were removed. If the government did not adopt complementary policies to decrease the money supply, cut back federal and provincial deficits, and avoid undue accumulations of economic power in private and public interest groups, I felt that wage and price controls would deal only superficially with Canada's inflationary challenge. The government could keep opposition to the controls temporarily in check by making exceptions for powerful interest groups, but what would happen when the controls were lifted? Would they ever be lifted when there were powerful interest groups for whom the controls were too useful to relinquish? I felt that Canadians were being condemned to a future in which liberal democracy and freedom would be in serious jeopardy.

Later, after the first round of wage and price controls had lapsed, I warned that we could be heading back to them again if we weren't careful. In "The market-based approach: A way to avoid wage controls" (*The Globe and Mail*, October 12, 1981), I expressed my unease with the prospect of new wage and price controls being imposed. I urged Canadians to think carefully about why such policies have so much appeal, why they never solve the underlying problem, and the form such policies might take if it was decided that they must be adopted.

The appeal of wage and price controls is easy to understand. They seem simple and effective in the face of inflation. At the time, inflation was rising, the public was becoming frightened, public pressure on politicians was growing, and economists were giving conflicting advice about what to do.

The problem in my view was that wage and price controls rarely have much effect in the short term and never work in the long term. The rationale for controls is to come to grips with alleged abuses by labour and management by limiting the amounts they are allowed to extract from the economy. But if we really want to curb excessive increases, what we have to do is limit the power of the groups making the demands. Otherwise, all we'll accomplish is an illusionary short-term result.

Setting up a review board to curb flagrant abuses and persistently above average rewards is tempting but flawed because, in the end, a review board's power depends on political will. How many politicians have you met who can stand firmly against powerful, vested, economic interest groups, the very groups most likely to contribute to election campaigns?

Instead of wage and price controls, I recommended looking at two options, a tax-based incomes policy and a market-based incomes policy. A tax-based approach would impose a 100 per cent surcharge on increases above a pre-determined, specified level. The problem, of course, is where to set the levels. A market-based approach could freeze all business costs and incomes except for labour, goods, and services in short supply relative to demand. There are problems with this approach, too, for example, serious administrative difficulties and the expense of monitoring and enforcing them. On balance, however, I felt that the market-based approach was more likely to strengthen the interactions of supply and demand, focus on abuses of economic power, protect the competitive nature of our economic system, and guard against inflation.

Friends & Foes

Many of my experiences with the labour movement were friendly and mutually supportive. I often lent a hand, for example by working with the CLC to restructure what is still a very divided and fragmented labour movement, to develop a code of behaviour for international unions in Canada, and to fight for full-scale bargaining rights for public sector workers. I appreciated the occasions when labour's reaction to my work was positive.

One of those moments came when Ed Finn, the Public Relations Director of the Canadian Brotherhood of Railway, Transport and General Workers, praised my book, *Industrial Democracy in Western Europe: A North-American Perspective*, in *The Toronto Star* ("A lucid look at shop-floor democracy," *The Toronto Star*, May 22, 1978). He began by describing me as "one of those rare academics who not only has made industrial relations his specialty, but can also speak and write about it lucidly, bluntly—and often colorfully." He went on to describe my book as informative and lucid, saying, "It is a crisp and readable account of the many forms of co-determination, economic, consultation, worker representation on company boards, shop-floor democracy and job enrichment that have transformed European industry in the last few decades. It is also an analysis of the many social and economic forces that have combined to effect such sweeping changes in traditional managerial decision-making methods in these countries. And it is, most importantly, a clear headed look at the implications of these European developments for industrial relations in Canada and the United States." He concluded by saying that I had tackled an immensely complicated and controversial subject without oversimplifying and that my book deserved to be read by everyone in positions of leadership or influence. These were fine words of praise indeed, and I treasure them to this day.

Personally, I get along well with many labour leaders. I don't know if they regard me as an ally or friend, but I think they respect me for my intellectual honesty.

Buzz Hargrove, President of the Canadian Auto Workers (CAW), is one labour leader I have always admired despite our many differences over a wide range of public policy issues. Buzz is a very able and articulate spokesperson for his cause and certainly has no equal in terms of public presence among his opposite numbers in the Big Three. At times, it seemed as if I was the only person in the country who dared to stand up to him.

We've debated frequently over the years but never as often and vigorously as we did over the 1997 round of Chrysler negotiations. At the time, I had a three-hour Sunday afternoon talk show on Talk 640 in Toronto. For a while Buzz was such a regular guest in person or by telephone that I began to wonder whose show it was. I distinctly remember one Sunday when he turned up unannounced. Suddenly, there was his face staring at me through the window of the studio. He had just returned from the Chrysler workers' ratification meeting in Windsor and was so full of himself that he just had to tell me all about it on the air.

I've known John for 25 years. We first met when we debated on a number of issues on television. My first clear memory of John is continuing the debate while I gave him a ride home after a television debate.

John has always been on the wrong side of the issues. For example, he said if we signed the Auto Pact, the Americans would take everything south of the border. The exact opposite happened. We've got a stronger industry producing higher quality cars than ever.

We never agreed on anything, but he's getting smarter as he gets older.

Buzz Hargrove, President, Canadian Auto Workers Union

Another labour leader who was a good friend was the late Joe Morris, former President of the CLC and the first non-governmental official to chair the Governing Council of the International Labour Organization (ILO), an international tripartite labour, management, and government organization which works on improving worker rights and standards around the world.

It was a great honour to be elected to this position, and Joe deserved it. It was also fortunate for me because at the time Joe was chairing the council, I was in Geneva for six months as an ILO Visiting Scholar.

There was no comparison in status, of course. I was a lowly soul holed up in a basement office without secretarial assistance or any other amenities. Joe didn't stand on ceremony, however, and he asked for me, paid a visit, and treated me like a long lost friend. This did not escape the attention of the ILO officialdom, and soon after his departure I was elevated me to a wonderful office overlooking Lake Geneva and provided with generous secretarial help.

But this was not the end of Joe's good deeds on my behalf, even if he wasn't always aware of them. I really needed his help again when I wrote the article every Visiting Scholar was expected to contribute to the ILO's *International Labour Review*. My piece strongly condemned Prime Minister Trudeau's wage and price controls. The ILO didn't want to publish it because it might offend the Canadian government, a risk the ILO didn't want to take because of our country's long standing support of the ILO. However, as soon I mentioned my intention to contact Joe about this censorship, which I knew he would oppose both in principle and practice, my article was printed as submitted.

Some of my experiences with the labour movement, however, were a lot less pleasant and got me thoroughly agitated. One really nasty one involving the Seafarers' International Union (SIU), which was as corrupt on both sides of the border as any union could be. Paul Hall was the leader in the U.S.A. and the infamous Hal Banks was his chief ally in Canada. What disturbed me most was the power the SIU had in the U.S.A. It extended all the way to the White House when John F. Kennedy, a hero of mine for a time, was President.

One of the intriguing aspects was why Hall had so much power in the States and how he was able to use it to protect Banks, who controlled the Canadian vote and who had contrived to put Hall in a position most useful to Banks. To maintain his presidency of the SIU, Hall needed the Canadian vote to protect him from the Union's east-west coast split south of the border. In turn, George Meany, the long-time President of the AFL-CIO, didn't need Banks but did need Hall because Hall controlled the maritime union votes. This in turn enabled Meany to block Walter Reuther of the Autoworkers from taking a real run at leadership of the federation. Also, in turn, President Kennedy needed George Meany because Meany controlled the bulk of the labour votes at Democratic Party conventions as well as labour funding of the Democratic Party's election campaigns.

How did all of these machinations affect Canada? When the Norris Commission, a federal Royal Commission investigating corruption and violence in shipping on the Great Lakes, found the Canadian wing of the SIU to be at the centre of a very corrupt relationship with Canada Steamship Lines, the Commission made the unprecedented recommendation that all the unions involved be placed under a temporary trusteeship. The Americans were so upset about this that they demanded there be at least one American, if not a majority of Americans, appointed as a trustee even though the trusteeship applied only on the Canadian side of the border. At one point, it seemed as if the Canadian government, then in the hands of the Liberal Party, was going to agree, but to its credit the CLC refused, stood firm, and forced the Canadian government to stand up to the U.S. on this issue.

While the CLC could be proud of this stand, its position with respect to SIU membership of the CLC itself was less admirable. Despite the best efforts of many people, including me, the CLC could not bring itself to expel the SIU for corruption. The CLC did eventually expel the SIU, but it was for another reason—raiding the Canadian Brotherhood of Railway Transportation Workers, which had fought the SIU corruption on the Great Lakes with the help of Upper Lakes Shipping. The practice of raiding is very common in the labour movement and seldom gives rise to expulsions. So the CLC was really expelling the SIU for corruption but didn't have the courage to do so directly.

My antagonistic relationship with the SIU didn't end with its expulsion from the CLC. When Hal Banks was allowed to flee to the U.S. to escape assault and battery charges, he was replaced by Red McLachlin, who was even more of a puppet of Paul Hall. When I continued my public criticism of the SIU for its corrupt practices, Red invited me to visit the SIU's Canadian headquarters in Montreal. I didn't think I could refuse, but I notified some friends in Montreal and the Montreal police to let them know when I was going and should be expected to return.

As soon as I entered the SIU's Montreal hiring hall, Red introduced me to the nurse on duty and told her I thought she was corrupt. I told her that I didn't know anything about her moral standards, but that I did know she was working for a corrupt organization.

Red finally took me into his office-boudoir, which combined many exotic features, as well as a folding wall at one end of the very large room overlooking the St. Lawrence Seaway. At the push of the button, the folding wall parted and there sat Red's Canadian Executive Board. We exchanged some inconsequential small talk, some pleasant and some less pleasant, and soon thereafter I left relieved that it was over.

The night after I returned from Montreal, my family was awakened by police pounding on our front door. When I called out from the upstairs window, the police asked me whether I was beating my wife or kids. I produced my family and showed that they were all safe and sound. The police cars that had descended on our quiet residential street left. Shortly thereafter, the fire department arrived in full force to tell us there was a report that our roof was on fire. Fortunately, this was not the case. The police then returned to ask if I had any enemies who might have been responsible for these false alarms. We speculated about my students, but since it was mid-term and I hadn't failed anybody yet, we dismissed student action as the cause. We all felt it was probably just a bit of SIU harassment, but we never had any proof.

Several years later, I was in Geneva and ran in to Red, who had ended up running the maritime workers' safety program for the ILO.

He'd been nominated to this sinecure by the Canadian government, which wanted him out of the country once he, like Banks, became an embarrassment to all concerned. For me this was another example of being looked after if you have enough dirt on those in power. Red surely had, especially about SIU contributions to the Liberal Party's coffers.

My more or less harmonious relations with the labour movement as a whole began to become seriously unglued when I started to side with governments against further wage and salary demands by public employees, although I still generally defended free collective bargaining, including strikes in the public sector. I began taking this position in the 1970s and 1980s, and I was still at it when Mike Harris and the Conservative Party came to power in Ontario in the 1990s. The advice I gave to Premier Harris (in "Public Sector Collective Bargaining Has Failed," *The Toronto Star*, February 21, 1996) was typical of what I had to say on the subject.

After reminding readers that I was a long-time defender of free collective bargaining in the public service and a consistent voice against any kind of wage and price controls, I admitted that my resistance was weakening. Why? Because I saw private sector workers absorbing significantly bigger pay cuts and more lay-offs than their public service counterparts during what appeared to be a recession without end. I noted that I opposed the social contract introduced by Bob Rae when he was Premier of Ontario because I felt across-the-board wage and salary rollbacks would be more fair overall.

I then turned my attention to Mike Harris's cutbacks in transfer payments to the MUSH (municipalities, universities and colleges, schools, and hospitals) sector. I had no quarrel with the general thrust of these cutbacks. In fact, I approved of them because I felt they were necessary if we were to deal with the fiscal challenges facing the province. But I felt that the loose way in which public service collective bargaining was then practised would prevent the public service from dealing properly with these cutbacks and the price would be considerable acrimony and bitterness. I also felt that the traditional recourse to arbitration was a problem because most arbitrators are more concerned with what I called their ABCs (acceptability, batting average, and credibility) than the merits of the disputes they were called upon to judge.

I recommended that the Harris government adopt a short-term strategy to short-circuit the lopsided collective bargaining system and a longer-term strategy to restore a degree of workability. In the short-term, I advised suspending collective bargaining in the public service on the grounds that the province was facing a fiscal emergency. The government should then order across-the-board wage and salary decreases as required to balance the province's books. I guessed that the decrease would be in the range of 10 per cent over two or three years. To prepare for the long-term, I advised that the government should permit strikes but ban compulsory arbitration.

I realized that I was contradicting much of what I had taught and written previously, but I believed that I was justified because of the inherent incompatibility between the province's fiscal needs and negotiating circumstances. As I expected, I was harshly criticized even though, as a professor in a publicly funded university, I would be directly and personally affected and even though I also proposed that an across-the-board rollback should be lower for lower-paid workers and higher for higher-paid workers like myself.

During the 1960s and early 1970s, John Crispo was seen as a friend of labour and I remember well his steadfast defense of free collective bargaining. However, into the late 1970s and beyond, John sharpened his views on such matters as inflation and free trade. His friends in the trade union movement did not change theirs and the honeymoon was over.

John Fryer, President Emeritus,
National Union of Public and General Employees

BREAKING RANKS

Although my changing views on public service collective bargaining got me into trouble with the labour movement, the coup de grâce came when I split with labour over free trade. I was an early and vigorous proponent of freer trade between Canada and the United States for both practical and theoretical reasons. The Canadian labour movement, however, was dead set against it for what I thought were basically ideological and political reasons that had a lot to do with Canadian labour's antipathy towards the U.S.

As the debate over free trade ignited around 1985, I found myself more and more at odds with the Canadian labour movement. I had many public debates with their senior leaders and spoke and wrote many times against their position.

In February 1986, I was commissioned by Simon Reisman, Canada's chief negotiator, to prepare notes for a speech to be delivered by Prime Minister Brian Mulroney. The draft was titled "Free Trade with the U.S. and the Labour Movement," and it fully set out my own position on that controversial issue. I don't know if the speech was ever delivered or, if it was, whether it was delivered as I wrote it.

My draft dealt with the Canadian government's commitment to free trade and the Canadian labour movement's reaction. Free trade, I said, was vital to Canada's future well-being and its long-term benefits would far outweigh short-term adjustment costs.

My case for freer trade included recognizing the growing protectionism in the U.S. and the devastating effects it would have on Canada, given that more than 20 per cent of Canada's Gross National Product (GNP) was derived from exports to the U.S. and that the U.S. consumed some 80 per cent of Canada's exports. Broader free trade arrangements under the General Agreement on Tariffs and Trade (GATT) would help but would be less effective in protecting Canada's interests than a bilateral free trade treaty with the U.S.

After dealing with the benefits to Canadians (lower prices for consumers, more opportunities for producers, increased employment, a higher GNP for Canada, a higher standard of living for Canadians, and a greater capacity to care for disadvantaged Canadians), I turned to the attitude of organized labour.

Labour, I noted, seemed to believe that Canada could live with the status quo. However, the choice wasn't between the status quo and freer trade; the choice was between freer trade and dealing with growing U.S. protectionism. Even if Canada could stick with the status quo, it wouldn't solve our unemployment problems and deal with our declining standard of living.

I also tackled the ideological and political character of organized labour's objections. After noting that various business groups were pro- or anti-free trade depending on their individual economic interests, I pointed out that organized labour as a whole appeared to be anti-free trade regardless of the consequences for any segment within the movement. For example, the CAW was spearheading the opposition, yet its members were benefiting daily and munificently from free-trade-type provisions under the Canada-U.S. Auto Pact. Why were Canadian auto workers, who enjoyed such immense advantages from a somewhat similar arrangement, denying comparable advantages to workers in other industries? The reason, I suggested, had to be ideological and political rather than practical or realistic.

Organized labour did have some legitimate concerns, however, and one of those was that comprehensive free trade might eliminate more Canadian jobs than it generated. My view was that this pessimism was unwarranted and simply reflected Canadians' inferiority complex, which leads us to underestimate our native entrepreneurship and quality of workmanship. Given assured availability to the massive American market, I was convinced that Canadians would do extremely well.

As for organized labour's contention that free trade would interfere with Canadians' ability to make decisions about a range of socio-economic issues, I was dismissive. The free trade agreement would not touch Medicare, other universal social security programs, our cultural identity, or pose any threat to our political sovereignty. In fact, I said, free trade would strengthen our most cherished institutions and values because it would strengthen our economic foundation and, thus, our capacity to protect them.

Finally, I dealt with the question of conditions and concessions. Canada would not pursue free trade at the price. It would not give undue concessions on anything relating to cultural heritage, Medicare and other universal social security programs, political sovereignty, or Canada's position as a separate country. We would insist on a flexible foreign exchange rate between the two currencies as a balancing mechanism should one or the other country be faring disproportionately badly in relation to the other. For example, if Canada was faring badly under free trade, the Canadian dollar would fall relative to the U.S. dollar, thereby improving our competitive position and correcting the situation. I also discussed the lengthy phase-in period, the joint machinery to oversee implementation and deal with later disputes, and the much higher penalties that would result for the U.S. if it decided it wanted to reverse or cancel the agreement.

I concluded with the assurance that the Canadian government would never do anything to jeopardize Canada's cultural, social, political, or national interests, and I urged organized labour to play a constructive and responsible role in the negotiations.

As I said, I don't know whether my speech was ever delivered by the Prime Minister, but I certainly delivered similar speeches across the country. One result was many ugly encounters with organized labour. One of the worst occurred at an OFL convention when labour's antagonism about free trade was at its height.

I had come to the convention with press credentials as usual and was sitting at the media table at the front of the hall when the trouble began. The first clue, which I missed, was that other members of the press who had been sitting with me seemed to evaporate. So much for media solidarity or support, assuming it ever existed.

A delegate grabbed a floor microphone on a point of personal privilege and announced there was a traitor in the house. He denounced me and, within moments, the entire convention was on its feet shouting, "Shame! Shame! Shame! Out! Out! Out!" I held my ground. As the volume rose and the atmosphere got tenser, an OFL official advised me to duck under the platform if things got out of hand.

The debate erupted. Old friends of mine, like Cliff Pilkey, President of the OFL, and Buzz Hargrove, President of the CAW, argued that it was an open convention and that I had press credentials permitting me to be there. The delegates finally began to settle down when Buzz told them I should be allowed to stay because I might learn something. Eventually, the convention resumed its regular order of business, and I departed as inconspicuously as I could. I would have stayed longer, but I had to teach a class back at the university.

I saved John's ass at an OFL convention. The free trade debate was at its height and the OFL was totally opposed. Somehow, John and Tom D'Aquino (of the Business Council for National Issues) got press credentials. When delegates saw John walking around the floor, they wondered how he had the gall. I wasn't surprised.

Anyway, one delegate got the microphone and demanded that John be thrown out. I got another microphone and said it was only fair to let him stay and maybe he'd learn something. The delegates voted to let him stay.

Buzz Hargrove, President, Canadian Auto Workers Union

Although public sector wage controls and free trade were the two biggest bones of contention, I also found myself at odds with the labour movement on other issues from time to time. A more recent one was in 1997 during Ontario's first province-wide teachers' strike. Although I felt that the Mike Harris government had handled itself poorly when it introduced Bill 160 and lost the public relations' war with the teachers' unions, I still tended to side with the government. For me, the critical issue was who should manage public education and the schools.

In 1980 and 1981, long before Bill 160 and the 1997 strike, I served on a three-person committee charged with reviewing Bill 100, the legislation then governing collective bargaining between teachers and their school boards. I was named by William Davis, then Premier of Ontario, and Dr. Betty Stephenson, then Minister of Education. In an effort to get a unanimous report for "Wild Bill" and "Betty the Bull," as I liked to call them, I compromised by backing off in my strong feelings that principals and vice-principals be pulled out of the teachers' bargaining units so as to ensure some management presence in the schools. I've regretted it ever since, and I suspect that my strong public support of Mike Harris years later on this issue was at least partly due to my urge to undo the past.

What I said in one of my articles during the Bill 160 brouhaha ("The Teachers' Strike about Control and Power," *The Toronto Star*, November 7, 1997) was that much as I sympathized with teachers, I was disturbed by the strike because I felt the goal of the teachers' unions and its leaders was simply to acquire more power and control.

I meant what I said about sympathizing with teachers. They have to deal daily with the results of poor parenting, cope with the problems of crime, drugs, and sex that society prefers to ignore, and compete for their students' attention in a world of instant electronic gratification, all while trying to give students a solid education.

I also meant what I said when I accused the teachers' unions and their leaders of seeking enhanced power and control under the guise of seeking quality of education and protecting the well-being of parents, students, and teachers.

I pointed out that most of the content of Bill 160 was precisely what the government promised to do when campaigning for election. Moreover, none of it is irreparable or irreversible. The proper course for the unions and the leaders is to mobilize teachers and other supporters to replace the government with one more to its liking the next time around. I also pointed out that few school boards are any match for the unions or their leaders either in contract negotiations or day-to-day administration. The imbalance results in most school boards ceding control to the teachers' unions because the boards have to be very selective about which battles they will fight.

Finally, I dealt with the issue of principals and vice-principals being removed from the teachers' bargaining units. Someone, I said, has to represent management in the schools and that can only be the principals and vice-principals. If the unions and their leaders object, it can only be because they fear that their control and power will be weakened by having to answer to management in the schools as well as to the management and officials of the school boards. I admitted that the government was fighting the same battle for power and control. The difference was that the government was elected and could be unelected by the public at large, while the unions and their leaders weren't and couldn't.

If the Harris government was so wrong-headed about its educational policies, I concluded, the proper course was to defeat it democratically through the ballot box rather than defy it illegally on the picket line.

Balancing Acts

I've written many articles explaining where I stand on the basic rules of the game governing labour and management relations. For me, it's a matter of balancing competing interests and trying to be fair to all.

One piece I wrote before I began work on these memoirs was in reaction to what I interpreted as Bob Rae's attempt to pay the debt he owed organized labour for its help in electing him as the Premier of Ontario, the first New Democrat to achieve this rank. I also used this piece as the basis for my testimony before the Ontario Legislative Committee Dealing With Proposed Changes in the Ontario Labour Relations Act in 1991.

Bob and I have a long-standing relationship that stretches back to his days as a graduate student at the University of Toronto. Although he wasn't my student, he spent two years as my graduate teaching assistant. I admire and respect him, but I was absolutely against his proposed labour code because I felt that he'd lost all sense of balance and fairness.

John was one of the first to understand the tensions between hard-nosed business unionism and the more politicized phenomenon, particularly in public sector unions. He always believed there were real limits as to how far private sector union members would go to support some political causes. John was farsighted and foresighted in this regard. For example, John was very sceptical about whether the average private sector union member would be comfortable with some political causes associated with the NDP.

What made John a little bit of a radical was his bombastic and iconoclastic style. He was different from other academics in that he studied and understood the labour movement. Many of his conclusions were cautiously conservative, but he remained an admirer of labour. He was totally unstuffy. He'd go to union conventions and get out on the floor and argue. That's what gave him his entrée.

The Honourable Bob Rae, Former Premier of Ontario
and now Partner, Goodmans LLP

Although I acknowledged that the proposed labour code had many positive attributes, including extending the labour relations act to cover previously neglected groups such as agricultural workers, domestics, and professionals, I questioned why others, like public servants and teachers, continued to enjoy the special protections of statutes covering them alone. My theory was that Bob owed his union allies a tremendous debt for the part they played in his rise to political power. I argued that to be consistent and to prove that he was not repaying a debt for services rendered, he should place all workers under the same law for collective bargaining purposes.

I also took issue with many of the provisions, such as those limiting management's right to operate during a strike. I felt that the right to operate during a strike should be permitted, subject to reasonable regulation. For example, management shouldn't be allowed to pay replacement workers more than it did regular workers either directly or indirectly. This type of safeguard would most certainly eliminate all professional strike-breaking activities.

I also objected to the proposed new certification procedure for unions, which could be done without a secret ballot if 50 per cent of eligible workers in a bargaining unit signed a card indicating they agreed to be represented by a particular union. Again, I felt that proper safeguards would prevent management from engaging in inappropriate practices to prevent workers who wanted to unionize from choosing to do it, just as other safeguards would prevent unions from forcing workers reluctant to unionize from refusing to do it.

My argument was choosing to unionize or not unionize was a critical choice and should be made as democratically, fairly, and honestly as possible. What disturbed me most was that the proposed legislation signalled that Bob and the NDP were just as lacking in principles as the old-line parties when it comes to backing their friends.

After the Conservatives defeated the New Democrats, one of Mike Harris's first commitments as Premier of Ontario was to rescind Bill 40 and replace it with something more balanced and fair. I declared my support, but encouraged Harris to be reasonable rather than vindictive. This article, "New Labour Law Needs to be Fair, not Extreme," was published in *The Toronto Star* on September 28, 1995.

My final words about the Canadian labour movement have to be an expression of disappointment and frustration. Ever since I wrote my monograph and book on international unionism, I have believed that truly international unions—as opposed to the bilateral unions we have between Canada and the U.S.—are the only means organized labour has of effectively countering the power of multinational corporations. Yet Canadian labour has been gradually moving away even from its bilateral links with American labour and has shown little or no interest in broader international unions.

Capital knows no boundaries, loyalties, or nationalities. But when it comes to union membership and solidarity, workers in Canada seem incapable of looking beyond very narrowly defined geography and interests. Meanwhile, union leaders speak fine, flowing words in international labour federations and trade secretariats for individual industries, while jealously guarding their status at home and refusing to yield any real autonomy or authority to an international labour body, even though it might well serve their members much more effectively in the long run.

I admit, however, that my fear about what would transpire if the CAW broke away from the UAW has not yet come to pass. I still believe, however, that what I wrote about this danger in 1984 is still valid. In "White driving a risky route for workers" (*The Globe and Mail*, December 10, 1984), I discussed Bob White, the articulate, bright, charismatic, Canadian Director of the UAW, and the danger I felt his stance posed to the well-being of the members of the Canadian UAW. I also felt he was exploiting differences between the Canadian and American members of the UAW rather than using his considerable abilities to bring them closer together.

I first met John in the early 1980s. I'd seen him around before, but that was when our contact started. During the Bill Davis government, we both spoke to changes proposed for the Ontario Labour Relations Act. They were minor, progressive changes, and I thought John was coming down on the wrong side of most of them, but he had great academic reasons for opposing them.

We got to know each other, and I spoke to his Industrial Relations class on several occasions. It was always a lot of fun because I'd cut John to ribbons first.

John was a fierce debater. I loved to be on T.V. panels with him. I always enjoyed it because John knew his stuff. Well, of course, he had all day to study it.

At CLC conventions, John worked the floor like a journalist. It was certainly unusual, but he was pretty successful in making contacts with the labour movement. I think he fundamentally believed in labour relations, but I'm not sure he encouraged a strong labour union.

We had a falling out at the time when GM was considering closing a trim plant in Windsor. John made a statement on radio that I didn't care about the workers, I only cared for my ego. It struck a sour note, and I was really angry. I called him and said it was over the top and I wouldn't speak to his class any more. Eventually, time healed the wound.

The best things about John are that he's challenging, engaging, energetic, and persevering. He's very interested in what's going on, and he has opinions about a lot of things. Some were really right; a few were really, really right.

John is an engaging character. I used to think that he would chose whatever side of the issue that was against the tide of opinion because it gave him his best chance of getting the most invitations to speak and the best media coverage because he'd be the lone voice. In fact, John came down on both sides of most questions, given enough time between them.

Bob White, Former President, Canadian Auto Workers,
and Former President, Canadian Labour Congress

In 1984, the issue was full autonomy for the CAW. White was arguing for it, and he was mounting a full, frontal media assault to help him win his case. In my view, he was looking for an excuse to break away from the international union for reasons that were not clear at the time. I speculated that he wanted to use a severed Canadian UAW as a nucleus to build a European-style metalworkers' union. In my view, this course of action could jeopardize further investment in the auto industry and the competitive labour cost advantage enjoyed by Canadian auto plants and undermine the Auto Pact.

Since Bob White's breakaway attempt in 1984, circumstances and conditions have changed for both labour and management. The Free Trade Agreement (FTA) and the North American Free Trade

Agreement (NAFTA) have rejigged the picture as have the increasing influence of global market forces. As borders dissolve and the nature of work evolves, perhaps my dream of effective international unions will emerge and crystallize into reality.

In the meantime, there is one issue on which labour and I have again found total agreement and common cause. The issue is the outrageous levels of remuneration that senior executives in this country receive, while piously telling unionized and non-unionzed workers to restrain their demands so that their companies can maintain their competitiveness and provide them with some income and job security. The result is growing disparities in distribution of income, especially between those at the very bottom and those at the very top of the economic scale. I believe this can and will undermine the degree of underlying social consensus which our type of socio-economic political system must have in order to survive.

I have condemned these executives as greedy, hypocritical, obscene pigs, with very long snouts deep in a trough which they refuse to share with others. Wouldn't it be ironic if those who end up destroying the basis for the success of capitalism turn out to be those who have benefited most from it?

I saw John in action recently (at a meeting in April 2001).We were having a struggle over the pension surplus at U of T.The main battle is between the retirees and the actives, more so than between the Faculty and Management.

We've been having great difficulty negotiating improvements in pension benefits in line with the large surplus (U of T hasn't contributed for years) and with benefits offered at other universities.The retirees and the actives have had trouble in the past. Retirees haven't been kept well informed and haven't been well represented. After about a year of bad blood, things got resolved at the meeting in a much more amicable way.

John gave a very statesmanlike speech. He helped to bring the two parties together. His knowledge and experience in Industrial Relations was really helpful. He said the worst struggles are usually within the union camp between factions. He helped bring the two sides together. He was an elder statesman and I thought him very effective. So that was "John the Peacemaker." He's also "John the Shit Disturber."

Peter Russell, O.C., Professor Emeritus,
Department of Political Science, University of Toronto

Chapter 3

Up and Down
the Corporate Ladder

My relations with the business community have always been ambivalent, complex, itinerant, and tentative, even during the many periods when I supported the positions generally held by corporate Canada on contentious issues, such as worksharing, equal pay for work of equal value, the National Energy Program, and free trade. In fact, throughout my career, corporate leaders have been wary of me and, at times, suspicious of my motives. This is still true to a considerable extent.

My guess is this is due to my long-standing, very close relations with the labour movement. Even after I parted company with organized labour, I found corporate Canada a chilly place to be and its representatives unwilling and unable to accept me without reservations. I believe this is because I make judgements based on principles and facts. I cannot and will not set them aside or close my eyes to rights and wrongs to avoid embarrassing friends or allies. More pliable thinking, however, is essential for being a good corporate team player, and people who aren't consistently good corporate team players are rarely admitted to the charmed inner circle. When they are admitted, it is with conditions and strings attached.

I also find it interesting that while I have long supported labour unions, it has always been in the context of supporting a hierarchy of institutions and values that centre on capitalism and free enterprise. My approach, therefore, has been intellectual rather than emotional. I am comfortable examining the hierarchy and debating the contribution of all its components. Lack of emotion is often equated with lack of commitment, however, and corporate Canada hates what it perceives as lack of commitment just as much as the labour movement. Both see it as grounds for suspicion.

Once suspicions are aroused, especially in the absence of hard evidence or absolute proof, it's doubly hard to set them aside or lay them to rest. In corporate management circles, suspicions about me have lingered from the beginning of my career in industrial relations, and I don't think they will ever be totally laid to rest.

And yet I have always drawn a distinction between labour unions and collective bargaining in principle and labour unions and collective bargaining in practice. I've always believed that the labour movement should be strong enough to balance the power of employers. But that doesn't mean that every workplace has to be unionized and every employee should be part of an organized bargaining unit. Far from it.

I used to tell my students that if I were an employer, I would establish above average wages, salaries, fringe benefits, and working conditions. I would hire topnotch human resource experts to help me create a corporate culture that not only ensured my employees saw no need for a union but also motivated them to join management in a common cause to build the enterprise to our mutual advantage. I would do everything possible to avoid unionization so as to retain the flexibility and freedom to operate efficiently and to avoid the fine print and work rules one finds in most collective agreements and which stand in the way of becoming more competitive and profitable.

I've found it both amusing and frustrating to watch the public, labour, and corporate perception of me move from pro-labour to pro-management. My own perception is that I have been pretty balanced and fair over my career and that any perception of me as pro-labour or pro-management or left-wing or right-wing is based on a single issue rather than a considered judgement based on my overall record.

My non-academic contact with John was watching him work with some young people in an incubator business. This is something to admire. He is the very opposite of a bully. He'll take on big people; at the same time, he's very supportive and patient with young people. He'll fight battles with those who are his match. People of integrity take on people who can fight back. Bullies pick on the weak. John's no bully.

Eric Kirzner, Professor of Finance,
The Joseph L. Rotman School of Management, University of Toronto

---

WORKSHARING

The first single, major issue that seemed to make observers think I was changing my spots from pro-labour to pro-management was worksharing, a notion that surfaces periodically as a solution to unemployment problems. Every time it pops up, I sound off against it, as I did in *The Globe and Mail* in 1984 ("Work-sharing: cure or curse?" *The Globe and Mail*, April, 24, 1984).

I refer to worksharing as a purported cure because by definition it is bound to do more harm than good. It seems so easy and so logical: Spread the available work among more workers and reduce unemployment, erase overtime, and give all workers who are able and fit to work an opportunity to earn a living. The problem is that worksharing tends to convert full employment for a smaller number of workers into underemployment for a whole lot of workers.

Not that I have ever quarrelled with the desire to work fewer hours and take more and longer holidays. Historically, this income-leisure choice involves a trade-off between making more money and taking more time off. As productivity improves, employers are in a better position to offer workers the opportunity to choose the way they prefer to receive their share of the proceeds—more time off or a wage or salary hike. The problem is that most employees want both. Yes, they want shorter working hours, but they also want to keep their incomes and purchasing power at least comparable to the level they have already reached and preferably continue to move up the economic scale.

Worksharing can be a useful tool in the short-term, for example, to avoid layoffs during a recession, technological change, or some other disruption. But when it's held up as a long-term solution to chronic unemployment, it won't work. The unwillingness of most workers to accept a proportionate reduction in wages and benefits is one fly in the ointment. Another bigger and more troublesome fly is the "lump of labour" fallacy. This mistaken idea holds that there is a fixed and immutable amount of work to be done at any given time and that it can simply be divided by the number of people willing to work to arrive at the number of hours each worker should work. The difficulty is that the amount of work ebbs and flows with external and internal developments, such as the state of the national and global economy, the value of the Canadian dollar compared with other currencies, the demand for a particular product or service, and so on. Also, of course, just having bodies available doesn't mean that all of those bodies, however willing, are able to do the type of work needed at that particular time. Are machinists, graphic designers, physicians, and C.E.O.s interchangeable?

EQUAL PAY FOR WORK OF EQUAL VALUE

Around that same time, the issue of equal pay for work of equal value started to push itself onto the political and social agenda in Ontario. My position made many corporate managers wonder whether I was as pro-labour as they had thought.

In 1985, I addressed what I called an attack on economic reality by the Liberals, who were then governing Ontario with the assistance of the NDP. (Work of equal value was one issue; the others were extended rent controls and opposition to free trade.)

The problem with opposing equal pay for work of equal value was that I was seen as denying that women were disadvantaged in the world of work. My position was that I was against equal pay for work of equal value because I was so aware of the disadvantages women faced. In my judgement, equal pay for work of equal value dealt with superficial symptoms rather than underlying, fundamental, chronic problems facing women in the workplace.

Systemic discrimination was still well-entrenched back in 1985. Although conditions for women had improved, relatively few were actively encouraged to think about careers beyond the stereotypes of the caring professions. Nor were they encouraged to think about rising to the executive suite, even if that executive suite was in a hospital where they started work as floor nurses. The old boys' network was firmly in control, which made it difficult even for self-employed women. Looking back, it seems hard to credit, but it was a given that to rise to the top of any ladder a woman had to demonstrate considerably more ability than the typical man climbing beside her. Sad to say, this is still true today, especially in business.

For me, the answer wasn't equal pay for work of equal value. It was ensuring that women were granted equal access and opportunity to whatever careers they wanted to pursue. It meant getting rid of the discriminatory barriers women faced in education and employment. It meant insisting that all institutions, beginning with public institutions, prove that they operate without discriminating on the basis of sex.

I didn't think that trying to equate the value of the work by a lower-paid female telephone operator with a higher-paid male parking lot attendant was to the point. I did think that it made much more sense to make sure that women could have equal access to jobs as parking lot attendants and not be held back by outdated, outmoded, and unfair ideas of what was appropriate work for women and what wasn't.

I also reasoned that equal pay for work of equal value does more harm than good because it pretends to attack the basic issues of access and opportunity without coming to grips with them. For example, if one assumes that everyone doing the same or a comparable job must be paid at the same rate, except for some allowance for merit and seniority, how does one deal with variations in demand within categories? The example I cited then was university professors. It would seem fair to pay all university professors the same salary, adjusted for merit and seniority. But universities draw on talent from a broad range of fields, and the income-earning potential in those fields varies dramatically. Is it fair to pay a professor of medicine at the same rate as a professor of industrial relations? Would a university be able to recruit any professors of medicine if it insisted on paying them at the same rate as professors of industrial relations? Quantity and quality are fundamentals that have to be accounted for. Equal pay for work of equal value skips over quantity and quality as if they didn't exist.

I argued that in the long-run, equal access to education and opportunity is the only solution to this systemic problem. Of course, I realized that it was cold comfort to women then trapped in the pink ghetto. But I still felt that equal pay for work of equal value was counterproductive at best and harmful at worst, and I urged the Liberal-NDP provincial government of the day to reject it.

Fifteen years later, as I watched the federal government dole out its multi-billion dollar pay-off to women in the federal public service in the name of equal pay for work of equal value, I realized how prophetic I'd been in 1985. What a pity that all those resources were wasted on comparing apples and oranges when they could have been used to ensure equal access, an issue that still hasn't been satisfactorily or fully resolved.

John saw all these stockbrokers with Grade 10 educations making all kinds of money. He figured he could, too, because he taught business. He had this idea that it was easy. First it was a company called RSI, a penny stock on the Alberta stock exchange. Then it was a yogurt company, an oil company, a smart card company, any number of ventures. None ever made money. He'd get everyone involved in his schemes, his friends, his brother, his mother, widows and orphans, anyone.

John Gilfillan, Q.C., Long-time Friend

TRUDEAU & INTERVENTIONISM
The idea of an all-encompassing industrial strategy for Canada was another issue that got me all worked up and seemed to mark me as more pro-management and less pro-labour. In 1981, I began speaking and writing on that topic and others related to the federal government's interventionism, including the National Energy Policy and constitutional reform. In fact, I set the stage for all my subsequent public policy work in a speech I gave to the Society of Management Accountants in Toronto in May of that year. That same year, I gave virtually the same talk to all of the Society's chapters across the country.

I began by dealing with the notion that if one is pro-Western Canada, one is judged as automatically against Central or Eastern

Canada. I regarded this as a false belief and noted that I felt that Central Canada's single most promising future market was in a prosperous Western Canada. (Bear in mind that in 1981 free trade wasn't yet part of the picture.) I also referred to the threat of separatism in the West, which I described as not imminent but not to be discounted entirely.

Canada, I said, enjoyed tremendous potential—land, space, water, virtually every other resource, the possibility of energy self-sufficiency, an educated people, a sound communications system, a solid transportation system, and ready access to the United States, the single wealthiest market in the world. The question was why Canadians weren't realizing this tremendous potential. My answer then was that we lacked certainty and confidence about the future in terms of a number of critical public policies. Energy and the constitution were two of them, but there were others as well—competition, inflation, trade, and the notion of an over-arching, federal industrial strategy.

I dealt with the notion of a federal industrial strategy first. The initial problem was to define it. I could accept a strategy if it was defined as that collection of framework or general public policies designed to ensure a high level of economic performance based on a private sector that is certain and confident and therefore more likely to be efficient innovative, productive, and profitable. It seemed, however, that the federal government had something else in mind—an industrial blueprint based on the view that government can distinguish potential industrial winners from losers and promote the winners while phasing out the losers. I questioned whether politicians are better equipped than the market to make the distinctions and, even if they were, whether they would have the political will to discard the losers. My fundamental concern was that Ottawa's notion of an industrial strategy wouldn't work but would distract Canadians from dealing with the real challenge of addressing fundamental policy needs.

One of those fundamental policy needs was energy. I was appalled by the announcement of the National Energy Program (NEP), which I felt was perverse and wrong-headed. My greatest concern was that it didn't put self-sufficiency and security of supply first. As well, it called for unrealistically low rates of increase in the price of petroleum (the ultimate target was only 50 per cent of world prices), which would not generate the wherewithal to make Canada self-sufficient. Higher prices are one of the most effective ways of encouraging reduction in use and conversion to alternate forms of energy. Higher prices would also bring more money with which to reduce the massive deficit the Feds incurred east of the Ottawa River by buying fuel at the world price and then reselling it at half the price.

I also dealt with the NEP's means of pursuing an otherwise laudable goal of Canadianizing the oil and gas industry. I felt the NEP would be much harder on smaller Canadian companies that the larger multinationals. The result would be that Canadian companies would be swallowed by the multinationals or forced to shift their activity south of the border, which is precisely what happened.

What we obviously needed was a redirected national energy policy that would turn loose an industry that could provide major economic growth for the country as a whole. The policy must provide for rapid movement towards Alberta's offer of 75 per cent of world petroleum prices. I also felt the policy should embody a revenue-sharing formula that provided the industry with a return competitive with the return it could command in the U.S.A. As well, the producing provinces and Ottawa must, I said, renegotiate their shares of the proceeds.

After dealing with the NEP, I turned my attention to the Canadian constitution, which was then in the process of being repatriated. I acknowledged that repatriation should be an occasion for celebration, but I found it impossible to join because of serious misgivings and reservations.

While I favoured repatriation in principle, I objected to it in practice because the process was flawed. It began with what I interpreted as Prime Minister Pierre Elliott Trudeau's insistence that the Liberal Party pursue repatriation of the Constitution at just about any price as a condition for postponing his retirement. This was followed by Michael Kirby's memo setting forth how best to manipulate the provinces to ensure that Ottawa got its way and by the wheeling and dealing with Bill Davis, Premier of

Ontario, and Ed Broadbent, Leader of the federal New Democratic Party, to ensure that Ontario and the NDP were on side.

These manoeuvres rested on at least two major deceptions. One was Ottawa's claim that the Trudeau government wanted a made-in-Canada constitution. The other had to do with the rationale for rushing pellmell through the process. The made-in-Canada desire could have been satisfied by repatriating the constitution together with an appropriate amending formula. As for the pellmell pace, it was argued that it was necessary to assuage Quebeckers who had recently voted to stay in Canada. That sounded reasonable until one discovered that no provincial party and no French-language newspaper in Quebec favoured the patriation package.

Another assertion was that the provincial premiers had been debating a new constitution for years and would never be able to agree. This ignored the fact that two of the most contentious issues in the repatriated constitution—the Charter of Rights and Freedoms and the referendum for resolving future constitutional impasses—had never been discussed at any length.

For me, the Charter of Rights and Freedoms was then and still is the most disturbing feature. It left us with a discomfiting choice: rely primarily on the lawyers and the courts or on the politicians and the legislatures. My concern then was that relying on lawyers and the courts would have the inevitable effect of politicizing the judiciary. I also felt that the Charter as written was so imprecise and vague that the courts would be compelled to take a lead role in interpreting it. Looking back from a vantage point of 20 years, I believe that my fears were justified.

Another greatly disturbing feature was what the constitution lacked. It failed to deal with the need to federalize Ottawa, to make it a more true reflection of the inherent regional sensitivities in the country. I recommended that we reform the House of Commons by injecting a degree of proportional representation and form a House of the Provinces to replace the Senate.

As well, I was greatly concerned about the potential for disunity and discord. Although the provincial premiers had contributed by failing to achieve consensus on constitutional change, the federal government had made the situation worse by changing the rules of the game unilaterally and without warning. I felt that renewing and reshaping the constitution should be a time of coming together, not pulling apart. Canada, I declared, is first and foremost a federation in which good faith and good will are essential between the two key levels of government.

I concluded by saying that Ottawa should start thinking more about what is good for this country and less about the next game it can win. I also said if Ottawa did so and the provinces replied in kind, there would be no holding back this country. I still believe this, and I still believe it is as unlikely today as it was back in 1981.

FIGHTING FOR FREE TRADE

If the business community ever wanted evidence of my propensity for making decisions based on principle rather than long-standing loyalties, it has only to look at my history with free trade. I took up the cause early, and I spent years defending it and fighting for it in the face of fierce opposition from the labour movement. My first major move into the debate was in 1982, when I addressed the Annual Convention of the International Foundation of Employee Benefit Plans. Then, in 1988, at the height of the debate, I took a two-month, unpaid leave of absence from the University of Toronto in order to focus on it full time.

By the time I hit the free trade public speaking circuit in a big way, I had been virtually banned by both CBC and CTV public affairs' producers because of my outspoken criticism of what I regarded as their one-sided, anti-free trade programming. At one stage, the CBC's *The Journal* allowed Bob White, then head of the CAW, to veto my appearance on the major town hall debate the CBC staged. Bob was furious with me because I had called him a double-dealing hypocrite for condemning free trade while he and his union members were benefiting from the Auto Pact. Tom D'Aquino, President of the Business Council on National Issues, was my replacement and spoke very ably for our side, but he was not as emotional or forceful as I would have been.

Tom, by the way, is so articulate and smart, he can take care of himself under any circumstances. During the free trade debate, we tried to figure out how to deal with the phony criticisms aired around us by some of the most inaccurate but media savvy characters this country has ever produced. Even though we often stood together, Tom got used to the fact that I would always find a way to differentiate our positions, however slightly. He understood this was my way of keeping my distance and independence. I think he forgave me because of our common cause and because he knew I had some honest differences of opinion with the business community on other issues.

If John Crispo did not exist, we would do well to invent him.

No Canadian I have ever known in the past 25 years has tackled public policy issues with the same passion, certainty, and irreverence.

His missiles have fallen like rain on hypocrisy, arrogance, and self-interest. But this indefatigable warrior has carried out his crusades with bountiful wit and good humour. And unlike Don Quixote, he has managed to skewer more than his share of windmills.

Thomas d'Aquino, President and C.E.O.,
Business Council on National Issues

Getting back to free trade, I was very effective on the subject, perhaps the most effective I've been on any subject. Those on my side wanted me fully involved even though I was denied access to much of the national electronic media. So, after Brian Mulroney lost the debate with John Turner, I was paid by a group of business people, very few of whose names I learned, to crisscross the country to speak in favour of free trade. But although they financed my cross-country tour, they didn't quite trust me to be out there on my own. They hired Sandy Millar, who was Michael Wilson's constituency office manager, to act as a combination shepherd, coach, mentor, scheduler, and watchdog. For more than a month, she orchestrated an average of two or three debates or speeches a day and an average of a dozen local media broadcasts and interviews.

This experience gave me a taste of what life must be like for politicians during major campaigns. I believed fervently in free trade, and I was on a personal, adrenaline-fuelled high throughout my intensive campaign for approval. But when the campaign ended, my adrenaline level dropped like a stone. I was utterly exhausted and drained, and all I could do was sit passively while waiting to learn the outcome of the 1988 national election. When the results rolled in, I was immensely relieved. It was such a close call. The Tories got just 46 per cent of the popular vote. If the opposition hadn't been split between the Liberals and NDP, the FTA could easily have gone down the drain.

Back in 1982, when I addressed the Annual Convention of the International Foundation of Employee Benefit Plans, I laid the foundation for my part in the free trade campaign to come, but I most certainly wasn't aware of how big the fight would be or how visible a role I would take.

The Foundation's convention is a huge gathering of thousands of Canadian and U.S. labour and management representatives who serve as trustees on various kinds of medical and pension plans. In my speech, "A Latent Continentalist Comes Out of the Closet," I began with a discussion of some biases on the subject of Canadian-American relations. I reminded the Canadians in the audience that we were lucky to share a continent with Americans, who were more benign and palatable than some other alternatives on the international stage. I also talked with optimism about our respective long-term futures, acknowledged that the United States needed Canada less than the other way around, and declared my belief that we would both benefit by working together.

After dealing with aspects of our common heritage and mutual irritants, I discussed two major concerns of the time, acid rain and the Auto Pact, and then tackled the issue of trade. The United States was, I noted, Canada's natural trading partner, and the logical flow of trade was north-south. Yet Canada had always been reluctant to pursue closer economic ties with the U.S., preferring instead protectionist measures. These measures had always benefited certain private vested interests, which were quick to wrap themselves in the Canadian flag and exploit legitimate concerns and fears that many Canadians have about drawing closer to the U.S. Those fears included control over resources, cultural sovereignty, political sovereignty, and, at the extreme end, even Canada's continued existence as a separate entity.

The challenge, I said, was to get our act together. For Canadians, this meant getting over our unwarranted inferiority complex, recognizing the economic facts of life, stepping forward into a closer relationship with the U.S., deciding what kind of deal we wanted, determining what we were prepared to trade in return, and then getting ourselves to the negotiating table.

For Canadians and Americans together, the mutual challenge was to work out our common destiny. Whether we liked it or not, we were inextricably and irretrievably bound, we couldn't escape our mutual dependence, and we would harm ourselves if we failed to find satisfactory accommodations.

I concluded with a plea for everyone to join in a process to bring our countries and peoples closer together.

My speech was a darned good one, so good, in fact, that it became the template for hundreds of other addresses I gave over the years to come. It also got me kicked off the Board of the Foundation because the union members found my position absolutely unacceptable.

FREE TRADE: THE REAL STORY

By the time we got to the peak of the free trade debate in 1988 in Canada, I was doing as much as anyone in the country to further the cause. As well as campaigning across the country, I edited *Free Trade: The Real Story*, which featured essays by 16 Canadians and one American, all well-versed in various facets of the Agreement. (*Free Trade: The Real Story* was published in 1988 by Gage Educational Publishing Company.) All 17 contributors favoured the FTA, but most had some concerns about various facets of it. For myself, by then I was totally committed to it, a position I made clear in the introduction and conclusion I contributed.

While I and others were trumpeting the virtues of free trade, others were arguing equally forcefully against it by fair means and foul. In *Free Trade: The Real Story*, I countered by concluding: "The articles in this book speak for themselves. Given half a chance, so does the Canada-U.S. Free-Trade Agreement (FTA). The problem is that few Canadians are taking the trouble to find out for themselves what this historic agreement is all about. Instead many are allowing themselves to be deceived and misled by those who are determined to scuttle the FTA, regardless of its merits."

I then tackled the anti-free traders head on: "Rather than reviewing and summarizing each of the foregoing chapters, this concluding section will concentrate on the misconceptions that naturally exist and the misrepresentations that have been spread about the FTA. Distorted and misleading accounts of the contents of the FTA have gained far more credence than they deserve, due to the highly emotional nature of much of the attack on the FTA. This has been aided and abetted by powerful nationalistic elements within the media.

"Many of the critics and opponents of free trade have charged that the FTA represents a sellout of basic Canadian interests and will turn Canada into the fifty-first U.S. state. As this book has proven, these charges are not supported by the facts about the FTA.

"A well-known academic has said that the FTA will generate more crime and drugs on Canadian streets. A celebrated author has said that the FTA will result in the pillage and rape of Canada. One politician has even suggested that it will lead to more surrogate motherhood in this country. A publisher has claimed that the FTA will force Canada to accept nuclear weapons on its soil and to participate in the U.S. Star Wars program. All of these charges represent ridiculous commentary.

"Other ill-informed critics and opponents of the FTA claim that it will take away Canadians' jobs—particularly from women—and their culture, medical plans, and pensions, not to mention their sovereignty, if not their very existence. The truth about the FTA obviously counts for absolutely nothing in many quarters.

"The anti-FTA exponents are allowed to exploit their alarmist warnings to the fullest because of their network of sympathizers in the media. It would appear that the FTA has no hope of receiving a fair review from many media representatives. Many people are thus being turned against an economic treaty that could be instrumental in shaping a better future for all Canadians.

"The most appalling example of this lack of journalistic integrity is embodied by *The Toronto Star.* Unlike *The Globe and Mail,* which editorially favors the FTA but features almost 40% anti-free-trade commentaries on its op-ed page, *The Toronto Star* was at one point running more than 90% anti-free-trade material in its unrelenting campaign against the agreement. And it was doing this in the critical southern Ontario market—which it dominates—where, partially as a result of the *Star's* role, there is more fear and suspicion of the FTA than in any other part of Canada.

"Far more unforgivable is the similar approach being pursued by the Canadian Broadcasting Corporation in its national radio and television programming. As a publicly owned broadcasting system, the CBC has an obligation to be more balanced and fair in its coverage than any other media outlet. Yet the CBC plays up anti-free-trade stories while playing down anything running the other way.

"A typical example of this deliberate strategy was evidenced by the CBC program *National's* handling of the reaction by the Council of Canadians and by the Canadian Alliance for Trade and Job Opportunities to the final version of the FTA. The Council's negative reaction was the second item on *The National,* with no contrary flak running either before or after it. In contrast, the Alliance's subsequent positive reaction was the fifth item on *The National* and was preceded by an item featuring a distorted account of the purported job loss due to free trade and followed by an undistorted account of the legitimate fears of Okanagan fruit and vegetable farmers after their twenty-year seasonal protection expires.

"The media in general revealed themselves at their worst, during the House of Commons committee hearings on free trade. Whenever the critics of free trade appeared, the media showed up in droves and duly reported the critics' opinions, with particular emphasis on the more sensational of these. Then when the proponents of free trade appeared, the media virtually abandoned the hearings and reported little or nothing of their more factual presentations. There was a deliberate, unmistakable pattern to this totally unprofessional treatment of the two sides of this critical national debate before the committee...."

John and I had our adventures together. John is irrepressible, and sometimes it gets him into trouble. During the free trade debate, we were invited to be on a panel at York University, Atkinson College, on a Saturday afternoon. We were speaking to the pro side; the other two panelists were speaking for the anti side. The room was filled. It was a huge crowd. I was surprised because it was a Saturday afternoon.

Even though the audience was mostly negative, I thought we'd done a pretty good job and we were winning. Then John blew it. During question period, someone got up and got a hold of a microphone and wouldn't let it go even though the Chair asked him several times. He kept skipping around the room, carrying the mike, making speeches, and so on. Eventually, Security was called and took him and carried him out. As this was happening, John said, quite unnecessarily, "One of York's students, no doubt." Someone from the audience called, "No, Professor Crispo, that's one of our professors."

Ed Safarian, Professor Emeritus, Faculty of Management,
The Joseph L. Rotman School of Management, University of Toronto

---

After this one-two punch, I dealt with the six major misconceptions and misrepresentations promulgated about the FTA itself. The grossest, I said, revolved around dispute settlement, the auto pact, energy, investment, services, and Canada's sovereignty. After discussing each, I turned to a final assessment:

"The Canada-US FTA clearly could not and obviously did not yield Canada everything it wanted. It is quite naturally the net result of a complex series of tradeoffs that could not possibly satisfy everyone on either side, let alone both sides of the border. It is a comprehensive but not complete free trade deal because some exceptions remain—some at Canada's request and others at the request of the United States.

"There is no general code of fair-trade behavior that sorts out acceptable and unacceptable subsidization practices in the two countries, although there is a commitment to work out such a code during the first five to seven years of the FTA. There is only the beginning of a general government procurement policy, ensuring national treatment of suppliers in both countries when bidding on all levels and types of government contracts.

"Despite these shortcomings the FTA is a good deal for Canada. It enhances and protects Canada's access to its major foreign market. It introduces an effective bilateral dispute-settlement mechanism that should eliminate U.S. abuse under its countervail and anti-dumping laws. By these means, the FTA benefits virtually all parts of Canada, from its industrial heartland to its resource-based regions.

"It does all this without jeopardizing the major non-economic elements that are the essence of Canada. Except for two relatively modest concessions, Canada's cultural industries were exempted from the agreement. Moreover, Canada's social policies are in no way adversely affected by the FTA. While there was some compromise of Canada's sovereignty in a few areas, the country may have improved on its overall position vis-à-vis its giant neighbor.

"The FTA is far superior to any other alternative that is available in terms of Canada's trading relations with the United States. Furthermore, it could provide an encouraging example and precedent for the world and thus help break the logjam that has been holding up a GATT breakthrough and thereby threatening a worldwide trade war. Finally, the FTA provides Canada with a hedge against any such disaster, since it assures Canada of much-improved access to its most important market.

"One of the keys to the success of the FTA from a Canadian point of view stems from the unprecedented effectiveness of the consultative mechanisms that were put in place to advise and counsel the Trade Negotiations Office throughout the negotiations. Canada's able negotiators regularly consulted a host of industry and provincial representatives, and their collective views were reflected in a very meaningful way in the final agreement.

"The result is an agreement that Canadians should support. By ensuring Canada more ready and secure access to the U.S. market the

FTA will allow this country to realize its full economic potential. In so doing it will enable Canadians to provide more support for their important cultural, regional development, and social-security programs. The combination will produce both a stronger and more vibrant economy and a more caring and compassionate society."

During the course of the great free trade debate, I became a member of the Apparel Sectoral Advisory Group on International Trade (SAGIT) and then the International Trade Advisory Committee (ITAC), the umbrella advisory body chaired by the Minister of International Trade.

The Apparel SAGIT was chaired by Peter Nygard, one of the most colourful entrepreneurs I have ever met. I believe Peter and I both played a part in bringing the labour members of the Apparel SAGIT to meetings. Moreover, they played quite a constructive role, a marked contrast to the boycott by the labour movement of most other SAGITS.

Peter and I became quite good friends, and after the free trade debate was over, he invited me to accompany him on a trip to his native Finland. I accepted with alacrity because I'd never been to Finland and knew I'd never have another opportunity to see it from the vantage point of what amounted to a royal tour. Peter was treated as a conquering hero because of his success abroad, and we were fêted everywhere.

Labour attendance to ITAC was sporadic, except for the President of the Canadian Federation of Labour (CFL), because the CFL had a fairly good relationship with the government. Bob White of the CLC, however, had a much more combative relationship both with the federal government and the Trade Negotiations Office (TNC). So when Bob, the TNC, and John Crosbie, the Minister of International Trade, all showed up, things got very interesting. John used to rely on me to take on White and company, something I relished because I love a debate and felt they were so very wrong on the free trade issue.

John and I always got on very well. One of my warmest memories of the free trade debate, in fact, is John waving a copy of *Free Trade: The Real Story* in the House of Commons and declaiming that it told the truth. But I had been an admirer and champion from long before, when he was Minister of Finance during the short-lived Joe Clark government. I vividly recall John's efforts to persuade Canadians that they had to get rid of the National Energy Program, which forced the West to subsidize oil and gas prices in the rest of Canada. He was also right in his attempt to stem the fiscal hemorrhaging which was multiplying our national debt at a disastrous rate.

Soon afterwards, John ran for the leadership of the Progressive Conservative Party, and he came close to winning. I think he would have beaten Brian Mulroney had John been bilingual. When pressed on how he would deal with French Canadians when he couldn't speak their language, John answered in his typical honest style that you didn't have to speak Chinese to deal with Chinese people. You can imagine how well this went over with the French-Canadian delegates at the convention.

I got to know John best when he became Minister of International Trade under Brian Mulroney and led the charge for the FTA. John was always his charming, irascible self, and I will never forget his encounters with Sheila Copps and others who drove him crazy with their ill-informed, unfounded ranting and raving over this Agreement. He's a great Canadian, and it was a wonderful experience to work with him.

John Crispo was a very positive ally in assisting me I carrying out my assignment from Prime Minister Mulroney, which was to steer the Canada-U.S. Free Trade Legislation through Parliament and to sell the Agreement to the Canadian people. At the time of my appointment, there was a tremendous amount of fear mongering spread by the opponents of the Canada-U.S. FTA creating misapprehension and fear and completely distorting what the nature of the Agreement was and what it was designed to accomplish for Canada. Crispo was an able political economist with a good reputation in academic circles, fearless and ferocious in expressing his views, which were usually calculatingly controversial when he was seeking attention or seeking a platform, and having the ability to goad the anti-free trade conspiracy theorists, left leaning, mendacious, nervous Nelly, fear-creating vacuous, anti-American hysterics into apoplexy whenever he spoke up or wrote to explain why the U.S.-Canada FTA should be supported.

At an early stage in the free trade debate, Crispo wrote and had published a cogent, clear explanation of the U.S.-Canada FTA and why it should be supported. It was clearly a case of Crispo by name and Crispo by nature. The left wing, professional wing nuts who opposed the FTA wished that Crispo was frying in hell's fiery furnace and there, done to a crispo. As I am greatly attracted by those who are unafraid to be frank, controversial, and obnoxious in a good cause, I received a tremendous boost from the activities and opinions of John Crispo, a Canadian of intelligence and conviction, not given to surrendering to the usual bunk and hypocrisy of the typical pusillanimous, prissy but pushy carnivorous Canadian cultural naturalist.

Crispo was a member of what is known as the ITAC or International Trade Advisory Committee set up to advise the Minister of International Trade on international trade matters generally and his private opinions expressed at these meetings were always cogent and to the point.

In the matter of public opinion where help for the free trade side was greatly needed, Crispo was a valuable ally. Never the academic pussycat, he was a veritable academic alligator, tough skinned and dangerous both from the jaws to the armour plated tail. He later was appointed by Prime Minister Mulroney to the CBC Board of Governors where he again performed fearlessly, unafraid to disturb the beatitudes of the baffle-gabbing bureaucrats of that august institution.

The Honourable John C. Crosbie, Former Minister of International Trade

---

INTO THE LION'S DEN

Although I allied myself with management over issues like free trade, I never lost my critical faculties about the corporate sector, and I spoke out on a number of issues, including bank mergers, executive compensation, and the growing power of multinational corporations.

Around the time I retired from the University of Toronto, for example, I dived headlong into the debates surrounding the proposed mergers of four major Canadian banks to form two giant-sized megabanks. Early in the game, I expressed my formal opposition before the National Liberal Caucus Task Force on Financial Institutions. Shortly afterwards, in October and November 1998, I published two pieces in *The Globe and Mail*.

I had grave reservations about the proposed mergers. One was that the major beneficiaries of the mergers would be the senior officers of the banks. Another was that the banks had jumped the gun on the federal government's task force on financial institutions, which the banks had asked for and which was due to report in just a few weeks. A third was that the banks' assurances that there would be no job cuts, no cut in services to customers, and no changes in service charges were not credible. But mostly my concern was the banks had not proved their case— that to survive they simply had to realize major economies of scale and they could achieve this only by merging.

A few years ago, when the Canadian banks were attempting to merge, John told us a story about a dinner party he had attended over the weekend. The dinner party included several senior bank executives and their wives. They were anxious as to whether the mergers would go through. John said he didn't think the mergers should be allowed. They turned on him. One woman said it was because "You don't have as many bank shares as we do." John's reply was, "Now I know why you think the mergers are in the public interest."

For me, this was the first time I saw John exhibit some suspicions of the capitalist side as well as the labour side. It was some indication of the broadening of his point of view.

Ernest Sirluck, Ph.D., Professor, Dean, and Vice-President, Retired,
University of Toronto, and President, Retired, University of Manitoba

---

I was supported in this last concern by *The Economist*, which reported (in its October 31, 1998, issue): "Huge, broadly diversified banks are not, on average, any more profitable than less far-flung ones. Economies of scale often taper off quickly with size…. Nor does a ubiquitous branch network seem to improve profitability. Most troubling of all, the economies of scope that are meant to come from bringing a variety of financial institutions together have proved elusive."

Another of my concerns was that if the mergers were approved, the federal government would resort to increased regulation in order to protect Canadians from the resulting, much more concentrated banking industry. In fact, when the task force on financial institutions did report, it called for a consumer watchdog group and annual reports by the banks to Parliament, in other words, increased regulation.

My position was that the only way to protect consumers and the public in the face of megabanks would be to open Canada's banking industry to foreign competition. My fear was the federal government would go along with the mergers, with some conditions attached, just to make the decision palatable to voters. As it turned out, Minister of Finance Paul Martin resisted the banks' demands in 1998, but the rumblings and the pressure continued and the banks are bound to push forward again.

Another major issue about which I am greatly concerned is the growing disparity in income between those at the top and those at the bottom of Canada's income hierarchy. According to Statistics Canada (as reported in "The Wealth Gap," *Maclean's*, August 28, 2000), Canada's middle class, lower middle class, and working class have seen their incomes shrink by four per cent, 13 per cent, and 17 per cent respectively in the decade spanning 1989 to 1998. During the same period, Canada's upper middle class and richest Canadians have seen their income increase by one per cent and nine per cent respectively. In 1998, the average annual income of the richest Canadians was about 15 times the average income of Canada's poorest citizens. This trend is showing no signs of stopping or reversing.

But to my mind what's worse is the hardening of attitudes towards the suffering at the low end. If people are poor, it must be because they don't deserve to be better off. If people are forced to subsist on welfare, apply for rent-geared-to-income public housing, or ask for other assistance, it's because they're drug-addicted, beer-swilling, lazy, good-for-nothings who deserve contempt rather than compassion.

What bothers me about all of this is that I believe the survival and health of any society depends on forming an underlying consensus. Part of that consensus relates, I suspect, to the distribution of income. If I am right, we should be doing far more to narrow the extremes. Yes, it is difficult for any country, and especially Canada, to do much about the obscene incomes at the top of its income hierarchy unless the U.S. also chooses to do so. One argument is that high-level talent now operates in an international labour market and will simply move to the highest paying bidder. While I do not fully subscribe to this theory, I do believe there is some truth to it, which is depressing because I see no disposition in the U.S. to care enough to do anything about disparity of income.

Even if the U.S. decided to act, I'm not sure what it should do. One idea I came across some years ago was that no institution should be allowed to deduct from its legitimate costs for taxation purposes more than one million dollars in total remuneration for any single individual. Regardless of how total remuneration is defined—I would make it very comprehensive, including salaries, bonuses, country-club memberships, and realized capital gains on stock options—this might lead shareholders to call a halt to the excessive awards, since the excess would come directly out of the shareholders' pockets.

In any case, I'm not holding my breath until the U.S. decides to do something. I think the odds of that happening are so small as to be invisible. However difficult as that makes it for Canada, there are still actions we can take. One of them is to ensure that all Canadians, however poor and disadvantaged, have access to decent food, shelter, health care, and education. No one should be left without the basic necessities of life. Of course, in return, Canadians must also be prepared to do everything they can to help themselves become more self-sufficient.

Internationally, I am concerned about the growing influence and power of multinational corporations, a natural outgrowth of the so-called global village that those of us who championed freer trade have fostered. My fears about these multinationals stems from their growing ability to play off countries against each other. It began in the Third World, where countries fought desperately to attract foreign capital and investment so as to improve employment, incomes, and standards of living. Now, virtually all countries are caught up in this process because multinationals and capital know no boundaries and respect no nationalities. All they seek is the most economic locations to mine resources, produce goods and services, or otherwise improve the return on investment.

The proposed Multilateral Agreement on Investment (MAI) was shelved in December 1999 in great part because the opponents of freer trade and globalization are beginning to catch the public's attention about the increasing potential for abuse by multinationals. This rising public worry is occurring even in Canada where we are already subject to a limited MAI under the NAFTA and little harm seems to have occurred as a result.

Mass public demonstrations are now a given at World Trade Organization (WTO) and G8 meetings. Unfortunately, once the public is aroused by demonstrators marching in the streets, it's just as hard to get them, as it is to get demonstrators, to recognize distinctions between the mandates of the various organizations and the objectives of the various agreements. It's also hard to hear the legitimate comments and concerns in all the din.

With respect to the WTO and the objective of multilateral trade agreements, I think the way to make such an agreement acceptable to the public at large will be to incorporate clauses dealing with labour, the environment, competition, and culture.

We need an international labour code that deals with procedure rather than substance. I believe international trade agreements of all kinds must eventually include covenants requiring member countries to respect the right of workers to organize into unions and, through them, to take collective action, including strikes, to better their lot in life. Going beyond procedural safeguards and getting into substantive issues, such as working hours and minimum wages, makes me uneasy. Specifics like these are the basis for comparative advantage, the tools countries use to attract investment and, ultimately, improve the standard of living for their citizens. The only exception I think should be considered is child labour, which probably should be subject to curbs on an international basis.

We need an international environmental code that goes beyond the beginnings built into NAFTA. The problem is that poorer countries cannot afford the standards we should be imposing on wealthier countries. The poorer countries have a good case for asking for and indeed insisting on differentials in standards to be met. After all, they know and we know that most, if not all, of the advanced countries attained their present higher standard the dirty way, that is, with little or no regard for environmental standards. Poorer countries can now quite logically argue that richer countries have an obligation to finance the difference in costs. I'd be surprised if the richer countries, Canada included, ever agreed because we are intrinsically selfish and short-sighted. But I believe it's a must if we are ever to make meaningful, world-wide progress on the environmental front.

We need an international competition code to control the power of multinational corporations using anti-competitive measures to dominate and even monopolize the market for their products and services. Few countries can afford to take on the Microsofts of this world. We also have to establish an international tribunal to ensure that we have effective competition on a world-wide basis or at least competition without unnatural barriers created by multinational institutions.

Finally, we need an international code to protect national and local cultures from the homogenizing influence of the American entertainment juggernaut. I believe we must develop an approach that allows countries to subsidize their own cultures, provided none of the products of these cultures are exported. Once they become goods or services for sale internationally, they should be regarded as any other good or service and not be permitted to take advantage of benefits or subsidies.

BOARD STIFF

During the 1980s, as I became more involved with the business community, I was drawn into the affairs of companies who leaders I respected. I was also curious to test my own theories about what it takes to operate a business successfully. Since retiring from the academic world, I have been deeply committed to and involved with a small number companies, several of them in the start-up stage. I cherish those relationships and treasure the experiences, but I remain critical of many business practices.

How corporate boards are formed and how they operate is an issue of intense personal and professional interest and concern. I began writing and speaking about corporate governance long ago. I began living it during the latter part of my professional career, and I continue to live it today.

In 1983, I wrote an essay for the Max Bell-Business-Government Relations Program at York University entitled "Public Directors on Company Boards." (In 1982, I'd received a research grant to study public members on corporate boards.) Since then, I've had a lot of direct and personal experience with corporate boards, and what I've learned has underscored what I learned and discussed at York.

In the Max Bell lecture, I said that reform of corporate boards receives far too little attention even when the boards' performances cry out for examination. As part of a comprehensive reform, I proposed appointing members of the public to corporate boards of directors to perform a special role. Both statements are still true today.

It's easy to understand why corporate boards continue to put reform so far down on the agenda it rarely sees the light of day. There are always many more pressing problems, like attracting capital and finding competent outside directors who are willing to served in a regulatory climate in which corporate directors are vulnerable to penalties for not discharging their duties properly and directors' liability and other insurances don't provide blanket coverage. Other problems include sidestepping potential conflicts of interest, which is extremely difficult in a world of interlocking boards of directors—where the same people and their friends keep popping up on each others' boards—and avoiding insider trading and other malfeasances.

Competition, market forces, the law, and the courts have been unable to curb corporate abuses. Appointing qualified members of the public—people who aren't part of the cozy insiders' club and who represent the public at large—could do the job by shining a light into the back rooms and board rooms.

The corporate board has a responsibility to reach beyond its managers to the shareholders. The board also has a responsibility to look out for shareholders' long-term interests and a duty to develop policies and implement procedures that identify conflicts of interest and ensure compliance with the law and principles of ethics at all levels within the corporation.

The corporate board is, by definition, the independent conscience of the institution it serves. Its directors must stand at arm's length from the daily work and relationships and be concerned with the values and the morality of the company's actions. The chief executive officer and other senior managers cannot play this role. It must be up to the board to examine and, if necessary, rule against the people who have transgressed even if they are perceived as too valuable for the corporation to lose.

Few corporations have truly independent boards of directors. On most, the outside directors are colleagues and associates doing duty as directors on a reciprocal basis. They know that if they ask pointed questions or stand firm on principle, they will be crossed off the list of directors to be trusted and also shut out of future business dealings not only with that company but also with any others associated with the board's members. Occasionally a token outsider, someone who really is an outsider, will be appointed, but that individual will have all the impact and influence of the window dressing he or she is.

If corporate boards are serious about reform, they must recruit directors with a much broader range of backgrounds, talents, and qualifications than they do at present. There is a wealth of talent out there, but nominating committees never see it because they don't want to look for it and don't want to be bothered with nourishing neophytes. If they looked just at academics, ex-politicians, and the women available at all levels in corporate Canada, for example, they could fill all board vacancies many times over with fresh faces and fresh points of view.

I'm not suggesting that every corporate board needs to clean house and start over. I am suggesting, however, that there are many effective steps that can and should be taken. For example, a corporate board could name a full panel of independent members from a cross-section of the community to act as advisors or sounding boards at board meetings. It's what I call the "full voice, no vote" method of bringing balance and insight. The independent panel could also be charged with preparing an annual report stating how well (or poorly) the corporation did in the light of existing laws, advertising claims, guarantees, warranties, codes of ethics, statements of mission and values, and so on.

As far as I know, no corporate board in the for-profit sector has ever dared to step outside the convention of "you scratch my back and I'll scratch yours." Maybe the dot-com generation coming up will be the one to meet the challenge.

John is always coming up with wonderful investment opportunities. I think of it as charity because I always lose my money. But he's so enthusiastic. If John buys it and backs it, you know it's going to fail.

Jim Gillies, Ph.D., Professor of Policy, Schulich School of Business,
York University, Toronto

My own brilliant career in business—inside and outside the board room—began long ago with a partnership that combined antiques and land speculation. I was lucky to emerge with the shirt still on my back. My erstwhile partner took off with our truck and our inventory. Yet years later, he had the nerve to call. Would I give a speech, free of charge, of course, at a fund-raiser for a politician he was backing? Tempting offer, but I declined just the same....

Since then, I've been involved in several more serious and costly ventures, including a promising computerized point-of-sale inventory control system; a yogurt company, whose fantastic product is still on the grocery shelves today, although under the label of another company; an oil company that found oil but also found it too expensive to get it out of the ground; a ground-pollution environmental clean-up process that may yet prove fruitful under a new owner's direction; and a long distance telephone service discounter. In two of those ventures, I could have made money if I'd sold my shares at the right time. But I held on to them because I was convinced their value would continue to rise. I was wrong.

During the last few years, I have become involved in several more businesses. I've taken ownership positions in some and I'm currently serving on several companies' boards.

One is The Brand Factory, a very creative and innovative marketing strategies group that's brought me into a close working relationship with such a hard-driving, likable, and talented group of young people that it may keep me young, in spirit at least, all by itself. It's exposed me to a whole new side of business life and taught me a great deal about business imaging, positioning, and strategizing. And even though I am a bit player, I may make some money at it.

Others are Engineering.com, which hopes to become the international centre for engineering data and resources, and KML Pre-Engineered Steel Homes, a pre-engineered, factory-produced, steel-house framing company that has made me marvel at the miracles of modern technology. Founded by some of this country's largest developers, KML has a leading edge technology that could become a world beater. I have helped with making international contacts and am assured that I will do very well if this product does as well as we believe it can.

PlanetWiz Inc., developer of educational games, such as the Bust-A-Bank CD-ROM game board, is a start-up venture. I'm enjoying helping these deserving entrepreneurs dig up the capital and contacts they need.

I wanted to go to M.B.A. school, but my résumé was a bit thin, so a friend and I came up with this business concept as a way of building up credentials. We invented this kid's game, but we couldn't find sponsors. I wrote to John Crispo, not really expecting an answer, and the next thing—three days later—I got this call. John gave us instant credibility, a Board, venture capital. Then the dot-com market tanked and we had to start over.

Now we're making more tangible games. We're really proud that we can do something tangible and multi-facetted. We take sharp concepts and content and produce them in whatever format is needed—CD ROM, book, play, television show. You name it. Kids take to our game as soon as they see it.

We launched the first one in India on June 4, 2001. It's called Bust-A-Bank and it teaches money math to kids from Kindergarten to Grade 5. What we're doing is introducing basic business concepts to kids in a fun and cool way. The heads of math at school boards love it because it's curriculum based.

We've got more Biz Kidz games in development. We're taking our methodology and going into other subject areas and age groups. Our next games are on shopping, commodities, stock markets, and spelling. We'll be introducing them over the next few weeks.

David (my business partner) used all the Biz Kidz hoopla we built to get into M.B.A. school at Western. Me, I'm looking forward to quitting my day job.

John has been a major influence on me. We're now close friends. It's the perfect story and a rare thing. And it's all happened (the game business success) because of his will power. If it wasn't for John, I wouldn't be in this position. No one would take me seriously. Period.

Ahmed Naqvi, President & C.E.O., PlanetWiz Inc., Toronto

eBox Inc. is another favourite. This fantastic service solves the fulfilment problem through unattended night-time delivery guided by GPS-equipped trucks. The service is going to solve a whole lot of problems for everyone from dry cleaners to department stores and grocery stores struggling with the logistics and expenses involved in home deliveries when there's no one to answer the door. The system also solves the tremendous problems with returns, particularly with such items as women's apparel. It is so promising that eBox has signed up several major Canadian organizations for pilots, including Canada Post, Sears, The Bay, HMV, and Chapters/Indigo. All have delivery problems to solve and all see the extraordinary potential in the eBox system. eBox is also well on the way to facilitating business-to-business transactions, which has even more potential than residential deliveries.

I also have consulting relationships with other companies for which I am sometimes paid in kind although I usually do it for free. Working with these companies has taught me more about entrepreneurship and what goes into it than I could have learned any other way.

I wish I'd had all of these experiences before I began teaching my Introduction to Business course at the University of Toronto so many years ago. During my last few years of teaching, I used to tell my students that I might even be sufficiently knowledgeable and qualified by the time I retired. At least I was aware of my inadequacies, which is why I brought in so many highly qualified guest speakers.

John asked me to make a presentation to his famous Commerce 101 class. I think there were about 250 students in it. The first time I lectured, John came, probably for quality control purposes. After that, he booked me without ever bothering to come. He'd have one of his assistants meet me and film it for future use. He was famous for that. He'd book a couple of dozen speakers every year and be off in Montreal or somewhere while they lectured to his class. And you know, he never paid me a nickel. I think he bought me a Coke once.

Anyway, I guest lectured for a number of years. Then John asked me for the name of a really good entrepreneur. I suggested my son-in-law. Jeff came and spoke to the class, first with me and then on his own. After that, John stopped inviting me. One of these days I'm going to have to pay him back.

George Fleischmann, President and C.E.O.,
Food and Consumer Products Manufacturers of Canada

Most of my experiences on corporate boards have been wonderful—enlightening, interesting, and exciting. But I've also seen the dark side in a way that's made me realize that corporate board reform is still a pressing need.

I worked for several years with one company that I think has a winner of a product. It should do very well. It already is in certain international markets. I was proud to play a critical role on the Board. The problem was that a few key investors in the company had ethical standards and business practices that are very different from mine and some other members of the Board. That led to a lot of battles in the boardroom, a lot of expenses for the company, and the need for a lot of morale boosting for the staff, who naturally got wind of what was going on and were rightly concerned about the future of the company.

For example, one major investor forced the company to hire a relative's advertising firm, which charged us far too much for services rendered. A small example but indicative of attitude.

Another example: the same major investor kept promising to ante up cash to pay the company's bills and then coming up with new conditions to be met before the cash would actually be forthcoming.

The final straw came over hiring a new senior executive. I was on the search committee, and we found somebody fantastic. But this major investor refused to allow us to release certain information to the candidate, information which he needed to make a proper decision, before he actually accepted the job and arrived on site. I said this was immoral and unethical and I wouldn't be a party to it. This major investor said I was sabotaging the company. I said I was being fair and honourable to a fellow human being. And round and round we went.

What followed was a sneak attack on me. It took place over about 16 hours on a weekend by telephone. I was shut out. Basically, the other Board members were told they had to go along with getting me off the Board or this major investor and his group would pull out and bankrupt the company.

When I finally heard what was going on, I decided it was time to step aside. I didn't want the founder and the employees of the company to lose everything. So I arranged to negotiate my withdrawal. I was mad and sad because I was convinced this company is going to succeed and I wanted to be part of that success. Also, I'm angry about the shenanigans in the boardroom. This is one company that would benefit enormously from an independent panel assessing the board's ethical standards and practices.

What has happened since I left is even more disturbing. Those now in control of the company seem to be jeopardizing its future by finding a way to squeeze out minority shareholders so that the major investor can take over the company completely, turn it around, and get the full value of its assets for the investor. There seems to be no way to stop it. I find it appalling and frightening.

Now, I contrast this experience with the other many good ones I've had in the corporate sector and with serving as President and Chair of the Board of the Board of Directors of the Devil's Glen Ski Club. In the Spring of 2001, the Board persuaded 72 per cent of the Club's members to support, by a secret ballot vote, a $4 million expansion. I saw a good group of people working together as volunteers in common cause, with no hidden agendas, no vendettas, no rivalries, and no expectations of personal gain. The Directors worked hard and listened to each other and the members. We knew what the big issues were, and we agreed and adjusted our proposals accordingly. It was great.

Maybe it's unrealistic to expect corporate boards to operate in the same altruistic fashion as volunteer boards. But it isn't unrealistic to expect corporate boards to operate ethically and honourably, to avoid conflicts of interest, and to serve the executives, employees, and share-holders equally well. We have a long way to go in Canada before we can assume this is taken for granted.

In 1987, I headed a public company called Ryde Industries Inc. We were in the frozen yogurt business, and we needed a Chairman of the Board. I prepared a list of every prominent person in Canada. I didn't know any of them. John wasn't on the list. I didn't know him either.

Then I read a notice in a local newspaper that John would be speaking about free trade at a breakfast meeting in Calgary. I bought a ticket. My first impression was tremendous. He's a dynamic, charismatic guy. He's got great wit and humour and genuine warmth. Within five minutes, I threw away my list and persevered on getting to know him.

I stuck like glue. I sat next to him at breakfast and complimented him on the healthy breakfast he'd chosen. I hung around through the media interviews afterwards. I offered to drive him to the CBC-TV studio for a live interview. Then I invited him to dinner. Finally, I served him my frozen yogurt for dessert, and he said, "I give up."

Since then, John has been chairman for all of my businesses. After I sold Ryde to Ault Foods, we were in oil and telecommunications. Then we got into water. The product is first class, our major client base is in the U.S.A., and it's very sensitive from political and regulatory standpoints. John's given us tremendous leadership throughout.

John has the deepest sense of fairness of any man I've met. He has an ability to look at all aspects of a situation and come up with some alternatives. He's still my sounding board. I only call him about five times a week now. It used to be much more often.

John is a tremendously supportive guy. Once he's on your team, you couldn't have anyone better in your corner. I admire him tremendously.

Randy Von Hagen, President, Island of Cuba Co. Ltd.,
and President, Tempatations Beverage Co. Inc.,
High River, Alberta

Chapter 4

Immoral Authority

Early in my career, I was very much involved as what could be termed a neutral intervenor in everything from labour-management disputes to broader political, social, and economic problems. Frequently, I was an arbitrator, conciliator, or mediator, and I participated in several Royal Commissions and Task Forces. Despite some wonderful experiences working with the likes of Carl Goldenberg and Bus Woods, the overall result for me was cynicism and disillusionment. I concluded that intellectual honesty is too great a handicap in those farcical spheres.

I quickly learned that Royal Commissions and Task Forces were like giant rugs under which politicians could sweep problems too hot to handle any other way. They could postpone action until the problems disappeared of their own accord or the politicians got through the next election campaign. I became convinced that these delaying tactics were intellectually dishonest hoaxes designed to give the impression that something was being done on its merits when in fact the over-riding imperative was political expediency.

Eventually, I became both thoroughly disenchanted and totally unacceptable to most of those who might have continued to use my services. By 1975, I was so fed up with the deceptive and phony games social scientists and politicians play that I began burning bridges.

I first met John when I moved up from Harvard to the University of Toronto in 1963 as Professor of Political Economy. I must have met John almost immediately, likely over coffee at Sidney Smith Hall. Later, we met often for lunch at The Trough. It wasn't called The Trough at the time, mind you. I gave it the name during the time of the student troubles because in the eyes of the radicals we were capitalist pigs with our snouts in the academic trough.

John and I were both very good lecture hall performers. It helped us stand up to the student radicals during the governance troubles. The kids just ate us up. We felt most secure with 150 to 200 students in our lecture halls because we knew any student radical who made a peep would be destroyed by the other students.

We differ in one respect, though. John is more of the Minister type, while I am more of the Deputy Minister type. I like working behind the scenes, making things happen, while John revels in being an out-in-front shit disturber.

My first impression of John was fabulous, and I never thought of changing it. John was a supremely practical academic, and that, coupled with his charm, is what appealed to me. I still admire John for his absolutely abiding respect for the core values of the academic enterprise coupled with his marvellous sense of humour and profound sense of excitement and enthusiasm.

J. Stefan Dupré, O.C., O.Ont., Professor Emeritus, University of Toronto

PAYING THE PIPER

My first eye-opener came in 1961 when I was Director of Research for Ontario's Royal Commission on Labour-Management Relations in the Construction Industry. The sole commissioner was the late Senator Carl Goldenberg, CBE, QC.

Carl was an admirable person, and I remain indebted to him. He gave me a free hand to look into the corrupt and exploitive practices in Ontario's construction industry, and he asked me to draft a report on the situation and what should be done to remedy it.

I wrote a very strong report, which Carl seemed to appreciate, but it was at that point that things turned upside down. In keeping with his efforts to educate me about public commissions, Carl kindly offered to take me to his meeting with then Premier Leslie Frost. The purpose of the meeting, it transpired, was to clear what I thought should be our conclusions with the Premier.

I will never forget that meeting. Carl began by asking me to review what I believed were our mutually agreed conclusions. When I finished, Carl and Leslie negotiated what should go into Carl's final report. The gist of their discussion consisted of Carl pushing the Premier as hard as he could and the Premier shoving back in terms of his view of his own political realities. Their shared idea was clearly to have Carl look as determined and independent as he could while allowing the Premier to implement a majority of his recommendations as long as they were politically palatable.

I was shocked and chagrined. I respected Carl, who was rightly known as Canada's Mr. Royal Commissioner because he was involved—usually as chair—in far more Royal Commissions and Task Forces than anyone in else in our country's history. I also realized that he liked and respected me enough to show me how these things were done so that I could do a lot more of this work in the future on my own.

Something nearly as disillusioning happened with the Prime Minister's Task Force on Labour Relations, which followed on the heels of my work with the Goldenberg Commission. The federal government claimed that it implemented a majority of our recommendations. If you counted strictly by number, this was true, but if you looked at the weight or importance of the recommendations, it wasn't. The brutal fact was that practically all of the major recommendations and key findings were rejected out of hand. Bryce Mackasey, then Minister of Labour, and his senior advisors didn't like our report. They turned it into a bland and innocuous piece of legislation that didn't accomplish anything but didn't ruffle any important feathers either. The unfortunate byproduct was a residue of unsolved labour relations problems that were bound to hang around haunting us.

Later, when I told my academic colleagues about the Goldenberg-Frost encounter and the Mackasey result, they were incredulous at my naïveté. How, they asked, do you think difficult decisions get made and implemented? Serious problems, they argued, had to be dealt with in a manner politicians in power can swallow.

I've accepted that this is the case, but I still wish we could be more honest and open and spare ourselves the expenses involved in only for-show Royal Commissions and Task Forces. Mind you, some other way would then have to be found to reward individuals friendly to the government of the day.

As a footnote to the Goldenberg affair, I should note that in 1967 he and I edited a volume on industrial relations in the construction industry for the Canadian Construction Association. The Association was celebrating its centennial, which happened to coincide with Canada's centennial. We were much more forthright and strong in recommending what should be done to clean up a very troublesome situation. But this time neither of us was on the government's payroll and both of us were working with like-minded, free-thinking contributors.

I've known John Crispo for 25 years or more. We've worked together often, written articles together, served on commissions together, and so on. I regard John as a professional controversialist. He's a complicated person.

We worked together for six or eight years from the early 1960s. We both served on the Woods and Goldenberg Commissions, and we collaborated on articles and papers for learned societies. Eventually, we drifted apart as our interests diverged.

John was famous for poking a finger in someone's eye and then saying (later), "They'll never ask me back." And finally people did stop asking him back. Ultimately, his voice in the wilderness became accepted orthodoxy. His views came into fashion. However, I believe a great number of people respect him. He is an honest, engaging person and I feel affection and admiration for him.

The last time we worked together was in the mid-1970s. We suddenly got a call because two federal ministries, Labour and Consumer Affairs, had got into a quarrel over proposed labour legislation. We were asked to mediate in Ottawa between the deputy ministers and their staffs. We both agreed on how to settle the issue, that is, we mediated between ourselves without much difficulty. I remember the incident because it reminded me how practical and honest John is. This is at variance with his public belligerence and extreme positions. When the chips are down, he'd figure out a way.

Professor Harry Arthurs, Osgoode Hall Law School, York University

CALLING THE TUNE

On November 20, 1975, I delivered a commentary to the National Social Science Conference in Ottawa. In "The Mutual Prostitution of Politicians and Social Scientists," I aimed at the jugular, focussing on the use and abuse of social scientists by politicians and the public service mandarins. What disturbed me most was the exploitation of social scientists by government to serve narrow political ends. I was also disturbed, however, by the collusion of social scientists who were co-opted willingly and very quickly neutralized as independent critics. As I put it then, "Whether as consultants or researchers, royal commissioners or task forcers, more and more purportedly independent social scientists are on the gravy train or are trying to get on it."

I castigated hired intellectual guns, who might as well have been wearing labels announcing "Have Brief, Will Accommodate," who swagger into town to participate in the ritual dance that surrounds so many Royal Commissions and Task Forces. I called it mutual prostitution because the politicians and mandarins selected social scientists with complementary preconceived notions or who could be counted on to avoid contentious positions. On the other hand, accommodating social scientists understood their role, if they were to continue to receive calls from people in power, was to "take time, appear fair, open, and studious, do the government's bidding or close to it, and retire in silence to await another charge. Above all," I added, "they must not defend their efforts afterwards if this in any way embarrasses those who appointed them."

I made it clear that there were outstanding exceptions to the rule and many individuals serving on Royal Commissions and Task Forces who never compromised their integrity. In fact, I named some. But I believed then and still believe today that the majority are biddable, obedient, and pliable. They are acutely aware of who's in charge of the call list.

I believe the reason for this unfortunate situation is a fundamental incompatibility of roles. The politician and mandarins must be interested first and foremost in political survival. The social scientist must be devoted to the search for truth. The two tracks rarely mesh. When they must run in tandem, one must conform to the shape of the other. As a rule, the social scientist is the one to adjust to the realities of power. When objective reports or studies are submitted, governments often ignore them unless by happy coincidence the recommendations support the pre-determined path.

The remedy is just as elusive today as it was in 1975. Many social scientists fail to perceive a problem. Those who do must compromise their integrity and engage in the ritual or pay the price of isolation from those in positions of power and influence. The stark truth is that if you want to work with politicians and their confidantes, you must adopt their standards. If you choose that route, you must discard any idea of intellectual integrity as so much excess baggage.

The great thing about John Crispo is that he is not the captive of any interests…he speaks his mind with a clarity that offends some, pleases others, but always educates and broadens. His impact on public policy and ethos, by raising the unpleasant but essential issues others tiptoe around, make him the quintessential Canadian original…of which we need many, many more.

Hugh Segal, President, Institute for Research on Public Policy

---

CONSULTING & OTHER BOONDOGGLES

The Royal Commission's evil twin is consulting. Many academics—not just social scientists—become so involved as consultants to corporations and government, and so dependent on the resulting incomes, they can no longer speak freely in their areas of expertise for fear of offending clients and losing fees. This situation is exacerbated with the chronic underfunding of universities. If the public refuses to underwrite the research and other work of the institutions, private parties will—and exact payment.

I've been a media commentator for years, a role I admit I relish. But there are times when I'm not the best choice for an interview. In those instances, I refer media to academic colleagues with more expertise. I lost count long ago of the hundreds of times I've been told, "Oh, we've already contacted so-and-so but he or she has declined to comment because of commercial entanglements with one of the parties involved."

These same academics are the ones who claim they must have tenure to ensure the freedom to speak frankly on issues relevant to their areas of research and teaching. For myself, I regard this as an intolerable conflict of interest.

My initiation by fire into the world of consulting came in 1972 when I agreed to help the Canadian Brewers' Association figure out why it was taking such a beating in almost every round of collective bargaining with its unions. The answer, I quickly found, lay in the unions' divide-and-conquer tactics. The unions stood together and were very effective. The breweries used to stand together in collective bargaining, but after committing nefarious marketing practices against each other, they no longer trusted each other in any sphere of activity, which made them easy pickings for the united unions.

I got to the bottom of this distrust only because of my interview with the President of the Moosehead Brewery in the Maritimes. He was furious because the three big brewers had welshed on a marketing deal.

At the time, Moosehead was a strictly regional brewer, and it couldn't afford to go head-to-head in a national advertising campaign. As a gesture of good will, the big three had agreed to stay out of the local tavern bribery business in the Maritimes. This allowed Moosehead a monopoly on buying refrigeration equipment, paying for redecorating and signage, and sending tavern keepers to the Grey Cup and other festivities. But the big boys had begun to violate the terms, and Moosehead's President was so angry he decided to tell me all. He spilled the beans not only about what they were now doing to him, but also what they were doing to each other all over the country.

In my half-day session with Moosehead's President, I learned everything I needed about competing with non-differentiated products and how that kind of competition can undermine all faith and trust among otherwise honourable competitors. I then made the rounds of the presidents of the big three breweries. I told each what I knew about what his brewery was doing to the other breweries in various jurisdictions. Each president quickly proved very willing to tell me what nasty things the other two breweries were doing to *his* company.

Armed with all these insights into how their unethical marketing practices were undermining their ability to work together on industrial relations or anything else, I presented my findings at an October meeting of the brewery presidents and their vice-presidents of industrial relations. They were astonished at how much dirt I had dug up, and they were in no position to disagree with my conclusion that their underhanded marketing practices, all done in the sacred name of sales, shelf space, and tap space, prevented them from co-operating in other areas, like collective bargaining.

By mid-morning, they'd had more than enough of me and my findings and called a brief adjournment after which they informed me that they felt they had learned all they could from me and would require no more of my services. My only regret is that I never wrote an article on these findings because I was not bound by any confidentiality agreement. I was doing so many other things at the time that I just never got around to it. Or maybe I was worried about the impact such an article could have on any other consulting activities which might have come my way. If this was a factor (I don't think it was), it wouldn't have mattered because I had few consulting opportunities thereafter.

Doubtless, the word that I was a potential menace as a consultant made the rounds very quickly. As a consultant, you are expected to underscore what those employing you want to say but don't feel they can say themselves. Unfortunately, I could never manage to do this. But it's a lucrative practice from which many continue to benefit very handsomely.

One sequel to the brewery episode is also interesting. The consultants of Ontario were then in the midst of forming their first union. They preferred the term association. Since I was then Acting Dean of the University of Toronto's School of Business, I was invited to the founding cocktail party and dinner. At the gathering I was accused of unfair competition, with some justification. Many had heard of my experience with the brewers and were angry because I could afford to take on the assignment at what they obviously believed was a lower fee than they could. After all, as a university professor, I had little or no overhead costs. This was becoming a growing matter of concern among private consultants, especially when they found themselves up against entrepreneurial professors in technical fields who could draw on a university's expensive laboratory facilities to further their consulting careers.

At this same consultants' gathering, I was also admonished for blowing what could have been a very long and lucrative consulting relationship with the brewers. I was told that you always staged these engagements so that you could draw them out for an extended period of time. Aside from being more subtle—which was and remains impossible for me—what I apparently should have done was begin with a tempting analysis of the problem to entice my brewer clients to engage me to try to come up with some possible solutions. After enough time to warrant a high number of billable hours, I should then have offered some alternative approaches, which should be intriguing enough for them to want to try under my guidance. This would obviously require diligent monitoring on my part, something which I gathered from the professional consultants present could consume a lot of my time and effort and provide billable hours for years. So much for the integrity of the consulting fraternity, who made this approach to work an art form. No wonder the term consultant is now so often used with a sneer. (One of my favourite jokes is the definition of a successful consultant: A person who comes in to a situation to help solve a problem and stays to become part of it.)

I first met John in 1950 at Upper Canada College in Toronto. We've been friends ever since.

Believe it or not, John was a very quiet, scholarly, observant type. In retrospect, I realized that he was learning about life. I was always surprised years later when people described him as loud. John knows when to be quiet, observe, and learn. I believe he is still a very good observer and listener.

My earliest memories are of three of us—John Crispo, John Elliott, and me—going to Lake of Bays in Muskoka to John Elliott's cottage. John Elliott and I would come roaring out of the Friday afternoon exam, totally mindless and raring to go. John Crispo would come out wringing his hands and saying, "I did so poorly." Then he'd get a mark in the high 90s. He always set extremely high goals and standards for himself.

What makes John such an interesting person is the diversity of his interests and his intensity of focus. On the one hand, for example, his education and professional career are intellectual and scholarly. On the other hand, he is a very practical, hands on person who becomes totally involved in restoring the original stained glass windows of his farmhouse.

John is an extremely intense, front and centre, on stage, under attack kind of person when speaking at a conference or on a television panel. Then compare this with his joy in riding his horse, with or without company or conversation, in absolute quiet and contentment for hours at a time. He does both with the same intensity and focus.

John approaches everything with absolute focus and interest and the drive to do the best he can for everyone involved. He is self-centred, but it is in his focus rather than in himself. This may be perceived as selfish or self-centred, but it isn't. In fact, I couldn't ask for a more honest, loyal, trustworthy friend.

Douglas B. Skelton, P.Eng., Retired Consulting Engineer and Long-time Friend

CONCILIATION & MEDIATION

To my mind, conciliation and mediation are the more benign and constructive labour-management intervention processes. Compared with arbitration, they are less damaging, less destructive, and more honest. The essential difference is that arbitrators render binding awards that may be appealed only on the most narrow legal grounds, while conciliators and mediators try to broker settlements between the contending parties and cannot impose anything on either of them against their wills.

Mind you, some of the things that go on in the name of conciliation and mediation are quite amusing. When he was Minister of Labour, Bryce Mackasey styled himself as the Babe Ruth of Industrial Relations, meaning he never struck out in the sense of not settling a strike. This particular story started in the bar of the Château Laurier Hotel in Ottawa during a major strike by the National Association of Broadcast Employees and Technicians (NABET) against the CBC. The hour was late when Bryce turned up to brag to me and several reporters about how successful he was as a settler of disputes. We all knew he was in the hotel with his senior staff to try to settle the strike, and one of the reporters challenged him to show us how he was going to resolve this one.

Bryce swallowed the bait, hook, line, and sinker. He invited us to join him in his room—the bar was closing anyway—so he could demonstrate just how he went about settling such a tough strike. Once we were settled, he picked up his telephone and called the CBC President at his home. By now it was about 2 a.m. but that didn't bother Bryce. In fact, it helped him. He told the groggy CBC President that Prime Minister Trudeau was fed up with the strike and wanted him to come up with another nickel by early morning to get this strike off the government's back. Sure enough, Bryce got that extra nickel the next day and, as he knew from his officials, it was enough to buy a settlement.

In major disputes in the federal sector Bryce had issued standard orders to the federal conciliators that nothing be announced by way of any settlement until he was present to preside. On one occasion he was photographed standing before a sink with his shirt hanging over his pants and shaving as if he'd been up all night negotiating the deal in question. Everybody knew he'd been sleeping one off, but he knew how to make good theatre for himself no matter how limited his role was. Neither previously nor to this day has there been anyone like him either federally or provincially as a minister of labour.

On the provincial level, one of Canada's greatest conciliators was Bill Dickey who became Chief Conciliation Officer in the Province of Ontario. One of his most remarkable capers occurred during one round of negotiations between the autoworkers and one of the big three auto manufacturers. After one long day of difficult negotiations, he told both sides separately he was going to meet with the other side in the morning in a last ditch effort to find the makings of a settlement. The next morning, he went out for a game of golf, leaving both sides stewing over how difficult it must be proving to get any more concessions out of the other side. By the time Bill got to one and then the other side in the afternoon, they were both in a mood to move towards a resolution. As I recall he wrapped the whole thing up late that night largely by keeping the two sides apart and letting them sweat it out.

My most amusing experience arose in 1969 when I was named the first-ever mediator between the Metropolitan Toronto School Boards and the Ontario Secondary School Teachers' Federation, both of whom were relative neophytes when it came to collective bargaining. My task was greatly complicated by the fact that the School Boards had foolishly offered a 10 per cent increase right off the top to demonstrate their good faith. In fact, 10 per cent was all the teachers deserved that year and it was all they ended up getting. But it took me the best part of three weeks to get the teachers down to that amount.

To get there, I had the School Boards throw in several joint committees to study everything from lunch-time duty to pupil-teacher ratios. None of these committees meant anything beyond a show of consultation, and it was like pulling teeth to get the teachers to reach an accommodation. In the end, just to stall things, the teachers had one of their number—an English teacher—dot i's and cross t's that no one else ever noticed were needed.

Finally, totally exasperated because the ski report for the weekend was fantastic, I told both sides that Friday night was the deadline for a settlement. I even turned up in my ski clothes because I just knew they would make it a late night for me and it would be hard to get home in time to change for an early start on Saturday morning. When the teachers' union finally agreed, subject to a couple more dotted i's and crossed t's, I took it back to the School Boards. Once they acquiesced, I went back to the teachers to announce we had a deal. Their chief negotiator interrupted me to tell me there was no deal. In shock, I listened to him harangue me about the fact that they were still at 10 per cent and all I'd got for them was a bunch of phony consultative committees. I began to blow my cork, telling them their word was their bond and that a deal was a deal. They all began to laugh, and, as I sputtered to a halt, their spokesman said something to the effect, "Don't worry, John, you still have your deal. We just wanted to see how good an actor you were. And you're not bad."

What he said is so true—not so much about me as about all those involved and the entire process, even when you are dealing with relatively sophisticated people like school trustees and teachers. This is because the process is often as important as the result. There was a happy ending to this case, however. I made it to the ski hill by nine the next morning.

I've known John for a long time, but I knew him best for the 10 years I was at C.D. Howe. John is the quintessential, irrepressible, and happy warrior. He helped to light up the place. We had regular conferences of just academics or of academics and very, very senior business and government people. He would stand up in the midst of these solemn occasions and say, "I probably don't know what I'm talking about. I don't do my own research any more. Thank God, I'm at a place filled with other people who do." And then he'd launch into a denunciation or assertion. John was always irreverent. He broke the ice and engaged people who were sitting on their hands. It always resulted in a better debate because of John.

John's strength was enlivening the debate. He's a formidable debater, but also a gentle one. There's no edge or nastiness. He's always good-humoured.

When I left C.D. Howe, I arranged for John to have a free, lifetime membership because he made a big difference. He's the only person who ever got one.

Thomas J. Kierans, Former President & C.E.O., C.D. Howe Institute, Toronto

ARBITRATION

Way back in 1968, the Prime Minister's Task Force on Labour Relations offered a significant and wise alternative to compulsory arbitration for major disputes. Basically, it was to form an independent, three-person commission, composed of informed members of the public and reporting to the Prime Minister. The commission's role would be to decide when a dispute actually posed a threat to the public interest and to recommend one or more of a variety of possible measures for dealing with it. The commission's reports would be treated as public documents and final authority would be exercised by Parliament. The Task Force's recommendation weren't adopted, and the result has been many subsequent arbitration-related troubles.

Arbitration is a process made-to-order for the money- and power-hungry and intellectually corrupt. When an arbitrator makes a ruling, it is final. Grounds for appeal are extremely limited, little other than exceeding one's jurisdiction or violating due process. Another reason to be troubled by the use of the arbitration process, at least when applied to contract disputes, is that employers are forced to abdicate fiscal authority over their enterprises.

Mind you, arbitration is good for something—making a very good living. If one wishes to make a lucrative practice as an arbitrator, however, one must observe the commonly accepted rules and practices. One is to bill by ratio rather than by actual time. The result is usually to bill for much more time than it actually takes to write the award or report. When I was active in this field, for example, the commonly accepted ratio was 2:1—charge for two days of contemplating and writing a report for every one day of hearings. Now, I'm told the ratio is closer to 3:1—charge for three days of contemplating and thinking to every one day of hearings. No wonder some of those who practice this art become millionaires. And to think they have so-called professional associations and meetings to try to make their activities look respectable and responsible.

One must also protect the opportunities for extending assignments. I learned this during my very first case as an arbitrator. It was the mid-1960s, and I was so green I kept calling short breaks so that I could dash to a telephone and call Bora Laskin for advice. In this case, all parties had agreed in advance that we would require two days of hearings. Half-way through the first day it became clear that we were going to be able to wind up the hearing in one day. Yet after lunch the lawyers for both sides came to me together in consternation; they said they could both call some additional witnesses, thus extending the proceedings to fill the allotted time, and, of course, ensuring that they would meet their self-determined quota of billable hours. As arbitrator, I had the power to rule. I declined their offer and threatened to tell the parties involved what they were proposing. I assume word about this spread through the legal profession and helps to explain why I became less and less acceptable as an arbitrator.

Another rule is to avoid offending either party unduly, something at which I did not excel. Once, for example, I undertook a major arbitration between the Government of Ontario and what was then the Civil Service Association of Ontario (CSAO). The CSAO had the usual long list of demands, which it refused to rank until I threatened to call a press conference to announce my resignation as the arbitrator because I was dealing with a union which could not tell me what its priorities were. The

CSAO negotiators reluctantly agreed to comply but never forgave me for forcing them to assign weight to the many competing and conflicting claims of their highly diverse membership. Yet that is precisely what a responsible union leadership has to do in any bargaining situation.

In another instance, I was mediator and final offer selector for a couple of years for disputes between Ontario Hydro and what was then called the Society of Ontario Hydro Professional Engineers and Associates, which is one of those organizations that likes to walk, talk, and quack like a union, but not be called one. My instructions were to try brokering or mediating a settlement, but if that effort failed, both parties were to put their final positions in writing and I was to choose one of those positions as the binding agreement. This method, known as the final offer selection, is one of the least corrosive forms of arbitration because it tends to draw the parties closer together as they vie to attract the final offer selector's attention by appearing to be the more reasonable.

I failed to mediate the dispute, and I ended up selecting the union's final alternative even though it was slightly higher than the position I had persuaded Ontario Hydro to offer in mediation on the grounds that I thought it would settle the matter. Both parties ended up angry with me, Ontario Hydro didn't understand the difference between trying to broker a settlement on any terms and deciding which final alternative deserved my support on its merits. The union felt it had to come too close to the final offer I had extracted from management or I would go with management's position. In the end, both parties separately exercised their independent right to veto me for the next round of mediation and final offer selection. In my mind, that mutual rejection is a badge of honour. As it turned out, this was my last assignment as a mediator, arbitrator, or conciliator.

It's because I feel that the arbitration process is intrinsically corrupt that I believe it should no longer be used. In 1974, I was raising the alarm. (See "Collective Bargaining in the Public Service," *Canadian Public Administration*, June 1974.) In 1999, I was still advising against it. (See "The Corruption of Arbitration," *Saturday Sun*, May 8, 1999.) Although in those instances I was writing specifically about public service disputes, what I said also applies in the private sector.

Why do I call arbitration corrupt? Because of the corrosive effect it has upon collective bargaining. Because arbitration is such a lucrative field that practitioners are less likely to rule on the merits of the case and more likely to concern themselves with protecting what I call their ABCs—acceptability, batting average, and credibility—so as to guarantee further assignments. Because arbitrators have to worry about the score cards labour and management are bound to be keeping. Because arbitrators can quickly become the scapegoat whipped in fierce public relations wars by disgruntled parties. Because the practice of using a standard set of criteria to determine settlements (for example, changes in the cost of living, productivity improvements, and internal and external comparisons with comparable workers) has not been expanded to include more relevant economic criteria. In some instances, governments have felt compelled to order arbitrators to consider such criteria. For example, some years back in Alberta arbitrators were found to be recommending what were thought to be extraordinarily high awards for police and firefighters. The arbitrators were ordered to add to the standard criteria two entirely new ones—what the employer could afford to pay and how difficult it was to recruit and retain employees—both extremely important factors. My impression is that this had little or no effect as arbitrators in that province and elsewhere remained focussed on their ABCs.

In my view, it's too late to save arbitration. Instead, I favour final offer selection. Using this process can avoid strikes, draw the warring parties closer together, and limit the damage an arbitrator can do.

However, if the arbitration mechanism is deemed too useful to dispense with entirely, I think it should be improved by broadening the grounds on which appeals of decisions can be made. I would extend this approach to all quasi-independent tribunals as well, such as labour relations boards and human rights commissions, which have gradually accrued extraordinary powers and autonomy they often deploy arbitrarily and capriciously.

The problems with appeals—whatever the grounds—is that the dispute then ends in the courts. The judiciary cannot be expected to have the range of expertise needed to deal with all the specialized matters that land in their laps. In fact, that was why special tribunals like labour relations boards and human rights commissions were created originally. Another problem is volume; our court calendars are already jam-packed.

In addition, my problem with the courts is that they have become all-powerful since Trudeau foisted the Charter of Rights on Canadians. This desperate accommodation—that is, more ready appeal to the courts—flies in the face of my fundamental concern about them, that there is no appeal from their decisions.

When the debate began, I favoured a very comprehensive and well entrenched charter. But shortly afterwards I found myself spending time at a First Ministers' meeting with Allen Blakeney, then NDP Premier of Saskatchewan, and Sterling Lyon, then Tory Premier of Manitoba. They came at me hard with left- and right-wing perspectives on the perils and pitfalls of an American-style Supreme Court, so hard, in fact, that I changed my mind and started speaking against the concept.

Well, we have the Charter and we have the American-style court that was the inevitable result, but what we don't have is a U.S.-style appointments procedure. In the U.S., the Senate has to approve all presidential nominees to the Supreme Court. Although this sometimes results in a terrible abuse of the nominees with all sorts of special interest groups appearing to testify for or against them, at least there is a degree of public scrutiny. In Canada, the Prime Minister has a virtual monopoly on appointments.

With the lower courts there has been one encouraging development which began in Ontario and is spreading to other provinces. In Ontario, anyone who wants to be a judge or wants to nominate someone for a judgeship places his or her name before a non-partisan vetting committee. The committee passes judgement on candidates' abilities and places the names of those thought fit to serve on a list for the province's Attorney General. It's a vast improvement on giving the Bar Association sole status as an advisory body because it allows for something beyond a narrowly defined legalistic perspective. However, it hasn't prevented the use of judicial appointments as rewards for political services rendered. Under Premier Mike Harris, the Ontario government has led the way in delaying filling judicial vacancies because the committee-approved list hasn't featured names of Tory friends Harris wants to reward in this way.

As you may have gathered, I am thoroughly frustrated both by my earlier experiences with third party interventions and by the apparent lack of change. So much of what goes on is still based more on show than substance. The basic faults with arbitration are no better known or understood by the public at large today than they were in 1974. Those benefiting from these highly rewarding activities, mostly lawyers, certainly aren't ever going to admit how unprofessionally, and essentially dishonestly, they are really behaving. As for the move to elevate Alternative Dispute Resolution (ADR) to some higher moral ground, complete with expensive courses of study and professional designations, I think it's just another way of carving out a piece of territory and marking it "For Experts Only."

Recently, I've watched John's involvement in U of T pension issues. A small group of us took early retirement in 1995 and 1996. There was a good golden handshake. Just after we did, U of T announced a policy that kept us below what we were entitled to due to changes in the income tax laws. It turned out U of T knew these tax law changes were coming but didn't say a word. We wouldn't have taken early retirement had we known our pensions would have been thousands of dollars higher had we waited another year or two. Many of us protested quietly with letters. Some of us hired a lawyer. John said, "I'm going to nail them in public because this is very wrong."

Around that time, there was a special event fund-raiser where Rob Pritchard, the President, was present with an official party. John was there, too, and Pritchard took cover. I don't think John was going after him, but Pritchard certainly thought he was.

Anyway, John's speaking out quickly turned the tide. Within a few weeks, the University admitted what it had done and righted the wrong and repaired the damage. I think it was mainly because of John. He did it his way. We all benefitted.

Peter Russell, O.C., Professor Emeritus,
Department of Political Science, University of Toronto

ANTIDOTE

The most open, honest, and above board third party intervention process I've seen to date is the equivalent of Canada's Royal Commissions, Swedish-style. The Swedish method is to give each political party the right to name members proportionate to the party's representation in Parliament and also give the country's major interest groups involved—often labour and management—the right to name members. Majority reports may not be the result, and profound divisions may not be bridged, but phony efforts to paper over huge cracks and defects can't succeed. Honesty prevails. Canada could do worse than follow this lead.

Chapter 5

Feet to the Fire

My relationship with the media has swung from one extreme to the other. At times, it was a love-in; at others, it was very strained and stressed, especially during the 1990s when I was on the CBC's Board of Directors.

In some ways, this chapter is more the story about the CBC than it is about me. But it's also the story about how I believe the media in Canada shape the news and, with it, the views of Canadians about the issues of the day and their country.

I've been deeply interested in the role of the media in our society for as long as I can remember. I have always believed the Fourth Estate has more influence and power than it cares to acknowledge without much in the way of checks and balances to ensure responsibility and accountability. As early as 1975, I was writing about investigative reporting and other issues that reflect this long and abiding worry.

In *The Public Right to Know* (McGraw-Hill Ryerson Ltd., 1975), I discussed the role of the media in keeping the public informed about all developments that affect their daily lives. I described investigative reporting as the media's first duty and obligation and stressed that the media had two responsibilities: to bring out all the facts on a given issue of public concern and to ensure that all major, contending points of view were fully aired. Otherwise, I said, the media could be charged with using its privileged position in society to advance its own point of view. I warned that this should not be tolerated in a free society, even if putting an end to the practice might entail an inherent threat to the freedom of the press.

I also urged the media to maintain its new-found interest in investigative reporting and media scrutiny in a day when the trend of politicians and others trying to manage the news was gaining momentum. It would be irresponsible of the media not to probe every conceivable source of information to get and report all the facts. If the media failed in its duty, how could citizens be expected to vote intelligently or make other critical decisions?

Despite my reservations, however, I had no trouble enjoying a long and satisfying relationship with the media. The glorious, golden years lasted until the mid-1980s when I got involved in the debate about free trade. After that, it was pretty well downhill, at least from my point of view. It's been a wild and exciting ride. Yes, I have a few regrets and a degree of lingering bitterness, but on the whole, I wouldn't have missed it for the world.

How did it begin?

One day in the mid-1960s, I got a call from a fellow in Sault Ste. Marie who was opening the first labour relations consultancy in the north. To celebrate this event, he was having a one-day conference. At the time, I was Dean of Osgoode Hall Law School. He asked me to come, and he said he'd pay my expenses and a modest fee. He named some other lawyers who'd already accepted and said John Crispo was going to be key note dinner speaker. So I accepted.

The day came, and we went up and had the day's seminars and everything went well. Then we appeared for dinner. When we were seated, a bagpiper piped in the head table: the Mayor, the local Salvation Army padre, several other local dignitaries, the organizer, and John.

John gave his speech and then the organizer said, "To show my appreciation I've arranged for some entertainment, the students of a local belly dancing class." The lights dimmed, the music started, and the aspiring dancers in diaphanous dress appeared and twirled. Finally, all of them came to rest in front of John. They wound him in their diaphanous scarves and led him to a throne-like chair. He sat there for a good 20 minutes while they danced around him. He looked embarrassed for the only time in his life.

I said to my table companions, "If this organizer is dumb enough to do this, he's going to stiff us for our fees and expenses." So, when I checked out the next morning, I made sure my hotel bill was sent directly to the organizer. And sure enough we weren't paid.

Professor Harry Arthurs, Osgoode Hall Law School, York University

MY RISE AND FALL AS A MEDIA PUNDIT

It didn't take me long to take the speech-giving skills I developed in the classroom out on the road. I was soon addressing groups all over the country and, for a time, abroad. I still do a lot of public speaking today, mostly in Canada but also sometimes in the U.S.A.

I've been told that my popularity as a speaker is based on my ability to present my serious concerns with humour and irreverence, seasoned with a touch of cynicism. I've grown accustomed to being introduced or thanked as the Don Rickles of the rubber chicken circuit.

In those early years of media work, I took to it with gusto, and I admit that I've always enjoyed the experience and the exposure. I began with work on radio, then moved to television, first as an expert in industrial relations and later as an expert on just about everything.

In those years, the CBC loved me. My theory is it was because I was one of the most pro-labour academics in Canada. Possibly, the CBC needed me to bring some balance to the subject. In any case, as I widened my fields of interest, I was able to build on my initial media experience in industrial relations to get involved in a much broader range of subject matter, and for many years, I was almost a fixture on the CBC at election time and during the various political party conventions.

I particularly enjoyed working with Lloyd Robertson when he was *numero uno* in CBC News and Public Affairs, a role he now plays on CTV. I distinctly remember covering a First Ministers' meeting with Lloyd when Pierre Trudeau was trying to get the premiers to support his infamous wage and price controls. Trudeau knew I was opposed to these controls, and he wanted to give me as little time as possible to sound off after the afternoon session ended. Lloyd and I both knew Trudeau was keeping an eye on us up in our broadcasting booth. We knew that he knew we wouldn't be given any time if he could manage to end the session just before the evening news went to air at 6 o'clock, but if he went beyond 6 p.m., we might be given much more leeway. As I recall, Trudeau left us with no more than one minute to wrap up before the news. I will never forget him grinning up at us, almost gloating over his timing. The next morning he confirmed my suspicions in a caustic aside of the type he greatly enjoyed.

Within a few years, my media work began to fade away. I believe I almost disappeared from the national electronic media, especially the CBC, because of the media's perception that I was moving from the left to the right of the political spectrum. I still believe that the CBC loved me as long as I appeared to be an articulate spokesperson of the left of centre and dumped me as I became an equally articulate exponent right of centre. As I've already said many times, I don't believe my perspective changed as much as the issues did, and, to be fair, I have been repeatedly told by CBCers that I was, and still am, paranoid and that the real reason for my demise on their airwaves was that I had become stale. You be the judge.

Mind you, I don't think I helped myself by becoming more and more critical of the media and especially of the CBC for its lack of balance and fairness in coverage of many events. I think I sealed my own fate during an interview about free trade on *Morningside*, Peter Gzowski's radio program. When he asked me why I thought my pro-free trade side was losing the debate, I said that the reason was the anti-free trade stance of the CBC. This led to an on-air set-to, after which Gzowski told me "never again." He was true to his word. I was never invited back to *Morningside*. But I really slammed and nailed the lid on my media coffin when I accepted Prime Minister Brian Mulroney's invitation to join the CBC's Board of Directors. That's a story I'll tell in detail later in this chapter.

In 1994 or 1995, there was a press conference to announce the funding for the new Rotman School of Management. Premier Bob Rae was there because the Province of Ontario was making a grant. The other money came from private sponsors and, of course, the Rotmans.

Bob Rae said, "Some of you will be surprised to hear that I approve strongly of this grant. I was a Teaching Fellow when I was a graduate student for Professor John Crispo." There was a great gasp from the audience. They didn't associate the left-wing Premier with the apparently right-wing Crispo.

Rae went on. "The Teaching Fellows knew John Crispo very well because we had a lot to do. He was very popular, and he travelled a lot giving interviews and lectures. We used to say, 'God was everywhere. Crispo was everywhere except the Faculty of Management.' "

Ed Safarian, Professor Emeritus, Faculty of Management,
The Joseph L. Rotman School of Management, University of Toronto

FREE TRADE, FOUL PLAY

My first major quarrel of substance with the media in Canada arose over the way it covered the protracted free trade debate in Canada in the mid-1980s. Although I was most irate about the CBC's coverage, I was upset with the media in general. I believed then, and still believe today, that the Canadian media were dishonest, disingenuous, and irresponsible.

In my view, the media deck was loaded and stacked against free trade, and I saw this as a disturbing, even frightening, phenomenon. For a start, I felt that most journalists of the time, in both print and broadcast media, were left of centre politically. Maybe it was because left wingers were more willing to settle for the lesser rates of pay customary in journalism than right wingers, who were more interested in making money and so less inclined to make their careers in the media. But I was still mystified by the narrow-minded nationalism the left wingers exhibited. I saw this as an historic reversal of their customary positions on the political spectrum. The left used to be more internationalist and outward-looking, while the right tended to be more parochial and inward-looking. At the time of the free trade debate, however, the two seemed to have switched sides. At the time, I speculated that most journalists in Canada were anti-free trade and even anti-American because they were unionized and that many of their unions were affiliated to a labour movement that was in tune with the anti-free trade, anti-NATO, anti-NORAD, and anti-American stance of the NDP.

In the print media, although the majority of newspaper editors and publishers of the time were pro-free trade, the reporters bringing in the news cast a negative slant on most free trade stories. (An exception to the editors and publisher pro and the reporters con was *The Toronto Star*, where everyone was virulently anti-free trade.)

In the broadcast media, especially in national news and public affairs, the anti-free trade bias ran unchecked. Almost every panel, for example, featured one pro and two anti politicians or spokespersons. Both the CBC and CTV would invite one Tory in favour and two others against, usually one from the Liberals and one from the NDP. More insidiously, the anti-free traders would always be more articulate.

Accident? Coincidence? Possibly, but unlikely considering the frequency with which it occurred.

Worse still, when it came to the Free Trade Agreement itself, the media seemed unable to separate fact from fiction. They never developed any in-house capacity to understand the terms or provisions of the Agreement or the circumstances surrounding it. For example, at one stage the U.S. Senate Finance Committee expressed concerns about the ability of Canada's federal government to commit the provinces to the Agreement. The Senate Committee recommended that the President insist on Canada's assurances on this point. The Canadian media jumped on this with both feet, labelled it a demand for compliance, and deemed it an insult and an affront to Canadian sovereignty and, therefore, by definition impossible. Yet, it was a perfectly reasonable concern on the part of the Americans, just as Canadians had every right to worry about Congress meddling with the results of Canada's negotiations with the American administration.

Around the same time, the Canadian media made totally irresponsible allegations about the purported loss of Canadian control over this country's day care, education, and Medicare systems. Yet, anyone who actually read the Agreement could see that these systems were exempted from the Agreement. What U.S. firms *could* do was bid on contracts to manage these services if, and only if, the appropriate Canadian authorities decided to call for contracts.

For me, the most galling display of one-sided coverage was during the press coverage of the House of Commons Committee hearings. Whenever a left-wing nationalist appeared to berate the Agreement, a mass of cameras, microphones, and scribes would magically appear to record the inflammatory statements. But when a defender of the Agreement showed up, the media would melt away.

Another favourite tactic was selective reporting. A classic example was an experience Simon Reisman, Canada's chief negotiator, and I shared with the CBC. Early in the negotiations, the CBC's *The Journal* asked for an in-depth interview at my home. *The Journal's* team arrived about 7 p.m., just as my wife was leaving for a meeting. She was surprised to find the interview still in progress when she returned. When my wife asked why the interview was taking so long, I told her they were having difficulty finding anything I said that they could distort to serve their anti-free trade agenda.

The Journal's team finally left after 10 p.m. In the end, they got what they wanted. The next evening, all *The Journal* aired from our three-and-half hour session was a qualifying comment I'd made in the middle of a sentence, something to the effect that it would be hard to get a fair free trade agreement out of the Americans because they simply weren't that fair to deal with on anything.

The next day, I went up to Ottawa to see Simon, and he gave me an earful—which is putting it mildly—for taking such an anti-free trade position. When I explained what had happened, he wasn't surprised.

At that very moment, David Halton of *The National/The Journal* called about an interview with Simon. He put his hand over the telephone receiver and asked what I thought he should do. I suggested he say he would love to come on either live or unedited. David declined as I suspected he would. That night, on *The National*, it was announced that the CBC had tried to arrange an interview with the chief negotiator but that he had declined the invitation. It was typical of the deceitful and misleading CBC coverage of the issue, and I am still appalled.

The wonder of it all is that in the face of an unrelenting media campaign against the Free Trade Agreement, particularly by the CBC and *The Toronto Star*, 50 per cent of the Canadian public still supported it. I wonder how high public support would have been had the media been anything remotely balanced or fair.

I first met John in 1996. I was looking for a speaker on political and economic issues who was interesting, entertaining, and informative. When I told my brother-in-law, he told me he'd taken one of John's classes. He said it was the class he attended consistently because he never knew what was going to happen.

I remember speaking to a prominent Canadian journalist and I mentioned that John was on our roster. The journalist's response was, "Crispo's crazy!" But the journalist still signed with us.

All of our events (with John) have gone really well. In most cases the organizers wonder if he's going too far. Part of his strategy is to offend everyone and to poke fun at himself. It works. The response has been fantastic. He speaks his mind. But he has a good heart. As outrageous and outspoken as he is, he wants people to feel good and doesn't want to put anyone in an awkward situation. He just wants to stretch their thinking. The feedback is universally the same. It's always great. He makes people re-think their positions on things.

Nothing surprises me with John. He did a speech on the political and economic outlook here in Toronto for a U.S. client. When I suggested John, the client asked, "Are you sure he's not going to be a dry academic?" I remember John's opening remarks. He said, "I'm bringing greetings from the Prime Minister." This went over well. Then he said, "Actually, I don't have the Prime Minister's authorization. He didn't tell me I could, but he didn't tell me I couldn't and it's pretty well the way he governs." He cracked them up. I remember seeing the client's face. He wasn't worrying any more.

With John, what you see is what you get. It's a pleasure to work with him. As my brother-in-law said, it's the one class you don't want to miss.

Martin Perelmuter, LL.B., President, Speakers' Spotlight, Toronto, Ontario

On May 26, 1987, in the middle of this hot and heavy period, I wrote a letter to the editor of *The Toronto Star*, which was never published in its entirety. Since these are my memoirs, I'm taking the opportunity to publish it in full here.

Dear Sir:

I realize or at least strongly suspect that my reply to Carol Goar's spirited defense of your newspaper against Simon Reisman's charge of biased reporting of virtually all news on the free-trade-negotiations front will not receive anything like the same front page prominence her open letter received.

Nonetheless I feel just as provoked to rebut her convenient defense of your "nationalist rag," as I like to term it, as I felt moved to defend it. Not surprisingly her defense is quite selective in that it does not begin to review your long-standing concerted attack on free trade not only in your editorials but in what I would estimate conservatively is about seventy five per cent of your so-called reporting on the issue.

No one quarrels with your right to editorialize virtually non-stop against free trade anymore than one questions the right of *The Globe and Mail* to editorialize more judiciously on the other side of the debate. It is the lengths to which your commentators and reporters go—with the noteworthy exception of Jack McArthur—to support your editorializing.

Unlike *The Globe and Mail* which seems to feature just about as many anti as pro free trade articles you consistently feature a much higher proportion of negative than positive articles. I am not in a position to judge definitively whether this is by coincidence or design but I trust you will forgive me for thinking the worst.

My own experience with your newspaper on the subject of free trade has been most instructive in this regard. It began when one of your senior officers welcomed my suggestion that I prepare a major article defending the free-trade initiative to offset the steady stream of articles running the other way.

Enthusiastically I did so, only to run into a very cool reception. The major complaint or excuse was that my original draft was too long as it would fill at least a page. I found this reaction both frustrating and infuriating because at just about the same time your resident fanatical critic of free trade—one David Crane, whom I admire greatly for his style if not his substance—had just filled several entire pages with a series of four or five tirades against free trade.

As negotiations with respect to my article continued I was invited to join your editorial board for lunch. We had quite a battle that noon hour which did not bother me in the least. The concern I have been left with ever since, however, is that there was not one member of that board who had a decent word to say about free trade.

I deem it a journalistic tragedy when a newspaper of your supposed stature is so narrow-minded in its outlook that it cannot even bring itself to hire one free trade advocate against which to check your highly prejudiced views. That does not suggest to me a very high standard of journalistic accuracy, independence, or objectivity.

As for the fate of my own article I must concede that it did eventually appear in an abbreviated form, something for which I presume I should be eternally grateful. The fact that I am not reflects the experience I have had with a few of your more honest reporters when they have found themselves covering one of my well-received talks on free trade. As one of them said on one occasion, "Don't expect my story to appear in anything like its present form, if at all." Needless to say, it did not.

Earlier, I referred to your newspaper as a "nationalist rag." I think that is the kindest description one can apply to a newspaper which allows, encourages, and/or induces its editorial stance on free trade to permeate just about everything else it chooses to print on the subject.

Simon Reisman may not have had all his facts right when he attacked your brand of loaded journalism any more than you ever have all the facts right when you do your best to distort and twist every bit of news, good or bad, on the free trade front.

But he was dead right about your continuing blatant bias on the subject of free trade. It is a professional disgrace and mocks any claim you may think you have to any sense of journalistic integrity.

Yours very truly,
John Crispo

P.S. If you feel it necessary to edit—distort and twist might be a better way of putting it—this letter in anything but a minor way I would rather you not publish it at all. Not even among the obituaries or want ads where you would probably be disposed to publish it if you choose to publish it at all.

I don't recall when I met John. It must have been on a CBC program. I was aware of him when he had an intensive period on the CBC Board of Directors. I don't think I was at any CBC Board meetings when he was, but I heard the stories and I remember his assaults on the CBC. John claimed he didn't want to kill the CBC, and maybe he was telling the truth. Apparently, he felt the CBC was O.K. if only it would change itself into a form more to his liking.

John always loved the theatre of debate no matter how weak his case was. He didn't hesitate to use overstatement. I'm sure he had substance to his arguments, but he also tested the limits of people's endurance. Patrick Watson called him a cowboy.

Knowlton Nash, Broadcaster & Author

FREELY SPEAKING

During the free trade debate, I was agitated about the CBC's blatant biases, but my concerns about the CBC went far beyond that single issue. The Corporation played predictable roles in every contentious national issue.

During the GST debate, the CBC participated in a general media campaign against it just as the Corporation tended to oppose most forms of fiscal restraint. During the Oka debacle, the CBC began, like most of the media, by making heroes of a band of natives who had set up an illegal, armed encampment on Canadian soil. Later, it was shamed into providing more reasonable coverage only because of the largely exemplary conduct of the Canadian army compared with those it was confronting.

When it came to the Meech Lake Accord, the CBC initially led the campaign against it by providing more air and screen time to opponents than proponents. For a while, I thought Sharon Carstairs, the Liberal leader in Manitoba, and Clyde Wells, the Premier of Newfoundland, owned *The Journal*. Towards the end, however, the CBC became such a pathetic advocate of Meech Lake that I think there is only one explanation. I'm convinced its left-wing producers began to realize that if the Accord went down to defeat, it could mean the end of the country and, therefore, the end of their propaganda agency.

I used to say that CBC stands for Consistently Biased Coverage. One of the best examples was Peter Gzowski's Friday morning political panel on *Morningside*. It featured Dalton Camp, a red Tory, Eric Kierans, a pink Liberal, and Stephen Lewis, a tame New Democrat. Their points of view were so similar, they might as well have belonged to the same left-of-centre party.

One day, I listened to these three supposedly politically diverse characters agree unanimously that Canada should pull its armed forces out of

Europe and withdraw from NATO. Not one of them mentioned that, at the time, the European members of NATO were asking Canada and the U. S. to stand fast even if the Cold War seemed to be drawing to a close.

On another broadcast, I heard them unite in an anti-American, anti-Gulf War position. No one mentioned what Iraq had done to Kuwait. I felt as if I was listening to Radio Iraq instead of what purported to be three different political viewpoints in Canada.

The only occasions when I observed some semblance of balanced coverage was during the pre-election leadership debates.

Of course, the CBC wasn't and isn't the only guilty party. The media in general loves to sensationalize and simplify in order to attract and hold its audience. The question is what can be done to make the media more accountable without sacrificing the basic principle of freedom of the press. I suggested two remedies, one for the media in general and one for the CBC in particular.

For the media in general, I think it is long past time we considered an equal space, time, and prominence law to ensure that those attacked by the media have an equivalent opportunity to reply. For example, in the print media, editors allow aggrieved parties only abbreviated letters of reply, which they publish days after the perceived injustice. In the case of the CBC, at the time, I became so frustrated that I thought something more drastic was required, partly because I believed the CBC, as a publicly funded broadcaster, had a higher duty and should be held to a more rigorous standard of accountability.

I still believe the CBC should be held to a higher standard, but I have changed my mind about some of the details. For example, I thought then that the CBC's national and public affairs shows should have co-producers, one left of centre and one right of centre. Then, when controversial or critical issues came up, each producer would have the right to select and present the most effective champions of their respective points of view. The intent was to achieve meaningful, informative debates rather than sham encounters. Since then, I have rethought the idea of co-producing on the grounds that it could be unworkable and might be too expensive. But I still believe that, at the very least, the CBC should ensure its ombudsman is sufficiently independent to order the CBC to offer equal air time and prominence to any aggrieved group that demonstrated it had been unfairly treated or misrepresented.

Although I sometimes felt like a voice crying in the wilderness, I wasn't alone. The late Marjorie Nichols, a highly respected reporter, was one of many well-informed observers who shared my views. For example, in "CBC Right Out of Bounds trying to Kill Meech Lake," published on April 27, 1991, in the *Ottawa Citizen*, she cited a paper prepared by Queen's University professor John Meisel. She wrote that Meisel "disclosed that the CBC's national political editor decided that the Meech Lake Accord was a fraud on the people of Canada and was designed with the 'sole motivation' of feeding Brian Mulroney's ego. He thereupon set out to discredit the accord, scouring the country for critics, even sending a daily CBC messenger to Pierre Trudeau's Montreal office to solicit negative public statements." She went on to say that, "In abandoning its role as observer, the CBC stepped well beyond journalistic and democratic boundaries." She quoted Professor Meisel as saying, "I was aghast and shocked by what struck me as the appalling arrogant and facile stance of one of the most senior CBC journalists.... I am deeply troubled by any journalist in possession...of an immensely powerful instrument of opinion formation arrogating so critical a role to himself or herself, without being in any way accountable to anyone. My anxiety is all the more acute when the instrument is the public broadcaster."

Nichols concluded her article with this statement about accountability and freedom of the press: "Public corporations are accountable to their shareholders. Private corporations are accountable to consumers. Privately-owned media are accountable to their readers, viewers and owners. The simple truth is that a free press cannot be government owned. The political fetter is always there and it is naïve to believe otherwise.... A press owned by the government is a government press, not a free press."

John Crispo is a producer's dream. Because he has passionate opinions about many topics, he makes himself available to the media. In all the years I've worked with him, he's been unfailingly controversial, articulate, insightful, and refreshingly honest.

One of my favourite John Crispo stories happened while he was a regular contributor to NewsHour, a national news broadcast on the CKO radio network. Although on a skiing trip to Whistler (one of his passions), he had promised to be available, by phone, at the usual time. As the clock ticked closer to the time for John and host Robert Holiday to discuss the issues of the day, I began to get anxious. I'd heard no word from him and had no way of reaching him, skiing blithely on the slopes of Canada's most popular resort. Within just minutes of airtime, John called breathless, but ready for debate. "Where are you?" I asked, with some exasperation. "Oh, don't worry, I wouldn't forget," John replied. "I commandeered the ski patrol hut halfway up the mountain. They were very understanding when I explained it was an emergency. I had a live radio broadcast to do."

Linda Mackay, Producer

CRTC: 1, CRISPO: 0

About the same time Marjorie Nichols and others were sounding off about the CBC's biased news and public affairs programming, I decided to appear before the Canadian Radio-television and Telecommunications Commission (CRTC) to object to both the CBC's bias and inefficiency. The opportunity came during the CRTC's hearing on budget cuts proposed for the CBC. My case in a nutshell was that although I still believed in the principle of the CBC as a vital national institution, I had lost faith in the CBC's journalistic, professional integrity. I suggested that the proposed budget cuts were necessary as a notice to the CBC to clean up its act. If the CBC refused to address the biases in its coverage or its operating inefficiencies, then it should be abolished altogether. I made specific suggestions for ways the CBC could improve without cutting service.

I might as well have saved my breath. True, I probably didn't have much hope of influencing the CRTC anyway, but I shot myself in the foot by showing my contempt for the CRTC commissioners before I even began. (For that sorry little story, see Chapter 7, "Me and My Big Mouth.")

I also made more trouble for myself during my presentation. Just as I as getting to the substance, I saw Patrick Watson, then Chairman designate of the CBC Board of Directors, packing up his briefcase and preparing to leave. It was the last straw for me. I accused him of not being able to take even a little heat in his own kitchen. After all, he had basked all day in the accolades of the many CBC sycophants who had appeared before the Commission. I doubt if I had any friends left in the room by that time, but I was too upset to care. I was angry at myself for coming at all.

BIG FROTH, SMALL BEER

They say every cloud has a silver lining. My appearance before the CRTC was a very big cloud, and it came with a whopper of a silver lining. Or maybe it was just a cloud within a cloud. It depends on one's point of view.

Although I had no impact whatsoever at the CRTC hearing, my appearance caught the attention of someone in the Prime Minister's Office, who told Prime Minster Brian Mulroney he would enjoy my presentation and gave him a tape for his amusement. Apparently, he did enjoy it because the Friday evening after my appearance he called me and asked me to join the CBC's Board of Directors. In fact, the way he put the offer seemed more like a challenge. I agreed with almost indecent haste.

My wife immediately took me to task. Why had I not inquired about the ramifications? Why hadn't I asked about the time commitment, the remuneration, if any, or whether I could have a conflict of interest due to my commitments with other, private broadcasters? No question, she was right, so I tried to call Brian back, but, having taken care of this piece of urgent national business, he had left his office for the weekend.

I started to worry about the possibility of a conflict of interest, but all I could do was leave a message telling Brian not to take any action on my appointment until I could talk to him on Monday morning. I then spent *my* weekend talking to everyone from John Tory to Stephen Lewis. They all assured me that my private broadcast commitments wouldn't be a problem as long as I declared any possible conflict to the appropriate federal authorities, which is what I did shortly thereafter.

When I called Brian as promised on Monday morning, he immediately asked me if I'd lost my nerve. I decided to get back at him by telling him that I wondered whether he really had called me on Friday evening. I reminded him there was a guy on the Royal Canadian Air Farce who sounded more like Brian than he did himself, and since I knew everyone at the CBC had no love for me (or him, for that matter), I thought Air Farce might be pulling a fast one. I added that I had tried to call him back right after his call, and it made me very suspicious when I found he wasn't there. I'll never know for sure, but I think Brian believed my cock and bull story for a few seconds.

There has been much speculation about why the PM named me to the CBC Board. Much of it revolved around the little public spat he was then involved in with Patrick Watson. Patrick had been named as Chair of the CBC's Board by Mulroney just as he had named Stephen Lewis as Canada's Ambassador to the UN, as left wing appointments to prove he didn't just name right wingers to public bodies and positions. Maybe he had named me to the Board simply to aggravate and annoy Patrick, which it surely did, both then and later on, in spades. (Patrick and I subsequently fought about many things, especially *The Valour and the Horror*, but we managed to remain cordial and even friendly on a personal basis throughout our somewhat stormy relationship.)

Another theory repeated *ad nauseum* was that I was named to the CBC Board as a payoff for many years of service to the Progressive Conservative Party, or at least to the free trade debate. The fact is that I have never belonged to, or been loyal to, any political party, but I was totally loyal to the cause of free trade and I did endorse the Tories—as I would have endorsed any party—for battling what amounted to a political war of attrition to secure it. As for a seat on the CBC Board being a patronage appointment, I used to joke that "if this is what Mulroney does for his friends, I hate to think what he does to his enemies."

My appointment to the Board was greeted by what Lubor J. Zink described as an "orgy of vituperation." In his column in *The Ottawa Sun* of April 19, 1991, Zink started with a description of an interview I'd recently given to CBC's *The House*, referring to my admission that perhaps the language I'd used during my presentation to the CRTC had been a bit too strong.

"The attempt to mollify the badgering interviewer didn't, of course, ease the orgy of vituperation of the 'reactionary' professor by the outraged phalanx of guardians of correct progressive thinking," he continued. "But neither did it weaken the non-conformist professor's charges of CBC's all-pervading lib-left slant. In any case, if proof of validity of the fear from new criticism of CBC bias was needed, the trendy media gurus provided it by their frenzied reaction to Crispo's appointment to the Board of Governors of what some irreverent wits dubbed the Canadian Bolshevik Corporation back in the 'revolutionary' 1960's."

Zink went on to skewer Stephen Lewis, Patrick Watson, Dalton Camp, and others as "crypto-socialists" who were squealing like stuck pigs at the prospect of the "independent-minded, and therefore dangerous, professor" (yes, he meant me) challenging what he characterized as their uniformly biased, lib-left, conformist thinking.

Zink concluded with this dilly: "Challenges of that delusion from within the media pose no problem. Those who dare to point it out are, apart from being branded abominable reactionaries, simply denied effective mainstream platform for their 'despicable' views. But a challenge from an influential non-conformist academic whom the so far safely manipulable PM had the effrontery to appoint 'as something of a hired gun to the CBC board of governors,' as a venom-spitting Dalton Camp put it, poses a danger that must be nipped in the bud. Hence the fury of the attacks on Crispo and the commotion in the mutual admiration club of our lib-left mind-polluters."

For a number of years, John complained bitterly about the unfairness of the CBC, which he claimed was in the hands of radical lefties. Then one day he told us Brian Mulroney had called him and said, "I know you hate me, but I think you hate the CBC more, so I want you to serve on the Board of the CBC." John accepted and would then regale us with stories about the Board. The stories were always about John and one or two others frustrating the radical lefties.

Ernest Sirluck, Ph.D., Professor, Dean, and Vice-President, Retired,
University of Toronto, and President, Retired, University of Manitoba

Fortunately, others who were not right wing ideologues also came to my defence. One was Douglas Fisher, formerly an NDP Member of Parliament. In his column in *The Toronto Star* ("CBC hounds howl in unison," April 10, 1991), Fisher discussed the comments about my appointment by five columnists, Michael Valpy, Jeffrey Simpson, Dalton Camp, Gerald Caplan, and Allan Fotheringham. "Is an act bad when a pack of columnists rants at it?" asked Fisher, and then answered his question this way.

Valpy, said Fisher, was *The Globe and Mail*'s "all-purpose, caring columnist" whose emphasis was on my view of the CBC as "a left-wing propaganda machine for which he (meaning me) had only contempt."

Simpson, said Fisher, "was prompted by the 'devastating effectiveness' of Valpy's facts on the case, and he made more sport of Crispo than Valpy and mocked 'this thing' the Tories have about the CBC, starting from the top."

Noting that both Camp and Caplan had also been appointees of Brian Mulroney, Fisher said they "were even more cruel than Simpson" and he traced their connections with each other, with Stephen Lewis, who had also benefited from a Mulroney appointment, and with the CBC. Fisher quoted Caplan as describing my appointment as "simply more evidence of the government's moral corruption" and me as "irrelevant and trivial" and "...a dreary nuisance on the board...small beer" and sneering at me for my "exquisite talent for shamelessness."

Then Fisher tackled Fotheringham, whom he said was his "casually vicious self in mocking Crispo as a money-hungry professional loudmouth," but, Fisher added, Fotheringham was "less the moralist than his four confrères over the appointment, seeing it as a clever ploy by Mulroney just in time to catch some prairie eyes before the Reform delegates gathered."

Fisher then expounded his own view: "I'm chortling, not over one forlorn unbeliever among the CBC hawks, but because of what I wrote last week on the CBC.... Why no hullabaloo in the name of free expression at a government owned and funded crew becoming even more 'the grandest, most influential reportorial and agenda shaping force in the country?'

"My answer? The left triumphant! The silence 'reflects a now durable success in Canada of views held in a loose, left coalition. These liberally minded people are now far more numerous...than the conservatively minded right. They see the CBC as their kind of organization.'

"Any able critic who attacked the CBC's work in news, etc., I said, would be ridiculed 'by most who comment or editorialize for the privately owned news operations which, individually, are so puny alongside the CBC.'

"Witness came...from the five columnists!"

I only met John during the free trade debates in the mid-1980s when we would be on opposite sides on The National and The Journal. He and Tom d'Aquino did a good cop-bad cop act.

John struck me as a local phenomenon—another Toronto contrarian in that his arguments reflected his involvement in and resentment of CBC politics. Toronto is the only place in Canada in which CBC liberalism is really a presence, therefore, the only place in Canada where people find it useful to react against.

John MacLachlan Gray, Columnist, The Globe and Mail

Thanks to *The Globe and Mail*, I also had a chance to fight back. In a full-page article titled "Critiquing the Critics" (May 18, 1991), I began by expressing my surprise that the media outcry about my appointment had been even more negative than I had anticipated. Noting that the criticism came largely from what I described as a fairly well known cabal of largely Toronto-based media types who collectively consider themselves "the Canadian media," I addressed the matter of my style.

"I don't deny that my style sometimes gets me in trouble. I speak forcefully and sometimes with perhaps a little exaggeration and overstatement. When I appeared before the CRTC on the CBC, I spoke forcefully because I felt strongly. Undoubtedly, I did go too far when I said the CBC was 'a lousy left wing, Liberal-NDP pinko network.'

"My critics have repeated this hyperbole *ad nauseum*. But most of them have ignored the fact that I also said that I believe in the CBC despite my misgivings about its performance in news and current affairs. I also made it clear that none of my criticisms had anything to do with its drama, music, sports and other presentations.

"What most of my critics have chosen to downplay or ignore is my basic message about the media in general and the CBC in particular— to put it bluntly that they are potentially the most dangerous and evil force in our society. They are the single most influential force, yet are accountable to virtually no one.

"Just before I joined the board, I learned that the CBC does have an appeal mechanism to deal with claims of lack of balance and fairness. I have been criticized for not knowing such a mechanism existed, but I'm not alone in this. Virtually none of the groups and individuals who have complaints about the CBC's lack of balance have heard of it either.

"One of the first things I want to do as a CBC director is to see that the existence of this ombudsman is well publicized. I also want to ensure that he or she is as impartial, independent and objective as possible and has adequate power to provide remedies to victims of biased commentary and reporting.

"How successful I will be remains to be seen. It doesn't encourage me when my views on balance and fairness are so distorted by CBC insiders."

After discussing what I regarded as highly misleading statements by Dan Oldfield, then President of the Canadian Wire Service Guild, I moved on to the media coverage of my appointment.

"Michael Valpy got so worked up that he returned to the subject over the course of several columns. At least he tried to call me before he cut loose, which none of my other critics felt moved to do. Mr. Valpy seems to believe that no one who is strongly critical of the CBC should serve on its board. Building on this theme he made the more sensible suggestion that all such appointments be subjected to more parliamentary scrutiny than they are. Mr. Valpy was first off the mark, leading the way for many of his more lazy colleagues to simply crib his ideas. The worst was his colleague Jeffrey Simpson who followed Mr. Valpy's first assault. One of his silliest analogies raised the question, 'Would General Motors invite Ralph Nader on to the Board?' To compare the CBC to GM is ridiculous. The CBC is a public corporation; its board should reflect a range of public opinion.

"In *The Toronto Star*, Gerald Caplan and Dalton Camp attacked me in one edition. Mr. Caplan declared that I was irrelevant and trite, then implied that my appointment could mark the end of the CBC. The sleaziest attack came from Mr. Camp who speculated that I might have known of my appointment to the CBC board before I appeared before the CRTC and that the appointment might have depended on my doing a job on the CBC at those hearings.

"Later on *The Star* more or less made up for this tirade with an editorial cartoon of me interviewing myself on the topic of 'intellectual faggots in the media.'

"Allan Fotheringham, having nothing better to say, made up a story about my trying to take over Jack Webster's talk show in Vancouver while I was on a sabbatical leave at Simon Fraser University.

"The most mean spirited outburst came from Diane Francis, who accused me of ranting and raving and made the specious argument that because she and other right wingers sometimes appear on the CBC that proves there is balance.

"On the other side of the media ledger were Doug Fisher and Peter Worthington, among others. The first was Andrew Coyne, who had this as his opener: 'Anyone who attracts the scorn of Jeffrey Simpson, Allan Fotheringham, Dalton Camp, Michael Valpy and Gerry Caplan, all in the space of four days, can't be all good. Surely John Crispo has some faults worth mentioning?'

"He then went on to compare my plight with that of Susan Eng, a controversial gadfly somewhat to my left, whose appointment to the chair of the Metropolitan Toronto Police Services Board was also greeted with consternation. Mr. Coyne concluded: 'Eng can count on well placed admirers to fill the papers with sympathetic prose in her defense. Crispo just has me—and I don't even like him that much.'

"Doug Fisher recalled that he had written a column just the week before my case blew up, saying that anyone who dared to criticize the CBC's 'work in news' would be 'ridiculed' by the likes of critics who 'see the CBC as their kind of organization.'

"Mr. Worthington reinforced the cabal thesis: 'What is instructive in the case is not that some people are upset with the appointment—that's inevitable with anyone who has strong clear opinions backed by evidence—but the speed and intensity of the reaction.'

"Last but hardly least was Barbara Amiel. After reviewing her own experience with the CBC bias, she adds: 'Knowing John Crispo as I do, I believe that he will try simply to get the CBC to pull itself together and understand that it should not become a propaganda machine for any organized group.'

"The CBC's on air reaction to my appointment was mixed. The fairest in its coverage was *Midday*, which had a feisty debate between host Valerie Pringle and myself. I gather they ran our heated exchange unedited, which is as fair as you can get.

I knew John best when I was doing my radio program on CFRB. I think it was called "The Pringle Program," and I interviewed John on a different topic every week for several years. At the time, this was about 1981 to 1985, there were lots of commentators on the left wing, but very few great spokespeople to represent the right end of the spectrum. John Crispo and Diane Francis were about it. John was a regular on my program because he was so great, so provocative, so passionate. He stood out dramatically.

At the time, he drove a little red sports car. I remember raising my eyebrows when I saw it, and he deadpanned, "Mid life crisis."

He did love being on television and radio. He's a complete ham. We're not talking a minute ego here. But he's extremely likeable, very smart, very provocative, hyperactive. He has a great sense of humour and fun and passion. He's full of life. And he has a lovely boyish quality, so eager and keen.

I'm very fond of John. He's very honest, sweet, and sympathetic. He's also very wise, I think because of his background in industrial relations.

Valerie Pringle, Broadcaster & Interviewer

"Contrast that with my treatment by *The House*, with host Judy Morrison. It ran an item featuring members of all three parties attacking me with varying degrees of intensity. That was followed by what I felt was an unfairly edited version of an interview with me. During the interview, Ms. Morrison challenged me to point out a recent example of lack of balance and fairness on the CBC. I cited Peter Gzowski's show with his 'triplets'—Dalton Camp, Stephen Lewis and Eric Kierans—in which all four had a great time going over me. This part of the interview was edited out, just as I predicted it would be.

"On editorial pages I have fared much better. *The Halifax Chronicle-Herald* said: 'As a steward of so much public money the CBC has an obligation to listen to the views of its critics. What better way to ensure this happens than to put one of them in its boardroom?'

"*The Ottawa Sun* opined: 'Clearly, Crispo's three year term won't be easy…but anyone who comes along demanding balance, fairness and efficiency from CBC News and Information will have our support.'

"At the other end of the spectrum was *The Montreal Gazette*: 'The last thing that Canada needs is the presence of a cultural luddite on the CBC board, lashing out to smash what he does not like.'

"*The Edmonton Journal* put me on notice: 'The government, in its wisdom, has appointed Prof. John Crispo, a long time critic who now declares a commitment to the CBC that few would have surmised. Let's see him demonstrate that commitment.'

"The politicians also enjoyed something of a feeding frenzy. The NDP termed my appointment part of a scorched earth policy directed by the government against the CBC.

"Sheila Finestone did most of the speaking for the Liberals and resorted to misquoting me about the Prime Minister's motives in appointing me. She said on the aforementioned *The House* show that I had said that the Prime Minister was putting me on the CBC board to do a number on the corporation.

"On the same show, one of the Tories, in the person of Felix Holtmann, said he felt the CBC had been quite fair to him and his party, and that despite the fact that no matter who is in power the CBC regularly features three party panels with two against the one representing the government.

"What have I learned from the experience? That you can get into a pack of trouble if you speak your mind in this country. On the other hand, no one was paying attention to my concerns about the CBC until I did so.

"I've also learned that nothing Brian Mulroney does these days is going to be judged on its merits. It's almost as if he should advocate the reverse of what he wants in order to get it accepted. That's not healthy.

"Finally, I've learned that there is indeed a media cabal who believe they know what is best for this country. They tolerate criticism by one another but woe betide anyone who attacks the collectivity, this time in the form of their beloved CBC.

"If I had it to do over again, I'd probably tone down some of my overstated rhetoric, but not at the expense of making my basic point in a telling fashion.

"I know I won't be the most welcome addition to the CBC board. My fellow board members are bound to have misgivings and reservations. Then, too, many CBCers have a distaste for me which is quite disturbing.

"I did not accept this appointment to try to destroy the CBC. I think its news and current affairs programming could be more balanced, and that there should be an effective procedure to ensure equal time for all views. I also suspect that the CBC could make more efficient use of tax-payers' money.

"Meanwhile I will probably be appearing even less on CBC than I have in the recent past. Some of my few remaining friends there have told me nobody dares to use me for fear of being seen as kowtowing to me.

"This is why I will continue to do commentaries in the private media, even though some will doubtless suggest that this represents a conflict of interest with my membership on the board. If this is ever ruled to be the case I will resign, since nothing—not even the opportunity to help improve the CBC—is worth giving up my freedom to speak out on all manner of public affairs issues."

I think I met John at his first CBC Board meeting in about 1991 or 1992. As CBC Chair, I had publicly criticized the Prime Minister for a callous statement he had made about cutbacks at the CBC. Characteristically, he flew into a rage and instantly filled the vacancy on our Board with the first person he thought of who was a declared enemy of the whole idea of public broadcasting.

The President (Gerard Veilleux) and I took this with good humour, figuring that even a Crispo with his reputation for rough-and-ready, right-wing, anti-public-enterprise would, once involved in the intricacies of running the CBC, have a contribution to make. And this turned out to be the case.

However, at Crispo's first Board meeting, I think it was in Montreal, I had to openly reprimand him for his outburst against "those jerks!" in programming who had done something he didn't approve of, but also didn't really know anything about and, being the new guy, did not understand. A Board's relationship with a group of energetic and proud program producers was not going to be improved by that kind of language if it was allowed to pass without response from the Chair. So I made a formal reprimand and a demand for retraction. What was striking at that moment, and remained an important part of my personal profile on John Crispo, was the complete lack of resentment or indignation in his response to my chastising him formally in front of the Board, an expression of understanding that he had gone over the top, and an immediate and easy-going apology—while all the time reserving judgment on the issue, of course.

Another time I had to demand of him a public retraction for a damaging public statement that he had made about some current controversy (like many of those, this one pales into insignificance with the passage of time), and, when I pointed out that he had been misinformed and had told the press stuff that was simply wrong, he was instantly, undramatically, and straightforwardly apologetic and dealt with the matter in a decent and straightforward way.

We had lots of arguments in Board meetings and in private. But we had lots of good humoured exchanges, too. John has an appealing strain of self-deprecating humour. He also had a real capacity to slice through the bullshit, and from time to time—at the Boardroom table—was able to lift, in a way that was helpful, the essence of what we should be dealing with out of a dense and intricate discussion. I think a number of Board members who were gritting their teeth in anticipation of his arrival ended up feeling the same somewhat puzzled affection for him that I did.

There is a boyishness about John that undermines the instinctive hostility of some to his seemingly doctrinaire conservatism. This boyishness wins over many of those who are opposed to what he stands for and to the way in which he expresses himself, a boyish good humour and unpretentiousness that overcome what—with a person who took himself really seriously—would be an overwhelming impulse to tell him to bugger off.

On the personal side, one area of common interest we enjoyed was jazz, about which he is far more knowledgeable than I. Our tastes here were pretty convergent, and I recall with pleasure an evening off from Board duties in Montreal where he had sniffed out a good club, and we went and sat for a few hours and drank a few beers (well, I did; I'm not sure that John drinks any alcohol) and listened to some delightful jazz and had a totally companionable evening.

Patrick Watson, Broadcaster, Author, & Former Chair, Board of Directors,
Canadian Broadcasting Corporation

THE VALOUR AND THE HORROR

After the furor over my appointment, I might have expected things to calm down. But what happened during my brief term on the Board eventually led to more strain and stress than I have ever experienced in my life.

My term started peacefully enough. Although I am sure my fellow Board members had misgivings and reservations about me, all of them—including Patrick Watson—treated me with cordiality and respect. I got to know them, I grew to like many of them, and I remain grateful for their open-mindedness and generosity of spirit. In the end, however, I broke with virtually all of them over that despicable and dishonest so-called documentary, *The Valour and the Horror*, first broadcast in January 1992. To me, the story surrounding this documentary epitomizes what was and remains so wrong with much of the CBC's news and public affairs programming.

The Valour and the Horror was a three-part series I believe was designed to smear much of the Canadian wartime record during World War II. It was produced by Brian and Patrick McKenna, brothers of Irish descent I suspected of hating the English and any kind of war. The CBC provided them with an opportunity to vent all their spleen at the expense of Canadian taxpayers and did little or nothing to determine the accuracy of what was the McKennas' personal propaganda piece before it was aired. The ensuing outcry may have even surprised the CBC's raft of other propagandists who continue to use its airwaves to propagate their view of what is politically correct and what is not.

The outcry was led by Canada's veterans but was joined by many columnists and historians. To provide some flavour of the intensity of the debate, let me cite just one Canadian Press article which I believe is more than fair to the McKennas. Published by *The Edmonton Journal* on June 26, 1992, "Historians blast CBC producer for documentary about war" by John Ward reported that Brian McKenna had dismissed the criticisms of three historians as misguided. Ward also reported that supporters of McKenna, speaking before a Senate subcommittee, had characterized attacks on the controversial documentary as "unCanadian" and said they "smacked of McCarthyism."

Ward quoted Lieutenant-Colonel John English of the National Defence College as saying that "McKenna had behaved 'as a petulant flower child' during a battlefield tour that English conducted."

Ward then quoted academics Professor Reg Roy of the University of Victoria and Professor Robert Vogel of McGill University as saying that McKenna started with a certain point of view and tailored his research to fit. Vogel, who had written several books on Normandy and the battles in Europe, also said that the lack of context made the third part of the production "virtually incomprehensible" and cited a series of factual errors. Bill Carter, a military historian from the University of New Brunswick, was quoted as saying the documentary "is not good history, it is sub-standard."

The McKennas had supporters in Professor Michael Bliss of the University of Toronto and Professor Brian Villa of the University of Ottawa. Both said they were shocked at the way the McKennas were being treated by the Senate subcommittee. The CBC weighed in with a team led by Patrick Watson. As well, several prominent writers, including Pierre Berton, called the Senate hearing a "witch-hunt." Ward quoted Berton as saying, ""The Senate isn't composed of historians or people who can tell whether something's accurate or not, and they've decided in advance it's not."

While Patrick Watson and other high level CBC sycophants were appearing and speaking in defence of the McKennas, I talked to many historians about the injustice *The Valour and The Horror* had done to our wartime history, and I was getting more and more angry. I tried to contain my public utterances, but I was having difficulty because everyone who knew me also knew where I was bound to stand when someone deliberately smeared both our veterans and our war effort. After all, I wouldn't be here and I would never have had the freedoms I have enjoyed throughout my professional life had it not been for Canada's disproportionately high contribution to the defeat of the Axis powers.

Fortunately, the Board decided to refer the matter to one of the CBC's ombudsmen, Bill Morgan, a man I came to admire and respect as much as anyone I have ever known. I believe that without Bill Morgan, the whole issue would have torn the CBC Board apart, and I regret to say that I also believe the majority would have sided with the McKennas.

When I joined the Board in 1991, Bill Morgan was the network's English language ombudsman, yet I had never heard of him or his office. I had been roundly criticized for my ignorance by Patrick Watson and others, so I decided to test my knowledge against the knowledge of other Canadians. For more than a year, in speeches all over the country, I would ask audiences whether they knew the CBC had two ombudsmen—one for English language and one for French language matters. Based on the responses, I can assure you the existence of the ombudsmen was one of the best kept secrets in this nation.

When I found out about Bill Morgan, which was, by the way, well before *The Valour and the Horror* reared up, I called him. He came to my office at the University of Toronto immediately and we had a long talk. I can't tell you what he thought about me, but I was favourably impressed by him. He had excellent professional credentials as a former Director of CBC News and Public Affairs and as the virtual founder of CBC's Newsworld Network, and he seemed determined to ensure that CBC programming lived up to its own code of broadcast standards, something else about which few outside the organization knew anything. As I recall, Bill and I agreed to judge each other on our respective behaviour and merits. Neither of us had any inkling how intertwined our activities would later become.

Bill attended the Board meeting at which it was decided that he should assess *The Valour and the Horror* in the light of the CBC's own broadcast standards. I believe we chatted briefly at the time. I did not see him or talk to him privately again until after he reported his findings to the Board. This is important to note because later the likes of Pierre Berton and Knowlton Nash falsely accused me of unduly influencing Bill while he was preparing his report. They never retracted this blatant lie, which was part of their scurrilous and unworthy effort to smear both Bill and his report after he released his findings.

I made several attempts to correct the record. One was in the form of a letter to the editor published by *The Globe and Mail* on April 6, 1995.

"A recent article in *The Globe and Mail* reveals how far a big lie can travel and grow once it gets started. I wish to clarify the record on this lie.

"I refer to Ray Conlogue's *Globe and Mail* article entitled Media Howl Gives Impression Of Culturally Intolerant Quebec (Feb. 18), in which he claims that 'Crispo then abused his authority by making intimidating telephone calls to producers, journalists and even the CBC Ombudsman.'

"As his source for this outrageous lie, Mr. Conlogue cites Knowlton Nash, apparently from his recent book *The Microphone Wars: A History of Triumph and Betrayal in the CBC*. In that volume, Mr. Nash claims that I repeatedly tried to influence the ombudsman while he was preparing his report on *The Valour and The Horror*.

"There is absolutely no truth to that or any of these other allegations, as I hope and trust all those who served with me on the CBC Board will know. I fought hard for my belief in accuracy, balance and fairness while I was on the board, but I never stooped to the kind of behaviour imputed to me in the unsubstantiated public charges of Mr. Conlogue and Mr. Nash."

This is what actually happened when Bill brought his report to the Board. I had no idea what he was going to say. The first inkling I got was when Patrick Watson accosted me at the beginning of the meeting at which Bill rendered his judgment. Patrick asked me not to gloat. I was so relieved and satisfied that I don't think I was in a mood to gloat. Anyway, that was hardly the issue. The real issue was what to do about

Bill's disturbing and troubling findings, which I later learned he had been induced to water down considerably under tremendous pressure from the CBC brass.

William Walker's "CBC official condemns controversial war series," published in *The Toronto Star* on November 11, 1992, provides a good sample of the early reactions to Bill's report.

Describing it as a stunning move, Walker reported that the CBC's own ombudsman had condemned *The Valour and the Horror* as flawed and misleading. Noting that outraged veterans had complained that the series "improperly portrayed Canadian bomber pilots as drunken and leaderless, bombing Germany indiscriminately and killing innocent women and children because they had no clear military strategy," Walker went on to quote from Bill's report: "The series as it stands is flawed and fails to measure up to CBC's demanding policies and standards."

Walker then reported on reactions to the report, beginning with Pierre Berton, who said, "I find it very weird that the National Film Board (the series co-producers) would stand four square behind this film and the CBC would not." He also quoted Berton as saying that he understood I, whom he described as "a Progressive Conservative appointee" and "an enemy of the CBC," had lobbied strongly for the film to be criticized.

After Walker reported that then CBC President Gerard Veilleux had said the CBC's vice-president of news and current affairs, Tim Kotcheff, would be making recommendations to ensure "greater journalistic balance in the making of documentaries" in the future, Walker returned to Berton. He quoted Berton as saying that investigations of the film were inappropriate and that it meant "the CBC will be very reluctant to produce anything in the future that is the slightest bit controversial.... They won't be able to repeat this program, as they should, or show it in schools, as it should be." Berton then went on to gripe at the Senate's role in the affair. "Any time an appointed body (like the Senate) is allowed to probe the CBC, we are in danger. What's next? The sooner we're rid of these guys the better."

Brian McKenna claimed that he'd been shut out of what he called the CBC's closed investigation, adding, "It would have taken the courage of the early morning for the CBC to stand up for this series on the eve of Remembrance Day. That courage was not there."

I met John when I was at the Clarkson Centre for Business Ethics. On the research side, I'm studying Boards, and I've seen a lot of rubber stamp Boards. One theme is dissent. I talked to him about how corporate Boards operate and especially about constructive dissent. He is fearless. He speaks his mind.

I interviewed John about dissent after he came off the CBC Board. He was so impressive, I invited him to my class to talk about constructive dissent in the boardroom two years in a row (1997 and 1998).

Later, when I taught first year management students at Schulich in classes of about 350, I would always bring in John to debate Buzz Hargrove. John would never miss an opportunity to debate Buzz. The last time I asked him to debate was in 2001, but he refused. He said as he's growing older, he's coming to agree with everything Buzz said. There's no debate any more.

Summing up, I describe him as irreplaceable, provocative, a mentor, educator. He marries style and substance, he cares for students, and he cares very deeply for his craft, the practice of teaching. He always, always makes time for his students. He was always great with staff, too, always welcoming. He never looked down on anyone.

Richard Leblanc, C.M.C., B.Sc., M.B.A., LLB, J.D., LLM, Ph.D. (Candidate),
Corporate Governance Program, Schulich School of Business, York University, Toronto

---

BREAKING RANKS

For me, Bill Morgan's report on *The Valour and the Horror* also marked the beginning of the end of my term on the CBC's Board of Directors. I know what I did was worth the fight, but I do not want to go through anything like that ever again.

Late one afternoon while we were still at a Board meeting in St. John's, Newfoundland, the Directors were asked to approve the draft of a Board statement to accompany the release of the Ombudsman's report. We were told to read it over with a view to approving it as quickly as possible so that it could be translated and issued the next day.

I could see at a glance that the statement, rather than supporting the Ombudsman or his report, undercut both. The statement was a whitewash of the whole exercise in self-discipline. So, I declined to comment on the draft until everyone else had.

None of my Board colleagues had any serious objections to the statement, and I was so upset that I decided not to say anything substantive. I simply told the Board I would be strongly dissenting and wanted my dissent released with both documents—the Ombudsman's report and the Board's official reaction to it. I then left the meeting to draft my dissent and made several calls to people I could trust—none of whom has ever violated my trust in them that awful night—to make sure I was on the right course. Either late that night or early the next morning—I can't remember which—I was prevailed upon by some of the few Board members in whom I still had any real faith to review my concerns with the entire Board. I agreed, although reluctantly, because I knew they were right in saying that I had an obligation to do so.

We met in the morning. I told the Board I wanted six fundamental changes in the draft. Otherwise, I would indeed dissent and use the original draft as the basis for my dissent so everyone would understand the Board's position when I withdrew from the meeting. It was a very unpleasant session. At one point, I was accused by a Board member I liked of blackmailing the Board. But I knew I was right, and I refused to back down. As a result, and I truly believe on the merits of my position, the Board's statement was amended to reflect my views.

This should have put the matter to rest, but it didn't. All I knew at that time was that the Board did not dare release the original version of the statement if I was going to dissent and take the facts public. What concerns me to this day is that I know the Board would have gone ahead with the dishonest whitewash had I not been there.

The very next day, the CBC's professional staff—and I use the word professional sardonically—and its outside friends fought back in defence of the McKennas with every weapon at their disposal. It began with an article by Pierre Berton in *The Toronto Star* that described pretty accurately what had transpired at the Board meeting and blamed me for the Board's backing of the Ombudsman's report. Clearly, Berton and probably others were fully informed about what was going on during supposedly confidential Board meetings. We all knew the source of the leaks, but no one could prove it and nothing could be done about it.

For me, the last straw came when the CBC used its domination of the Gemini Awards to secure the top documentary prize for *The Valour and the Horror*. After trying and failing to get the Board to condemn this affront and travesty, I again broke ranks with my colleagues and published a lengthy and strong condemnation on my own.

As I said in "The Valour, the Horror, the Travesty" (published in *The Toronto Star*, March 9, 1993), "*The Valour and The Horror* received this award in spite of the CBC ombudsman's well-researched finding that parts of it were inaccurate, distorted and pure invention; in spite of a critical, well-reasoned report from a Senate sub-committee; in spite of the military historians who detailed the various falsehoods the series contained; and in spite of the injustice the series has done to Canadian veterans.

"This award is the last straw for me. For too long now I have remained silent on the media frenzy over *The Valour and The Horror*. I kept quiet out of deference and respect for my colleagues on the CBC board of directors, whom I can only hope will understand why I feel I must speak out now....

"Why people like the supporters of this series feel they have to denigrate Canada's great and valiant contribution to the Allied cause during World War II in such an unfair way is beyond me. Perhaps what bothers me most about these programs—aside from the unwarranted hurt they have inflicted upon our veterans and their families—is that they exacerbate the traditional tendency among Canadians to diminish rather than celebrate their real national achievements.

"As strongly critical as I personally felt about the series, I recognized that there was no choice but to trust the CBC's ombudsman system to determine whether the series violated our media accountability standards. I counseled every veterans' group which approached me to do likewise.

"In the end, my faith in this system was rewarded, a matter of great satisfaction to which I will return....

"Perhaps the most outrageous charged leveled at us by those who sought to distract attention from what was wrong with the programs was the absurd claim that we were just doing the bidding of the government, the Senate Sub-Committee on Veterans' Affairs or this country's veterans. These charges were totally without foundation....

"By maligning the CBC's ombudsman, the supporters of the series were clearly hoping to silence not only him but any future independent authority who might point out and criticize irresponsible use of the airwaves. Regrettably, as I have said, massive numbers of our own producers and journalists joined in this cabal or conspiracy.

"Instead of condemning the CBC for upholding and acting upon its ombudsman's report on *The Valour and The Horror*, members of the media should have been praising the corporation for having the courage to be critical of itself....

"The CBC ombudsman's report represented a triumph for the concept of media accountability, for the integrity of the CBC as a public broadcaster and for professional journalism in general. It upheld the important principle that while journalists should be controversial and provocative, they must get their facts straight and not proceed on the basis of some preconceived notion or distort and make up evidence when they can't find what they are looking for....

"The courage and honesty the ombudsman has shown deserves the support not only of the CBC board but of the public whose trustees the CBC's board of directors are. In the end, our handling of this trying case will decide the future of media accountability at the CBC and whether the corporation is run just for the benefit of its staff and their friends or truly in the public interest.

"I believe that the CBC, its producers and its on air news and public affairs personalities can and must be both free and responsible. If this mutually compatible and essential combination is not rigorously maintained throughout the organization then the CBC ultimately will not survive.

"The CBC is a public trust, largely funded by public money, and none of us—producers, journalists, management or board members— should ever let ourselves forget it."

John is an academic who has interacted with the real world of business and labour. He brought to the real world the knowledge and insights of a well-trained university mind. He also brought the strengths and weaknesses of the real world's positions and exposed them in the classroom. He has the capacity and legitimacy to be listened to by all sides.

At the same time, John kept up with and contributed to his subject. He is a participant in the national debate of major economic issues. In a healthy, vibrant democracy, you need John Crispos engaged in issues of the day. He's lively and robust, and he also brings humour. He keeps them entertained. You don't see eyes glazing over when John Crispo gets up to speak.

Peter Russell, O.C., Professor Emeritus,
Department of Political Science, University of Toronto

AFTERMATH

The vindictiveness of the McKennas and their allies both within and beyond the CBC knew no limits. Perhaps the worst thing they did was virtually isolate the Ombudsman, despite—or perhaps because of—his courage, decency, and honour, attributes and qualities few of them could ever hope to match.

My own fate was mild in comparison. For a short time, a small cabal of Board members considered asking the Prime Minister to request my resignation. When I got wind of this amateur conspiracy, I contacted some of the Prime Minster's staff and suggested that if this ludicrous proposal should come forward they should instead have the Prime Minister ask all the other members to resign. My contacts loved the idea but chances are it would never have happened. In any event, calmer and saner minds prevailed at the Board level and no request for my resignation went forward. I confess I was disappointed.

Eventually, I did resign shortly before the end of my term. When I left, it was with memories that were not as fond as I would liked. I also left behind what I regarded as unsatisfactorily finished business.

One matter concerns the Board's refusal to sue the McKennas for slander. They and their allies subjected the Board, the Corporation, and the President—but not the Chair, Patrick Watson—to repeated scur-rilous attacks. Any self-respecting organization and group smeared by such blatant abuses and falsehoods would have fought back. My col-leagues would not. I never understood why.

The second concerns the CBC's obvious support of the Liberal Party during Prime Minister Chrétien's first election triumph. By the process of elimination, the CBC's producers apparently decided they had no choice but to support the Liberals. The Tories had already cut the CBC's budget, the Reform Party was threatening to privatize the Corporation, the Bloc Québeçois was prepared to break up the country, and the CBC knew the NDP was going nowhere. When the Board dared to confront key CBC public affairs staff on their obvious pre-elec-tion biases, we were told in two consecutive meetings that it was not the CBC's fault that the Liberals were running "a Teflon campaign" and therefore the Liberals' campaign was very difficult to attack. Several of us pointed out how non-teflon the campaign really was by citing the many holes in the Liberals' famous Red Book, but the CBC staff never let up in their support of the Liberals.

Many other observers noted this favouritism. George Bain's column in *Maclean's* was typical ("Soft on the Grits, hard on the Tories," November 29, 1993). He also brought out some disturbing features both about the media and about our supposedly non-partisan public service. Referring to what he called the old romance between the Ottawa press corps and federal civil servants, Bain wrote, "The natural Governing Party is back. Across the capital, the supposedly staunchly nonpartisan civil service is having trouble suppressing its glee. As one senior bureau-crat told a colleague the day after Chretien's Liberals swept into power, 'I feel like a kid abandoned by his parents for nine years and left in the hands of an abusive babysitter....'

"I am so choked up I am scarcely able to say that if the senior bureau-crat in question were willing to come out from behind the screen of anonymity he/she ought to be fired on principle, the principle being that the parliamentary system counts on a public service able to serve equal-ly whatever government the country gives it. Senior bureaucrats who aren't up to it, as this one can't have been, should be removed for their own protection, if nothing else....

"My only quarrel with (Gils Gherson) is that, in singling out the public service as one important segment of the Ottawa establishment that simultaneously looks upon the Liberals as the natural governing party and pretends to staunch nonpartisanship, he takes too narrow a view. The Ottawa press corps, another part of the same establishment, does the same....

"Just four days before the election, Peter Gzowski asked it, not quite in that form, of a media panel on Morningside. 'Perhaps the story,' he suggested, 'is the Liberal party. The consensus is that it is going to form a minority or a majority government. I don't sense it has been under the same scrutiny through the Liberals own choice. It has been difficult to get Mr. Chretien in for an interview. Where are his answers on what he would replace the GST with, or what his deficit plan is?'

"Two of his panelists, Jennifer Robinson, national editor of the Montreal Gazette and Dale Eisler, editor of Leader-Star News Service in Regina, thought Chretien had enjoyed pretty much a free ride. Eisler said there was a 'sort of comfort factor with Canadians and the media, with the Liberals.' He cited the natural governing party notion as a factor. Christopher Waddell, senior program producer at CBC television's Prime Time News, thought the Liberals had been 'held under a fair amount of scrutiny'—emphasis on the 'fair'—but allowed for some difference because 'Liberal policies do not predicate very much change from the way government has operated in the past few years.' (That was funny; a point made against Kim Campbell was that she wasn't change enough.) Robinson said: 'Yes, I think the Liberals have had a real free ride in the campaign, partly because Chretien has run a very intelligent campaign. He has managed to divert attention from mistakes he's made.'

"If these four were all representative in believing the Liberals got off lightly, how to explain why—why weren't reporters equally demanding detail of policies, and why weren't they equally critical when they didn't get it?

"But if the Tory campaign was weak enough in itself to earn defeat, which is debatable, the party's devastation clearly had deeper roots.

Certainly, over nine years they had their mistakes and messes, but what they also had to help them downhill was the most savagely judgmental press any Canadian government has faced, at least post–Second World War….

"In 1984, the Mulroney government was no sooner sworn in than it was under media attack. There was a vindictive air to it, and it never stopped."

Despite the cozy closeness of the media with its selected friends, I still believe that the media, by and large, try to act responsibly, and I try to give the CBC the benefit of the doubt. I also realize that during the period from the late 1960s to the early 1980s, when I was a fixture on the CBC and other broadcast media, I wasn't particularly conscious of any institutional bias. Perhaps it was because I was comfortable with the predominantly left-of-centre point of view. But once my eyes were opened, I couldn't *not* see the fundamental bias and lack of accountability. Nor can I accept the view that legitimate and honest criticism compromises freedom of the press.

In my view, media accountability is pretty much a paper tiger in Canada, and especially in the CBC. Why? Because the CBC's news and public affairs units are forces unto themselves. They're loaded with untouchables, like Peter Mansbridge, who are not subject to any real checks and balances. As Knowlton Nash said in an interview, I believe in 1994, "My role as a journalist is to establish the national agenda." If he and his colleagues and contemporaries believed that then, they probably still believe it now. And if they do, how will anyone who chooses to challenge them ever succeed in being heard? And if other voices and points of view are not being heard consistently and compellingly, then how can Canadians have any assurance that they are being told all sides of the truth that they need to hear in order to make balanced and reasoned judgements?

As I said in an article in *Maclean's* ("Crispo's Cure: A Vocal Critic Pleads for Fairness at the CBC," September 26, 1994), I realize that anything I say about the CBC will always be suspect if only because of the harshness of my past criticisms. I'm not surprised that some will dismiss me as simply bitter and paranoid.

To a degree of bitterness I plead guilty. But paranoid? No.

I am bitter because of the price I have paid personally and professionally for standing up for what I believed to be right, especially during the battle over *The Valour and the Horror*. Looking back, I realize I kept silent for too long. I had to learn the hard way that one should never hold oneself back from telling the truth, especially when one is a public trustee as one is when serving on the Board of a public corporation like the CBC.

I was hurt professionally by being virtually banished from the airwaves and the print media. Why? Because I was such an outspoken critic not only of the news and public affairs staff at CBC, but also of their peers.

My hope is that the CBC will revitalize itself as a broadcaster and become a more accurate, balanced, and fair news and public affairs programmer. I also hope that the CBC will lead the way for other Canadian media. Canadians should insist on no less. Our future depends upon it.

Travelling with John can be exhausting. It's hard to do without becoming an event. For example, a couple of years ago, we were skiing at Mt. Tremblant. We were on the gondola and two women were sitting across from us. One said, "You must be John Crispo." It turned out she had been a student of his, and we ended up having a long conversation.

Every meal starts out calmly enough, but soon becomes a debate involving everyone for six or eight tables around. John draws people into conversation. The more contentious it is, the better he likes it.

Douglas B. Skelton, P.Eng., Retired Consulting Engineer and Old Friend

---

I have long thought that the CBC—and indeed all Crown corporations—should be overseen by Boards of Directors appointed by each of our national political parties proportionate to their representation in Parliament. Years ago, I saw this approach working in Austria. I'm convinced that with all parties represented, the Board of the CBC would then have the clout to counsel and require much more balanced and fair coverage than the CBC is delivering to this day.

HOPE SPRINGS ETERNAL

Until the glorious day when Canadians have the privilege of being treated with absolute respect and scrupulous fairness, there are some remedies they can use when abused by the media. One is suing for libel, but it is an extremely costly business. Another is to appeal to the ombudsman where one exists. Some media outlets do have ombudsmen trying to keep them honest and fair.

Then there are the press councils. I didn't have much faith in these constructs until I tested the system personally in 1998. The body was the Ontario Press Council, and the occasion was objecting to the gutting of an article on the proposed megabank mergers by *The Globe and Mail*. I was conditionally against the mergers; *The Globe*'s editorial position was firmly in favour.

What happened? *The Globe* assured me that all my article needed was some minor editing. But when it was published on October 1, 1998, almost one-third of it was missing. The result was, among other things, that I was opposed to the mergers under any circumstances.

Here, for example, are two paragraphs that were cut:

"I would simply bar these mergers at least until after we attract new entrants who can compete effectively with our branch banking systems. Otherwise, we cannot be assured of enough competition to keep these proposed mega banks treating us efficiently and fairly.

"The only caveat I would add concerns the long run. If globalization and technological change continue to unfold the way they have been, we may well some day have truly world-wide banking for the full range of bank services. If, as and when that happens, we will have nothing to fear from unlimited bank mergers in Canada and probably much to gain. But let us not put the cart before the horse and gamble on something with too many risks for bank customers and the public at large."

Horrified, I wrote one and then another Letter to the Editor. *The Globe* declined to publish either one. I submitted my concerns to the Ontario Press Council. Under the Council's rules, the publication in question is required to try to work out the matter with the complainant. Shortly thereafter, I assume because of my appeal to the Council, *The Globe* very graciously agreed to publish a second, and I believe improved, article on the mergers. I was glad and relieved that our dispute ended cordially because, as you have probably gathered by now, *The Globe and Mail* has published many of my articles over the years without giving me any cause for concern.

And so, I end this chapter on an upbeat note. There is hope for balance and fairness. All we have to do, whether part of the media or a bystander, is remain vigilant, perhaps be a bit sceptical, and speak the truth as we perceive it...and keep speaking it until, eventually, all of our voices are heard.

John Crispo first came to my attention in the mid-1970s while I was News Director at CFTR-Toronto and he was a professor at the University of Toronto. He would, one of the staff reporters assured me, make an ideal commentator because he is saturated with good ideas and blessed with superb articulation but more importantly doesn't talk like a professor. And so began one of the longest, most rewarding professional friendships. Through the years John and I have debated many issues on many radio stations across the country and although his ideas are eminently challengeable, he is always entertaining.

Like all of us, from time to time, he suffers from political myopia, but his spirited defense of the most untenable positions is always interesting and many times quite compelling.

But of all the attributes that combine to personify John Crispo the man, I have been most impressed by his boundless energy and unceasing loyalty. It's unfortunate he never entered politics. The body politic in this country could use some snap, crackle, and Crispo.

Robert Holiday, Broadcaster

Chapter 6

Close Encounters
of the Political Kind

Throughout my professional life, I've been frustrated by my inability to take a consistently active part in party politics or stand for election. I came close twice but was rejected, first by John Turner on behalf of the Liberal Party and soon after by Brian Mulroney on behalf of the Progressive Conservative Party. In retrospect, I realize these rejections were my good fortune because, although I have politics in my blood, I could never accept the degree of party discipline required by Canada's parliamentary democracy. I've always joked that to be a politician in Canada you must be prepared to bray like an ass and flap like a seal on command of the Party whip.

Maybe if I'd been born in the U.S.A. I might have entered politics. South of the border there's so much more freedom within political parties. Americans have conservative Democrats and liberal Republicans, so there's room for just about any kind of politician, perhaps even me. I suspect I would have gravitated towards the Republicans, philosophically speaking, although there have been times when I could just as easily have been a Democrat.

The problem in the States is that private interest groups are the major source of funding for American political parties. Political action committees representing virtually every vested interest in the country channel money to candidates. The result is that nearly everyone running for office has to be on the take to finance his or her election campaign. The only question is the size of the bribe. If the views of the candidate are consistent with the view of the lobby offering the cash, the bribe will be smaller. If the views of the candidate differ from the lobby's, the bribe will be larger. So, I suppose I wouldn't have found a comfortable place in the U.S. political system either.

Although I've never been actively involved in any political party in Canada, I have at one time or another dabbled on the fringes of most of them. My relations with politicians of all stripes is as good a way as any to demonstrate my version of political involvement. Because I enjoy the cut-and-thrust of debate, I generally enjoy politicians with whom I disagree. I find it much more engaging and productive to argue with someone over honest differences of opinion than simply to reinforce one's existing opinions by talking with those who share one's views. This has nothing to do, of course, with the personalities of the individuals involved.

RAE DAYS

My most sustained interaction with any politician began with Bob Rae long before he surprised everyone, including himself, by being elected as the first NDP Premier of Ontario. I remember meeting Bob in the Royal York Hotel in downtown Toronto the day after he was elected. I was giving a speech and he was holding his first press conference as Premier. We compared thoughts on who was more taken aback by his election triumph.

Bob and I actually go back to the 1970s when he was one of the so-called radical students at the University of Toronto. At that time, I was moving from left of centre to centre, maybe even right of centre, and I deemed it very important to have a left-wing teaching assistant (T.A.) for my large undergraduate industrial relations course to ensure my students got a balanced perspective. For two years, Bob came to my classes and then led smaller group seminars for the students. He would contradict or disagree with almost everything I said in my lectures—and sometimes during the lectures themselves—thus helping me provide students with one of the most stimulating courses they probably ever had.

I never found Bob's equal as a T.A. By the end of my teaching career I couldn't find anyone resembling a left-of-centre T.A. because the student body in general became so conservative, due in large part to students' preoccupation with getting good marks so as to ensure their future employment prospects.

Dad and me before I could argue with him.

Grandmother's dock, Eastbourne, Lake Simcoe

Barbara, my wife, and me at a dinner with Brian Mulroney
during the free trade debate.

Golfing at Banff Springs, returning to old haunts,
now as a player as opposed to caddy.

Fishing in Bermuda after a successful day out on the Atlantic
with my son-in-law Brian, which is what led to our bonding.

Racing on Canada One in the Caribbean,
a highlight of a life of sailing.

On horseback with my daughter Sharon,
enjoying one of my favourite pastimes.

Me with my favourite dog, Lilly,
who is just a open as I am.

Me with my daughters Carol and Sharon at our farm.

Me with my wife, Barbara, on a cruise,
sharing a drink (hers alcoholic, mine not).

Grandpa Tractor with grandson Nicholas at the farm.

Barbara and I skiing at the top of Blackcomb Mountain,
Whistler, British Columbia.

Graduation, Bachelor of Commerce,
University of Toronto, 1956.

Left, top: Mother, Betty Gillespie Sifton,
and brother Martin. Eastbourne, Simcoe.

Left, bottom: Hiking with my stepson
Matthew near Whistler, B.C.

Above: Here I am with some of my favourite antagonists and friends on one of numerous post-election panels. Hugh Segal, Bob Rae, Francis Lankin.

Right, top: Me with Jean Marchand, the wisest of the three wise men Trudeau brought to Ottawa.

Right, bottom: One of thousands of public addresses in a career filled with such things.

Me, Barbara, grandson Nicholas in Bermuda.

I have no idea how many times or on how many issues Bob and I debated over the years, but I know we didn't miss many opportunities to take each other on.

I think Bob was still studying law at the University of Toronto when we ended up as antagonists on one of Pierre Berton's *The Great Debate* television shows in the late 1970s. I don't even remember what the topic was, but I do recall how Bob did a real number on me.

For a start, when Pierre introduced us, he highlighted the fact that Bob had been my T.A. for two years. I interrupted to protest that this might lead some of the audience to conclude that I was responsible for Bob. To underscore my point, I foolishly added that Bob had learned nothing while he was my T.A. There was a momentary pause, and then Bob said quietly, "There was nothing to learn." It was clear that Pierre loved Bob's riposte. Pierre then turned to me and said the ball was now in my court. I replied limply that I thought the ball was in a puddle and couldn't be retrieved. There was no comeback at hand.

But that was just for starters. On *The Great Debate*, the live studio audience voted on the question both before and after the debate. What I didn't know was that Bob had packed the audience with members of the University of Toronto's NDP Club. Before the debate, they all voted on my side of the question. After the debate, they all switched sides, creating the impression that Bob had won hands down. Whether or not he had didn't matter. In those cases, appearance is all. What a guy.

It took me years to get back at him. In 1992, when Bob was Premier of Ontario, his government decided to provide major funding for a new building for what was then called the Faculty of Management at the University of Toronto. To mark the grand occasion, Rob Pritchard, the greatest President U of T ever had, presided over a reception on November 27, 1992. Many dignitaries spoke—rather dully, I must say—including the Premier himself, who wasn't as dull as the others, if only because he took a gratuitous shot at me. He said it was rather out of character for me to attend such an occasion or any other university function for that matter.

Well, I couldn't let Bob get away with that, so I pushed my way to the podium and wrestled the microphone out of the President's resisting hand. I'm sure everyone was convinced that I was going to say something so offensive to Premier Bob that he'd withdraw the grant posthaste. Far from it. I simply wanted to explain the real reason why U of T got the money. I told the august assemblage the "There was nothing to learn" story and suggested that Bob had been feeling so guilty about what he'd done to me that he'd been waiting years to find an appropriate way to make amends. I further suggested that he'd finally found the way by providing the Faculty of Management with new facilities. I got a lot of laughs, but I think they were mostly out of relief that I hadn't blown the whole project.

Bob's and my most recent debate date was in June 1998 when we appeared at a charity event in Collingwood, Ontario. The topic was "What's Good for Bay Street is Good for Main Street," and I was expected to take the affirmative. The thing was I couldn't possibly argue for it because the banks had just announced their proposed mega mergers, and I was strongly opposed. When we got to the event, I suggested to the audience that Bob and I change sides on the grounds that Bob was now fronting for a major Bay Street law firm. Bob sagely declined my invitation, and we ended up having a discussion rather than a debate.

During Bob's premiership, our differences widened to some degree. I tried to be fair to him, but I was concerned that he was now in a position to do real harm and not just talk about it. Consequently, I spoke out against many of his initiatives.

My view was that Bob got to be Premier because the Tories had blown the election and the Liberals had missed the opportunity by being too confident and cocky that they were next in line to govern. Bob and the NDP were the default choice. They looked attractive, beguiling, and innocent to a disenchanted and disillusioned electorate.

The problems started immediately, however, because Bob was pretty well a one-man show who wasn't backed up by a sufficiently talented caucus. Also, the NDP lacked coherent programs and tried to move too far too fast on any number of issues, from the budget and auto insurance to a long list of legislation dealing with labour. To be fair, Bob was hampered by a recession, with its accompanying plunge in government revenues. This is what made him recognize how serious a fiscal situation the province was in well ahead of his caucus.

It's interesting to speculate on what would have happened had Bob been elected to a second term. That might have given him time to regroup, upgrade the quality of his caucus, and build some bridges to the outraged business constituency. He had the capacity to be a much better premier than circumstances permitted him to be. I've often wondered how high his star would have risen if he had been more opportunistic and joined the Liberal Party instead of tying himself to the NDP.

I got to know John Crispo when I came back from Oxford in 1974 for law school. I needed a job and my friend Peter Russell referred me to John. We talked and agreed that I would work for him as a Teaching Assistant, which I did for a couple of years. Then, in 1976–1977, when John was on sabbatical, I taught in his place, which was a lot of fun. We've been friends ever since. I have a lot of affection for him.

John was an outstanding lecturer, very funny, very irreverent. He moved around a lot and was always joking. But his jokes were never set pieces. They always came from the moment.

He had terrific rapport with his students. Never underestimate his dedication to his students and his seriousness about teaching. At the same time, he was always conscious that it was a performance. He understood that. Many of his colleagues didn't and don't. That's also been the rap on him. He was dismissed as so much of a showman.

John and I have always separated our friendship from our political views. We have never agreed on anything in politics, and he was never helpful to me when I was Premier of Ontario. Absolutely not. Mind you, I didn't ask for help and I don't know what he may have said in private. Maybe he was going around saying, "Rae's not that crazy."

The Honourable Bob Rae, Former Premier of Ontario
and now Partner, Goodmans LLP

"WILD BILL" DAVIS

With his baby face, benign look, and ever-present pipe, William (Bill) Davis looked like everyone's favourite grandfather. But "Wild Bill," as

I used to refer to him, was expert in reading the public mood and a master of political timing. I think he may have been the shrewdest politician I have ever encountered.

I knew John Crispo as an irascible critic of just about everyone and everything in politics. He didn't even spare me but I have to admit that I sometimes benefitted from his caustic but constructive criticisms. Luckily, however, many others were more often his targets than I.

The Honourable William G. Davis, P.C., C.C., Q.C.,
Former Premier of Ontario and now Counsel, Torys

Just before every election, he'd throw a bone to various constituencies to buy their co-operation or at least mute their opposition. I remember the year he threw organized labour a really juicy bone—requiring an agency shop in all collective agreements, thus ensuring the automatic deduction of union dues from the pay of all organized workers. Bill's Tory caucus rebelled at the very thought of such a bone, so he offset it with a bone for management—the final offer ballot. This allowed the employer to call for a vote, by secret ballot conducted by the labour relations board, on the employer's last offer before a union could go on strike.

While Bill was wrestling with his caucus over this trade-off, he told the Ontario Federation of Labour (OFL) and, more important, the NDP, then led by another of my friendly antagonists, Stephen Lewis, that they would have to support his package in the legislature or it was all off. They readily agreed because the agency shop was so important to them and the final offer ballot wouldn't be used that often.

This set the stage for Stuart Smith, then leader of the Liberal Party in Ontario, to pull a fast one in the House. When Bill brought in his package of bones, "the Psycho" (I always referred to Smith that way because he was a psychiatrist) moved an amendment striking the final offer ballot management bone from the package. It must have been quite a sight to see Stephen Lewis and his band of pro-union NDPers vote against this pro-labour amendment, which they had to do in order to keep their pact with Bill and his Tories.

Although I sometimes carped about Bill's government, he was always very accessible and open to me. I particularly recall one occasion when I was all worked up about something Bill had in the works. Hugh Segal, Bill's executive assistant at the time, called to say the Premier wanted to hear me out. The only time we could find was during Bill's drive in to work from his home in Brampton. So one morning I joined Bill, Hugh, and the chauffeur, and Bill and I had a very full discussion. Years later I learned from Hugh that I had had more influence on Bill's thinking than was apparent at the time and certainly more influence on other occasions than I ever appreciated.

I did temporarily jeopardize my relationship with Bill when I came out very strongly against his possible candidacy for the leadership of the national Progressive Conservative Party. Hugh and I ended up on the CBC debating whether Bill would be appropriate. I couldn't lose because Bill had sided with Trudeau on the National Energy Program, which meant Bill would never be acceptable in the West. At that time, I also felt it was hopeless because Ontario was still seen as the big bad ogre by most of the rest of the country. Any Premier of Ontario was guaranteed to be hated by voters in all the other provinces.

I met John in the mid-1970s when I was Premier William Davis's Legislative Secretary. John would call to express his concerns about the lack of direction in economic policies and I said that he should meet the Premier directly. One morning, when I went as usual with the OPP to Brampton to pick up the Premier, I invited John to come with me. John gave the Premier an unvarnished and insightful earful. He made a very strong case regarding infrastructure investment, and it had a significant impact. John was the inspiration for the BUILD program, which was the centrepiece of Mr. Davis's re-election campaign in 1990.

Most of my impressions about John are based on quasi-terrorist telephone messages. John would say something like, "The dollar may collapse next Tuesday if we don't speak," I always made a point of returning his calls, and without fail he would have some fascinating insight or fresh piece of advice.

John's utterly fearless. It's a rare quality. There's an expression "telling truth to power." In the public sector it refers to times when the Deputy

Minister tells the Minister that this is the Minister's dumbest idea ever. John is a tell the truth guerilla. No fence is too high, no power structure is too grand, and no poobah is too large to confront. He bombs power with grenades of truth.

Hugh Segal, President, Institute for Research on Public Policy

OTHER (ONTARIO) PREMIERS I HAVE KNOWN

My relations with David Peterson were never as cordial or constructive as they were with Bob Rae or Bill Davis. Peterson was the most reckless spender and taxer the province has ever known. Worse still—or so I thought at the time—he was unalterably opposed to free trade with the U.S.A. We briefly, informally, and superficially debated the free trade question several times at First Ministers' meetings and Liberal Party conventions. I think the most honest thing to be said of those encounters was that we just talked past each other. Nonetheless, we enjoyed jousting. For some reason, Peterson still claims I must bear a big share of the blame for his defeat by Bob Rae and the NDP. I've never understood why.

John's a media hound who has an opinion on everything. He has a pathological need for attention, and he's sort of spun this into making a living by being a media gadfly. As long as you talk about him, it doesn't matter what you say.

I don't remember when I first met John. I know I was aware of him for some years. He'd stand up and say horrible things about me. The truth is, I like John, but every time John took an opinion, I took the opposite.

The Honourable David R. Peterson, Q.C., Former Premier of Ontario, and now Partner, Cassels Brock & Blackwell LLP, Toronto

---

When Mike Harris swept to power, I already had a fairly well established relationship with him because I'd addressed a couple of Tory policy conferences in Ontario when the Party was still wandering in the wilderness. As I recall, the first of these province-wide events was held at McMaster University in Hamilton and attracted only about 40 delegates.

I liked Mike from the outset because he is a fairly simple and straightforward character. He certainly proved unique in the extent to which he implemented his election promises, something that amazed a lot of his supporters and annoyed some others. I was glad he was elected and then re-elected—someone had to call a halt to the Peterson and Rae excesses—but I haven't agreed with everything he has done, let alone with his methods. I'd have postponed the tax cuts until we got rid of the deficit, I believe he was totally wrong about cancelling photo radar, and I cannot believe the way in which he promoted gambling, one of the most regressive possible ways of raising public monies. But someone had to take back control of the schools from the teachers' unions and someone had to rationalize our health care system. I could only hope he would correct the mistakes he inevitably made in pursuing these laudable objectives during his first term.

Unfortunately, this didn't happen. During the summer of 2001, Mike was well into his second term and seemed to have lost steam and enthusiasm for the entire enterprise. He declared his determination to run for a third term and then, a few weeks later, suddenly announced his retirement. He had said in public that money would be no problem if that's what it took to implement his educational agenda. There's no telling what the view of his successor as Premier will be.

I spent a decade in opposition before forming the government in Ontario. And I always knew John to be non-partisan—he didn't hesitate to offer advice to both opposition and the government. Now, I didn't always take his advice...and I don't think any other Premier did, but we did value his passion for issues.

The Honourable Mike Harris, Former Premier of Ontario

FROM SEA EVEN UNTO SEA

During my career, I've had the pleasure of becoming acquainted with Premiers of many other provinces in Canada.

My Prairie baptism came when I was asked to deliver the keynote address to the Western Premiers' annual conference in 1987. The theme was free trade, which all the Premiers favoured even if some of their national associates did not. The conference was in Saskatoon, and there were large demonstrations against free trade outside the conference hall. Foolishly, I tried to confront the demonstrators. That's when I learned how earnestly and strongly activists in Saskatchewan take their politics. I was nearly hit on the head with a placard, and I was glad that police and hotel security were placed strategically around me.

One character I came to like was Dave Barrett, the first NDP Premier of British Columbia. I used to refer to him reverently as "the refugee from social work" because that was his background. We had a great debate over free trade before the Canadian Federation of Mayors and Municipalities. Our exchange was so heated, the audience apparently felt we hated each other. We were receiving a standing ovation at the end of our debate until we shook hands and Dave gave me a big bear hug. At that point the applause faded away quickly as everyone thought they'd been conned by two good friends.

John Crispo supported the FTA, NAFTA, and the WTO. Mulroney took his advice, and as a consequence, they are responsible for the WTO riots in Seattle. All this demonstrates again is Easterners' disdain for the West by staging such hopeless causes out here.

The Honourable Dave Barrett, Former Premier of British Columbia

---

Mike Harcourt, first Mayor of Vancouver and later the second NDP Premier of British Columbia, was another of my sparring partners on several, more informal occasions. The night of the Dave Barrett bear hug, Mike told Dave afterwards that he (Mike) would ruin Dave's reputation by reporting how he had embraced a right-wing fascist in public. Like Dave Barrett and Bob Rae, Mike was better than his party. All three appeared at times to have a better sense of fiscal realities than did their caucuses or party.

Even though Crispo is from Toronto, is a vitriolic, albeit witty, neo-conservative Neanderthal and therefore wrong, he's a friend. We forgive our friends' flaws—almost!

The Honourable Mike Harcourt, Former Premier of British Columbia

My most memorable brush with politics down East was in 1987 or 1988 when I addressed the annual convention of the Progressive Conservatives in New Brunswick. John Buchanan was the Premier at the time, and he introduced me on a stage thickly populated with dignitaries, many of whom were his cabinet ministers. About half way through my speech I noticed they had all abandoned me on the stage. I spotted Buchanan in the audience and asked him why he and all his colleagues bailed out on me. I must have been on a real tear that night because Buchanan replied from the floor that he didn't know whether it would be safe to sit near me. Nonetheless, I got a standing ovation speaking to the free trade issue and letting loose about my anger at how the federal Liberals were abandoning their long-standing, pro-free trade position simply because the Tories were then for it.

I also got to know Frank McKenna for a time when he was Premier of New Brunswick. On one occasion, Frank, Bob Rae, and I found ourselves in St. Andrews-By-The-Sea addressing different conventions in the same hotel. When I wasn't presenting or golfing, I'd while away some time monitoring Frank's and Bob's public performances. When Frank spotted me in his audience, he went out of his way to say that he was glad to see that Bob had brought his chief fiscal advisor with him. That prompted a great laugh at my expense.

I got to know Frank Moores a little bit when I did some work for him. He was Premier of Newfoundland and Labrador at the time, and he had a harebrained idea for a wage and price control regime for his province. But he decided he wasn't going to pay me because he didn't like my findings. Thankfully, his wife, who is now a Senator, intervened on my behalf and I finally collected my fee.

HOEING THE POLITICAL ROW

I began to prepare for what I thought would be a brilliant political career by developing my knowledge of and positions on key socio-economic issues. My year investigating varying national systems in Europe was a great influencer, and by 1978 I was staking out the basis for a life in politics by giving speeches in venues like the Canadian Club.

Some of those speeches had a distinctly melodramatic air about them. I would remind the audience that Canada was in a period of national soul-searching and that there was a great deal at stake because of the great question facing us—fashioning a new basis for confederation that would satisfy the Quebeçois and other forces for regionalism. I also warned about the need to put Canada's fiscal house in order, phase out wage and price controls, and preserve the free enterprise system and collective bargaining process. I also delivered dire warnings about the so-called industrial strategies leading to the corporate state and warned that corporatism leads to the centralization and concentration of power. Unless resisted firmly, the result for Canadians could be authoritarian, fascist, and totalitarian government.

About 10 years later, in 1987, I contributed a chapter to Mel Hurtig's *If I Were Prime Minister*. While some of the contributors didn't take Mel's invitation very seriously, I certainly did, partly because it came from Mel, a long-time and friendly protagonist, and partly because it gave me the opportunity to look back over the road not taken.

My essay showed considerable changes in my own priorities as well as those of the country. I argued that free trade with the U.S.A. was necessary if Canada was to become more competitive and that Canada had to come to grips with its massive deficits and the resulting huge debt servicing costs. If I were Prime Minister, I wrote, I'd rescind corporate and personal tax deductions until they were proved worthwhile for the country, I'd tax all social security payments once recipients' incomes reached a certain level, I'd institute tax reform aimed at taking the joy out of short-term capital gains, and I'd re-examine all research and development incentives. Privatization, deregulation, anti-inflation measures, more effective retraining and income maintenance programs, better managed health care, renewed commitment to NORAD and NATO, and linking foreign aid to respect for democratic principles and human rights were all on my "to do" list.

Between these bookmark years, I took positions on many other national issues outside my chosen academic field. One was on the cavalier way in which political leaders in Ontario treated the West, another was reforming the Senate, and a third was the challenge of finding accommodation with Quebec.

Western alienation is still a topic for discussion, although not so often and hotly debated now as it was back in 1980 when I first began raising my voice. In "Wake-up call for Ontario on Western Alienation" (*The Globe and Mail*, November 21, 1980), I summed up the state of my thinking by noting the West's feelings of bitterness and suspicion and Ontario's absolute failure to comprehend how it was perceived west of the Manitoba-Ontario border. I took all the political leaders of the time to task, including Prime Minister Trudeau, Bill Davis, Joe Clark, John Crosbie, Stuart Smith, and Michael Cassidy, who was then leader of the Ontario NDP. I reminded them that the West could separate and prosper for years by virtue of its access to and links with the American market. Today, with the NAFTA in place, the economic pieces have been moved around, but the same feelings of Western alienation persist and the same blankness of mind rules in Central and Eastern Canada.

My interest in Senate reform came partly as a result of my concern about alienation of the West. I dismissed the Senate as a decadent, disgraceful patronage bin for party bagmen, cronies, and hacks and as an anachronism that had no place in a self-respecting, democratic society. I cast my vote in favour of a new, elected chamber that would be more representative and therefore more responsive and sensitive to diverse national interests.

An obstacle to Senate reform during the 1980s was the Meech Lake Accord. If adopted in the form proposed, it would ensure that nothing could be done about the Senate without unanimous consent of the provinces. Another difficulty was the need to ensure representation by population while still providing a voice for provinces with populations much smaller than those of Ontario and Quebec. Deciding on the powers the new chamber should have and how the Senate's powers would balance the powers of the House of Commons would be, however, the greatest challenge.

Today, reforming the Senate is still a dream. It's entirely too useful a reward for any party in power—or any party with realistic hopes of gaining power—to give up. However, I still believe that Canada needs a regionally balanced chamber of reflective, serious, sober second thought that is not unfairly dominated by its two most populous provinces. Some day? I'm not holding my breath.

Finding an accommodation with Quebec also appears just as elusive today as ever. Over the years, I've waded into the issue in many venues.

I've always favoured a constitutional provision recognizing Quebec's different, special, and unique status, but even without that I believe Quebec is much better off in Canada than out of it.

I've also been consistently worried that a vote to separate would undercut both Quebec's and Canada's credibility and would result in pressure on the dollar, economic instability, political uncertainty, and, finally, a decline in the standard of living for everyone involved. Quebeckers would suffer first and hardest, but other Canadians would pay a price as well. The overall result might well be Canada's disintegration as a political and economic entity.

So, sympathetic as I have always been to Quebec's warranted aspirations within Canada, I believe Quebeckers would be very shortsighted if they chose to let emotion triumph over logic and ideology sweep aside reason. I still believe that if Bernard Landry, now Premier of Quebec, succeeds where Lucien Bouchard and others before could not, Quebeckers will be setting the stage for the disintegration of their own society as much as the break-up of Canada.

When Jean Charest left the federal Progressive Conservative Party leadership in 1998 to fill the void left by Daniel Johnson's resignation as leader of the Liberal Party in Quebec, I was all in favour with one caveat. I was convinced that Charest could never defeat Lucien Bouchard and the Parti Quebeçois as long as Jean Chrétien remained Prime Minister of Canada. I was convinced that with Chrétien out of the way, Charest could win the upcoming provincial election in Quebec. Even if Bouchard won, I thought we would be in a much better position with Charest as the Leader of the Opposition leader in Quebec and Paul Martin ensconced as Prime Minister.

Well, Jean Chrétien didn't resign and Jean Charest didn't win the

provincial election, but Lucien Bouchard surprised everyone by returning to private life, leaving the door open for Bernard Landry to move to
centre stage and sing another chorus of the neverendum referendum.
Like so many others, I remain committed to the concept of accommodation and perplexed as to how it may be achieved.

My first clear memories of John Crispo are reading his writings and seeing
him on television. He is clear and outspoken on fundamental issues such
as the role of government and the role of the state. I'm not sure I always
agree with him, but he is always thought-provoking.

I recall feeling quite good when one of my sons ended up in a Crispo
class at the University of Toronto. I thought that if anyone could make him
stand up and take notice of public policy, it would be John Crispo, and in
fact that is what happened.

Whether one agrees with him or not, any public policy debate is much
the richer for John Crispo.

The Honourable Paul Martin, Minister of Finance, Government of Canada

---

GRAND FROMAGES & OTHER POOHBAHS

I'm not sure when my interest in politics began but I do recall two
politicians who initially inspired me and later disillusioned me.

The first was John F. Kennedy whom I watched in awe when I was
a graduate student at M.I.T. as he mesmerized a full house in the Boston
Gardens. His assassination moved me as nothing else ever has until
September 11, 2001, and the unspeakable horror of the tragedy at the
World Trade Center. Still, it came as something of a shock to witness
him accomplish more in death than he likely would have in life. Lyndon
Johnson skilfully exploited Kennedy's murder to push through
Congress much of Kennedy's so-called Just Society legislation. I don't
believe Kennedy would have been able to do this himself had he lived
because of his rocky relationship with Congress. I was disillusioned
because I realized he would never be able to live up to his early promise.

The second was Pierre Elliott Trudeau, so articulate and eloquent
and seemingly so principled, who captivated me as no other Canadian
politician ever has. He soon revealed himself as a dilettante and a hypocritical, limousine socialist. That was long before he imposed wage and

price controls on the workers of Canada, but it was that 1965-era legislation that galvanized me and led me to a most interesting and stimulating confrontation.

Doug Hartle, a fellow political economist at the University of Toronto, and I organized a petition against wage and price controls. It was signed by about 25 leading economists from across the country. For our troubles, Doug and I were granted an audience with Himself, as I liked to term Trudeau, and his executive assistant Jim Coutts.

Trudeau arrived a little late from the House of Commons and promptly kicked off his sandals, one flying in one direction and one in another. He greeted Doug fairly politely and then said to me something like, "Crispo, you never show any respect and you're not going to receive any—agreed?" I don't recall even being offered a chance to reply as we quickly got into an often heated and often humorous discussion of what we were supposed to cover as well as everything from tenure for university professors to the relative worth of bank presidents and elevator operators. I distinctly recall Trudeau's concern about the latter because it allowed me to get in a crack about it being time he got to know the real world better. Elevator operators were a vanished breed.

Doug and I enjoyed our long and spirited debate even if it didn't accomplish much of anything. It was a challenge jousting with Trudeau because he had a very quick mind and tongue, but he was not about to change his policy. I think he had us in because he knew it would be stimulating and, if nothing else, he could humour us. We were also a welcome diversion from the House of Commons debates, which usually bored him to distraction.

There's a postscript to the wage and price controls affair. I continued to speak against the policy, and I believe I was being effective. Certainly, I was a featured guest on all the broadcast network news shows. After the wage and price controls had been in place for a time, I got another call from Ottawa, this time from a highly placed official in Trudeau's office. When I arrived, I discovered our meeting was to take place during a walk around the Hill rather than inside as one would expect. The official asked me if I wanted to be a consultant to the government and offered me a retainer of $300 a day, which was a lot of money at the time. I said, "What would I do?" The answer was, "There are so many issues you're involved in, we'd like your advice on all sorts of things." I said, "There's something going on here." And the answer confirmed it. "Well, obviously as a consultant to the government you should keep quiet." Did Trudeau himself authorize the attempt to muzzle me in exchange for money? I don't know and I doubt it, but I have a hard time believing that such offers could be made without at least tacit approval from the highest level. In any event, my disillusionment with Trudeau was complete.

My most fulsome interaction with a Prime Minister was with Brian Mulroney during the free trade debate. That political fight consumed me so intensively that I might as well have become a politician. Indeed to this day many people think I am a Tory because I stood firmly for so long with the Tories on that issue.

Two highlights stand out in my mind. The first was over that critical final weekend in the free trade negotiations, October 2 and 3, 1987, when Derek Burney, Brian's administrative assistant, and Michael Wilson, Minister of Finance, went down to Washington with Canada's negotiators on a make-or-break basis. I recall talking to Brian three times during that fateful weekend, constantly reminding him not to let our people agree to anything I couldn't defend. The crunch issue became a binding dispute settlement mechanism, which I knew was a must if we were ever to get fair treatment from the Americans under any kind of free trade arrangement. Thank God, we stuck to our guns. Without it we would have been in an indefensible position politically during the forthcoming election. As it turned out we only won the 1988 election—and I use the term "we" because for that election at least I was in effect a Tory—by splitting the opposition vote against free trade between the Liberals and the NDP.

During that make-or-break weekend, I took one of Brian's calls while I was in the barn on my farm. When Brian asked me what I was doing, I told him the truth: I was shoveling manure. I couldn't resist adding, though, that I thought he could use some of it in his next few speeches. He laughed heartily and asked me to send some along.

John was such a strong ally during the Great Free Trade Debate that I thought he should try his hand at reforming the CBC. I don't think he had as much success in that endeavour, but I know he tried hard to instill more balance and fairness in their public affairs programs.

The Right Honourable Brian Mulroney, Former Prime Minister of Canada

My other vivid memory of Mulroney has to do with Mila. My wife and I got to know her quite well because after we (there's that word again) won the free trade election, we (this time I mean my wife and I) were invited to several official functions. Both Brian and Mila displayed extraordinary charm and grace.

But I stray from my story about Mila, who invited us to a gala for the spouses of the heads of government of the Group of Seven when the Group held its conference in Toronto. The gala was held on June 20, 1988, at the McMichael Gallery in Kleinburg, north of Toronto. When we arrived a Mountie informed us that Mila wanted to see me. When we caught up with her, she asked me if I would do her the favour of escorting Nancy Reagan for the evening. I readily agreed after being assured that Mila had arranged for a handsome rogue to escort my wife to dinner.

I had a wonderful evening at the head table sitting between Mila and Nancy, both of whom turned out to be fascinating dinner partners. Mila told Nancy to be ready for anything from me, and Nancy proclaimed herself ready, willing, and able. We talked about everything from her palm reader in California to her views about Gorbachev's wife, and she was very forthcoming and frank.

When I asked Mila why she had chosen me for this great honour, especially when there were so many prominent Tory contributors and donors in the audience, her answer made me realize how politically astute and clever she was. She said she'd have been in far more difficulty if she'd picked one of them as Nancy's escort because the others would be jealous and resentful. By choosing me, she gave them the excuse to think it was merely some unaccountable eccentricity on her part rather than a slight directed at them.

At the end of the evening Mila said a few words of welcome and that seemed to be the end of it. I asked her if anybody was going to thank her and she said that was not the tradition and I must restrain myself if I had anything like that in mind. So, of course, I promptly rose to thank her on behalf of everyone present. I said that I owed her the most gratitude because of the great privilege of sitting between these two great first ladies. I added that I would never have the chance to sit between Mulroney and Reagan, but I'd much rather sit between their better halves. I'll never forget the look of relief on Mila's face when I sat down. She thanked me profusely for my thanks and for not doing or saying anything embarrassing, inappropriate, or untoward. People like her could give me a complex, if I was capable of absorbing one.

I guess I met John when I first entered politics about 20 years ago. I didn't know whether he was a friend or a foe. He was at the University of Toronto, very much associated with labour issues, and as outspoken then as he is now. Sometimes, he would sound like a rabid union supporter; sometimes, he would sound like a thoughtful, objective observer of the national scene.

My first clear memory of him is debating issues. He's always been very passionate and knew exactly where his thinking was. That's still the case. When I got to know him better, I realized he wasn't just a toady for the labour movement. He would get labour equally provoked. When he became supportive of free trade, he put his labour friends into orbit.

I got to know John better at the Mad River Golf Club after I left politics. He's the only guy I know who talks to himself in his own back swing. I always enjoy getting to the last green with him. When he has a three-foot putt at the last hole, he chokes up and misses as often as not. I must say I have great enjoyment because he yells and screams as he gives me the money. He does beat me occasionally, so it's not all one way, but if I'm winning or just a point behind, I spend a lot of time on the fairway walking to the last hole reminding him of past experiences.

John is a very active, entertaining person at the Mad River Annual Meetings. In fact, the Meetings wouldn't be the same without him. Some of us at Mad River have noted, however, that now that he is President of Devil's Glen Ski Club, he's more responsible in his interventions at Mad River.

John's an entertaining guy to be with because he always gives what's at the forefront of his mind. He's provocative, he gets you thinking, he's usually close to the mark, and he wears his heart on his sleeve.

The Honourable Michael H. Wilson, Former Minister of Finance,
and now Chairman & C.E.O., RT Capital Management Inc.

PROMISES, PROMISES

I have been asked to run under the banner of every national political party in the country except for the Communists and the Creditistes.

The first serious offer came from David Lewis, whom I admired very much during my earlier left-leaning years and continued to respect even as I began to move to the right of the political spectrum. He was a very articulate man who remained true to his causes. I loved his invention of the term "corporate welfare bums," which remains as appropriate today as when he first used it. My only real disappointment with him occurred one evening in Toronto when he badly lost a debate with William Buckley, a bright American right winger, whom I felt at the time deserved a good drubbing.

Years later, when Trudeau stepped down, I was approached by a group of young Liberals to see if I would run to replace him. Although they knew and I knew that I couldn't win, they thought with me in the race there would be a chance of ensuring that the real issues were debated. I came astonishingly close to doing so. I still have notes in my files about the pros and cons of jumping into the fray and brief policy statements on a broad range of issues. Stephen Lewis, surprisingly enough, was my main confidante at this time, and he urged me to run. Like the young Liberals who approached me, Stephen didn't think I could ever win, but he thought I could have a major impact on national policy. I was so close to going for it that I actually bought an airline ticket to get me to Thunder Bay where the first of a series of policy forums was to be held and the candidates for leadership could initially show their wares. I'm still not entirely sure why I chickened out.

My only real regret about this decision occurred when Stephen Lewis and I covered the subsequent Liberal leadership convention for what was then the CKO All News Radio Network. None of the leadership candidates performed well, and Stephen kept needling me about how easy it would have been to appear inspirational by comparison. It was a very dismal and disillusioning series of conversations. Stephen egged me on to many unrealistic flashes of the kind of impact, if not outright victory, I might have achieved had I entered the contest. In fact, given the way these conventions are run, I could never have carried the day, no matter how much more effective I may have been as a leadership candidate than John Turner or Jean Chrétien or anyone else. But it would have been fun trying, and I probably should have done it.

Shortly after Turner won the leadership and became Prime Minister, he called to ask whether I would ever consider running as a Liberal during the next federal election. Obviously still not cured of my political urges, I had a series of meetings with John, and I came close to agreeing. Eventually, before I came to my senses on my own, Turner rejected me.

Crispo and I disagreed on the Free Trade Agreement with the United States—but I had a great advantage over him; I had read the Agreement.

The Right Honourable John N. Turner, Former Prime Minister of Canada

---

Our first meeting took place at Winston's, a downtown Toronto restaurant famous for its rich and powerful clientele, where Turner had his own table. That meeting went extremely well. We more or less agreed that if I could get myself elected, I would become his Minister of Labour and serve on the inner cabinet. My job would be to pacify labour by affirming labour's bargaining rights in the public service and guaranteeing no more wage and price guidelines or controls. We also went over a wide range of issues and only felt ourselves at odds one or two times. We agreed that if the campaign got rough, he would take the high road and I would take on anybody who wanted to slug it out at a lower level. We thought we were on the verge of working something out, but we both should go away and think about it and then get back together again.

Our next meeting took place at Les Copains, a fine restaurant but one that was a bit of a step down from Winston's. I should have got the message, but I didn't. Shortly into that meeting, John told me that some of his advisors felt I was a bit of a loose cannon. I expressed surprise that his advisors had to tell him that since we'd known each other for years. I reminded him that this trait could prove very advantageous if I had to get into some low road campaigning on his, or the Party's, behalf. Matters deteriorated further when he asked me what I would do if he had to introduce some policy with which I could not agree. I reminded him of his commitment to me to be part of his inner cabinet and expressed the hope that any differences we had would be resolved there. When pressed, however, I had to concede that I would not be able to support any policy with which I did not agree in principle. I allowed that if it wasn't a major issue I would try to remain silent and arrange to be absent when the related vote took place in the House.

I'm not sure where our last meeting took place. I believe it was at a McDonald's on Bloor Street in Toronto. Whatever the venue, it indicated how quickly I was fading from John's schema. John conveyed the message that he couldn't accept someone who aspired to be a cabinet colleague yet couldn't commit to abide by whatever final policy choices he felt had to make. I could hardly blame him because, as I've already acknowledged, that's the way party politics work under a parliamentary form of government. I'm vain enough to think he made a mistake rejecting me because I might have been able to help save him from himself. But imagine what might have happened when the free trade issue came to the fore. Turner opposed it for both philosophical and political reasons; I supported it on philosophical and intellectual grounds. We would both have found ourselves between a rock and a hard place.

I guess, however, I'm either a frustrated or a slow learner, or both, because I'd hardly received my rejection slip from Turner when I agreed to come to Ottawa to meet with Brian Mulroney and Elmer McKay about the possibility of running for the Tories. When Brian first called me, I told him what I had just gone through with John Turner. I'll always remember Brian's reaction. He said something like, "John, I wouldn't have much respect for anyone who didn't check both sides of the street before deciding which one to work."

Anyway, up I went to Ottawa, and in one short morning we traveled roughly the same ground it had taken John Turner and me several weeks to cover. By the end of the session, Brian suggested that I was "a little too independently minded" and "that this Party can't stand another John Crosbie." I remember telling Brian he couldn't have paid me a higher compliment, because there was and is no other Canadian politician that I have admired more than John Crosbie.

I don't recall when I first became aware of John, but I imagine I first met him when he was on the International Trade Advisory Council in connection with the Canada-U.S. free trade negotiations. John was a literate and bright member of the Council. I paid attention to him because of his book on free trade. It was most helpful and useful in counteracting the propaganda.

I recall having Brian Peckford appointed to the CBC Board of Directors around the time Mulroney appointed John. Between the two of them, they stirred things up at the CBC. Generally speaking, I like shit disturbers, not the ignoramuses and yahoos like those in Seattle and Quebec City, but people not afraid to oppose the Establishment. John was one of them. He was a shit disturber on the CBC Board, aided and abetted on occasion by Peckford.

John is good value. He delivers opinions usually calculated to shake up the Establishment and the status quo or those who think they know everything. Speaking your mind is one thing. Having something sensible to say is another.

I have a very high opinion of John. I watch with interest what he's saying and who he's upsetting now. He's not afraid to speak up and make a vigorous point. He's an iconoclast. He's likely to be pushing against the current, whatever the current it. He's valuable and engaging and doesn't mind being controversial.

The Honourable John C. Crosbie, Former Minister of International Trade

---

Though actually somewhat shy, John Crosbie is blunt, humorous, and outspoken in public. I'd loved to have seen him as our Prime Minister for several reasons. I remember how sound his energy and fiscal policies were as Minister of Finance, before Joe Clark got his government defeated because he wouldn't make a deal with the Creditistes. And I recall John's valiant fight for free trade. I appreciated and enjoyed the many opportunities I had to stand with him. He would have added so much character to the Prime Minister's Office.

I can't resist adding just one story about John Crosbie even though I didn't witness it in person. John was involved in a debate with his nemesis, Sheila Copps, in Vancouver, and he got off to a politically incorrect enough start by suggesting that Sheila had arrived late because she couldn't find her broom. Then, in course of the debate, things went from bad to worse. The very dogmatic and ill-informed Copps actually suggested at one point that free trade would lead to more surrogate motherhood in Canada. This so provoked John that he promised he would seek an amendment to the free trade agreement if there was even a hint of such a thing in it. That was all right until he added that his proposed amendment, if needed, would require all women in Canada to keep their legs crossed. He doubtless thought this was funny, and normally I would agree, but the reaction was anything but. The media went berserk. The CBC's *The National* used it as its lead story. It was a perfect fit for the CBC's continuing anti-free trade tirade. I loved John Crosbie for always being himself, but more than once being himself cost him a real run at the Prime Ministership.

Anyway, back to John Turner and Brian Mulroney. Ultimately, I realized I owed a debt of gratitude to both of them. Heaven knows what would have happened to me had they not rejected me and had I become a member of either of their cabinets. I would have had to compromise my principles—with John over both fiscal policy and free trade and with Brian over fiscal policy—or resign or be fired or whatever. My lingering fear is that I might have succumbed to the same blandishments of power that have tempted so many other good men and women, who were probably equally as strong in their original convictions as I.

Still…. In the end, while I flirted with politics virtually all of my life, I never took the plunge into active involvement. I will always wonder if I made the right decision because I think I could have done rather well just by being myself. I may be wrong, but I refuse to believe that Canadians would reject someone who really leveled with them.

I remember vividly the first time I met John. I was doing my degree in labour relations and economics at U of T, and I walked into his second year Introduction to Business class. It was huge. It was full. John was there sitting at the front. No one said a word for 40 minutes. The class was only 50 minutes long. Then John started to lecture us. He said, "What's the matter with all of you? You're all losers. This country is in a shambles, and you just sit there quietly. You don't ask questions. You're useless. You don't have a future. Your lives are over." I thought to myself, "Who the hell is this wacko? Who does he think he is?"

Someone told me he had tenure and he could say anything he wanted. Sure, he had tenure and wrote all kinds of books and had his radio show. That's what you'd expect of a professor. But what really impressed me is he brought in all these top level people: the head of GM Canada, Bob Rae. They wouldn't come if they didn't have respect for him.

It was my favourite class. I learned an incredible amount. He taught me there's a lot more going on than in the textbooks. I learned from him if you say something controversial, you'd better have the facts to back yourself up. Another way he influenced me is to really research strongly. It really affected my accumulation of academic and business knowledge. He says, "You're just like me, a hot head. You can't say that. You have to back it up."

John tells the truth. He's a man of honour and integrity and principle. But if you disagree with him, it's good-bye, Charlie, unless you can show intelligent thought. Then he'll accept your opinion, but he'll never agree with anyone but himself.

He must be right. Even the Americans respect him. He's invited all over the United States to speak.

Ahmed Naqvi, President & C.E.O., PlanetWiz Inc., Toronto

Chapter 7

Me and My Big Mouth

There may have been times when I got carried away with my own rhetoric. All right, so there *were* times…and sometimes they proved to be embarrassing. Occasionally, I have done myself lasting damage.

I acknowledge that virtually every Dean under whom I served—as well as several Presidents—suggested more than once that I might couch what I had to say in more diplomatic language. This was probably more true during my earlier left-of-centre years, when I was thought to be too radical for a business school professor. Later, they questioned my style more than my substance.

Years after my fire-breathing, pinko years, I learned that Vincent Bladen, then Chair of the Department of Political Economy and later Dean of Arts and Science, used to talk to Harold Clawson, who was Vice-President of Industrial Relations at Stelco, about how they could save me from myself. Apparently, both felt I was reasonably bright but just a little too left wing and outspoken for their taste. However, my guess is that now at least one of them—Vincent Bladen—would think that I have swung too far right when it comes to my political positioning.

ROYAL BLUSH
My greatest verbal faux pas occurred at the Duke of Edinburgh's Commonwealth Youth Conference at Queen's University in Kingston, Ontario, in 1981. Because the focus was labour-management relations, I had the honour to be asked to co-chair with the Duke. All went well until….

The Duke himself, the Secretary of the Commonwealth, and Governor General Edward Schreyer all addressed the opening session.

217

I was incensed by Schreyer's remarks. This pathetic former NDP Premier of Manitoba was rewarded with the appointment to Rideau Hall because he had supported Trudeau's wage and price controls. Schreyer owed the truth to the young people who had come from all over the Commonwealth to hear the facts about the current state of Canada. What he told them was dishonest and misleading. His glowing words never hinted at the rumblings of the separatist movement in Quebec and the well warranted anger in the West over the imposition of the National Energy Program.

Anyway, I was under the impression that the first session, like the rest of the conference, was closed to the media. So, when I was asked by someone what I thought about the session, I did not restrain myself. In fact, I was so agitated that I not only spoke very frankly about Schreyer's remarks; I also threw in some gratuitous comments about the Duke and the Secretary. The Duke, I said, couldn't really say anything about anything in his position, and the Secretary of the Commonwealth occupied such a politically sensitive office that he was in the same position.

Unfortunately, the person who asked my opinion wasn't a delegate; he was a reporter for *The Globe and Mail*. The next morning, *The Globe and Mail* ran a front-page story that quoted me quite accurately as saying that the Duke of Edinburgh couldn't say anything of substance because of his position. It didn't really matter that the reporter hadn't identified himself to me. Nobody felt the least bit sorry for me on that score because I had already done enough work with the media to know that ethics, integrity, and media aren't words you find together when it comes to digging up a newsworthy angle. I should have known better.

When I learned what had happened, my heart, soul, and mind just dropped out of me. I remember thinking I would have to go to the Duke, apologize profusely, and withdraw from the conference. On my way to do the dreadful deed, I ran into Shirley Carr, President of the Canadian Labour Congress, and Lloyd Hemsworth, the senior management official at the conference. Both, rather wryly I thought, offered me their condolences.

The Duke received me quite calmly. I will never know what he really thought, although he did say he would prefer to be criticized for the substance of his remarks than for saying nothing. I offered to resign, but he told me emphatically I was not to withdraw. I had helped organize the conference, invited several speakers, and agreed to co-chair, and I was obliged to finish the job I'd agreed to do. But, he said, I could apologize to the conference as a whole for the embarrassment I had caused.

I should never have tried. My apology got me into even hotter water. I did apologize as profusely as I ever have, but I also told the delegates how angry, ashamed, and embarrassed I was that our Governor General had given them such a one-sided view of Canada and hadn't told the truth about the serious challenges we faced in both Quebec and the West. Afterwards, the Duke told me to remind him never to allow me to apologize for anything ever again.

In the end, I did fulfil my commitment as co-chair of the conference, and I did it fairly well, trying as the circumstances were. But I really regretted my indiscretion because it most certainly blocked me from being considered for comparable opportunities. I surely never got the chance to remind the Duke to forbid another apology.

Some years later, I had another brush with British royalty, but this time it was on the fringes and got me into much less trouble. In the early 1980s, I was invited to a Ditchley Conference, which is named after a famous British estate, to discuss the state of industrial relations in the Western world.

This conference could have proved very interesting had it not been packed with a bunch of British aristocrats who knew precious little about industrial relations or anything else of practical interest. I fell in with an intriguing American, Malcolm Dennis, who was then Vice President of Industrial Relations for the Ford Motor Company. I learned more from him than from the rest of the attendees combined. Both of us, however, became fed up with the ill-informed and pretentious guests who insisted on being addressed by their titles. We got the butler to give us their first names and from then on addressed them in that manner. This affront to these weak links in the royal chain was not well received.

Although I would have liked to have been invited to other, more informative Ditchley Conferences (Malcolm was not at all interested in a return engagement), the butler let it be known this was not likely to happen. We'd become quite friendly, although I could not get him beyond "Mr. John" in terms of how he addressed me. When I found him in order to say good-bye and express the hope that I would see him again, he said with wryly typical British understatement, " I would not anticipate an early return to Ditchley if I were you, Mr. John!"

I got a call asking for one of my five daughters to do a temporary, two-week stint as a receptionist at what was then the U of T School of Business. I ended up going instead. I was terrified. I'd never worked in an office and never been in a university.

At the end of the two weeks, I stayed on as Secretary to the Strategic Management Area and then as Secretary to John. Of course, I knew who he was. I was awed, but he was so down-to-earth. John got stuck with me, and I stayed 18 years.

John's full name is John Herbert Gillespie Crispo, but he hates the "Herbert Gillespie" and he hates the title "Dr." He's just plain old John.

John is a loving, caring man with passion. He's a sweetheart. I miss him.

Carol Brady, Secretary (Retired), Faculty of Management, University of Toronto

---

EATING CROW

Another indiscretion involved my exaggeration of a confrontation I had with the Editorial Board of *The Toronto Star*. It caused me much less public embarrassment than I deserved.

During the free trade debate, *The Star* was relentless in its campaign against the agreement, and I never missed an opportunity to attack the newspaper for its very one-sided coverage. As a result, in 1985 I was invited to meet *The Star*'s Editorial Board over lunch. We had quite a dust-up. I concentrated on what I thought would be useful for the editors—to appoint to the Board at least one pro free-trader whose function would be to make the other editors think about arguments on the other side of the question. As I recall, we agreed to disagree, strongly but with courtesy.

It was what I made of this encounter after the fact that was dishonest. I was shameless in the way I embellished it in subsequent speeches, and I got a lot of laughs from appreciative audiences. At my worst, I claimed that we'd never got to dessert. Sometimes, I went so far as to claim that I tried to pay for my lunch so that I wouldn't be obliged to *The Star* in any way. These embellishments were unwarranted.

Eventually, David Crane, *The Star*'s Financial Editor, tackled me on the topic, and I put an end to my unwarranted hyperbole. Neither David nor his colleagues ever went public about my post-luncheon nastiness, and I thank them for that.

The editors of *The Globe and Mail*, although generally much more supportive and friendly to me, did sometimes attack me in the editorial pages. Sometimes, the attacks were for excesses on my part that detracted from my basic message. Once, in 1981, I felt an editorial was unfair, although I also realized that I deserved the rough treatment. The editorial, which was titled "The Crispo Kid," skewered me for describing Westerners as anti-bilingualism rednecks while also proclaiming myself to have sympathy for the West's point of view.

The Globe and Mail had a good point. I do tend to exaggerate, and when provoked by the opposition, I tend to exaggerate even more. During the free trade debate, for example, when my opponents were making ridiculous claims about the FTA endangering Medicare and Canada's social safety net, I tended to reply in kind although not, I like to think, with nearly as much distortion.

During the 1980s, I was greatly provoked by the Liberal Party's reversal of its traditional pro-free trade position, and I began to criticize the Liberals for their highly opportunistic and pragmatic approach. I added, for good measure, that the Liberals lacked any convictions, ideals, principles, or soul and described them as just a very successful bunch of opportunists. For a time I felt a little guilty about these charges, but that guilt faded after Jean Chrétien became Prime Minister. He lied his way into office over both NAFTA, which he said he wouldn't implement without major changes, and the GST, which he said he would rescind.

Actually, I've since come to appreciate the Liberals more when they don't keep their election promises than when they do. They were wise not to keep their promise on NAFTA, and the country couldn't afford their promise on the GST. Two of the promises the Liberals did keep—to reverse the Pearson Airport contract and the helicopter deal—cost Canadians between one and two billion dollars in contract penalties alone. So I say be grateful to the Liberals when they don't keep their promises.

All right, all right, so maybe I'm still exaggerating some. I do find it very difficult to avoid even when I am apologizing or feeling repentant. And if I can't hold back, it means that either I didn't exaggerate in the first place (the interpretation I favour) or I am incapable of apologizing sincerely (which I don't think is true).

Someone to whom I never felt I had to apologize was Paul Martin, now Minister of Finance. At the time of the incident, he was an ordinary Member of Parliament sitting as part of Her Majesty's Loyal Opposition. One day in class, when I got rolling I lambasted Paul for not supporting free trade on the grounds that he surely knew better. What I didn't know was that one of his sons was in my class. He called home that evening to report what I'd said to his father. The next day I spoke at some big event in Windsor and spotted Paul Martin, Sr., in the audience. I asked him to persuade his son to endorse free trade because I knew he (Paul Martin, Sr.) knew better. As soon Mr. Martin got home, he called Paul to complain about how embarrassed he was at how I'd singled him out. The next day Paul called me. "Enough is enough," he said. I agreed to cease and desist calling upon members of his family to exert their influence with him, at least in public.

When I am dead wrong, I do apologize fully and sincerely. Once, during my many debates with Bob Rae about the free trade agreement, for example, I insulted him personally. I don't even remember what I said, but I do know it was uncalled for and so did the audience. I apologized immediately, and I still regret saying something so offensive to such an old and valued friend.

Very much more recently, when I started writing these memoirs, I called friends and acquaintances asking for comments. When I called

David Peterson, he almost jumped down my throat. He even muttered a mild oath. He was very upset because he had just heard from his son, a student at Queen's University, that I had called him (the son) a "yuppie twit" during a lecture I'd just given there. David quite forcefully and properly told me that he didn't mind what I called him but to lay off his family.

I finally figured out what had happened. David's son, who hadn't attended the lecture, had got the story second- or third-hand. I'd been discussing David's defeat by Bob Rae. I said I'd never found a satisfactory answer for that defeat, although at the time that the press had really played up David and his family's yuppie image and perhaps that had played a part in the election result.

The reason I got onto this subject at all was because I was regaling students with a story about a putdown I'd experienced in Saskatchewan shortly after Bob defeated David. I'd been asked to explain the election result and was having trouble answering when a member of the audience put me in my place. He said he was sadly disappointed that I didn't really understand what had just happened in my own province. He said that the answer was simple if only I realized what the NDP had come to stand for in Ontario. As he put it, what it stood for in that election was "No David Peterson."

I was so taken with this witticism I adopted it as my explanation for the Bob Rae triumph. But the anecdote got twisted when I told it at Queen's. It just shows how careful one has to be when one is telling or retelling a tale. Being careful and measured in public utterances is not, you may have gathered, one of my strengths.

John Crispo's ambition was to be a pain in the butt to every politician regardless of his or her party. He more than succeeded in his ambition.
The Honourable David Peterson, Former Premier of Ontario, and now Partner, Cassels Brock & Blackwell LLP, Toronto

---

I don't share the same remorse for calling Bob White, then President of the CAW, "a double dealing hypocrite" during the free trade debate. I've always liked White, and I still do, but I felt the epithet was absolutely accurate and deserved because he was viciously attacking the free trade agreement while the auto workers were benefiting greatly under the Auto Pact. As White properly argued, the Auto Pact was a form of sectoral managed trade quite unlike open free trade. But it still put him and his members in a very privileged position vis-à-vis the U.S. market. Worse still was that White would not acknowledge that the U.S. was so upset about how well the Auto Pact was working for Canada that Congress was threatening to weaken or rescind it. The free trade negotiations were designed in part to, and did, prevent this from happening.

TROUBLED WATERS

Actually, I've got into much deeper and hotter water with my academic colleagues than I have with outsiders. One of the first and harshest confrontations was in 1985 with an Acting Dean and Dean over an interview I had with the *Financial Times* and the subsequent fall-out in the form of a letter to the editor from David Orlikow, who was then an NDP Member of Parliament from Winnipeg.

Orlikow took issue with what I termed "obsolete work rules" for Canadian construction workers, which he compared with the work rules governing tenured university professors. He castigated me for throwing stones at organized workers from a privileged ivory tower.

My interview and Orlikow's letter prompted a note from a colleague and friend whom I shall not name because, despite everything, I still like and respect him. His note, dated July 9, 1985, said: "This is an example of the type of publicity that sometimes results from your public speaking engagements which bothers both *[name deleted]* and me.

"How can we get across the message that the purpose of tenure is to protect scholars engaged in scholarly activities?"

The next day, July 10, 1985, I wrote a memorandum to file. Obviously, the note from my colleague and other challenges I was experiencing at the time were bothering more than I realized. Here's what I recorded, although I have deleted the names of those involved, with the exception of Doug Tigert, who was Dean. Doug never seemed to be bothered by anything, which is why I feel able to let his name stand here.

"I started this file on Wednesday, July 10, 1985, after a series of disturbing events involving my position in the Faculty and University. I'd had some problems when Doug Tigert was Dean, but we seemed to be able to work them out—the issue being my mix of activities which features less academic and more popular writing than most of my colleagues and a lot of media and speaking, but no consulting—which is the complete opposite of most of my colleagues. I think what I do is valuable from the point of view of a professional school if only because I am one of the best known faculty members on and off campus. In any event, our acting dean for this year and our new permanent dean have made known their displeasure with my performance. The latest chapter is the note I received from *[name deleted]* about a letter written to the *Financial Times* about an interview I had with that newspaper. *[Name deleted]*'s note bothers me much more than David Orlikow's letter to the *Times*. I can't believe *[name deleted]* would write such a note given that tenure is the one protection people like me have to speak out without favoritism or fear.

"(Can you believe it – just as I was writing this note, *[name deleted]* calls me and ends by saying, 'one other thing—that letter to the *Financial Times*...'—I cut him off and said I would be answering it.)

"Have to leave for a meeting will continue this later.

"Just returned from one hour meeting with the Premier—not that *[name deleted]* or *[name deleted]* would care that I command respect even from among those I frequently criticize—anyway, I arrived back too late to catch *[name deleted]* for a meeting. Before turning to *[name deleted]* perhaps I should say a word or two about *[name deleted]*. Our relations have been strained for longer than I realized—at least with respect to the depth of strain on his part. *[Name deleted]* was mad when I quit as dean and has long resented my using economists as the butt for much of my humour. More recently he has grown increasingly upset about my role within and beyond the university. A few weeks ago he angrily, or caustically, told me I was lucky I had my tenure, or I might not be here anymore—all this in front of the main office staff. I went to his office and we had quite a heated discussion. To *[name deleted]*'s credit he told the then dean, Doug Tigert, that we had quite a set-to and therefore he could not be very objective about my merit increase. Heaven knows what this will mean when he is acting dean. As for *[name deleted]*, he made it clear to me at an earlier luncheon that he wasn't happy with my role. He went as far as to suggest that I go on half time.

"Enough said for the moment. I obviously have a different set of expectations for myself than either *[name deleted]* or *[name deleted]* do. I made the case for myself in my last letter to Doug Tigert. Where all this will end I don't know, but I think I better start making notes like this to myself lest they go off the deep end.

"I really believe a faculty like this needs at least one person around like myself. They don't, and therein lies the problem."

When John resigned his position at the University, I told him I was really sorry that he had ended up feeling that his non-conformist ideas were not compatible with continuing as Dean of the Faculty of Management Studies. All organizations and particularly academic institutions need people with strong, divergent, challenging views, and I told him we needed him on the inside where we would be forced to pay attention rather than hurling bricks from the outside. I suspect that I added that he might be even more effective if he could cushion some of the bricks with just a thin layer of padding! Today it's mavericks like John whose ideas are often critically important in helping an institution reshape its strategies and programs.

John R. Evans, Chairman of the Board, Torstar Corporation

Through much of my academic career, I was criticized for my many outside activities. Off campus, I was sometimes introduced as the Don Rickles of the industrial relations circuit or whatever other circuit I happened to be on. The first time I was described this way, I recall being somewhat offended, but later I took it as a compliment. I've learned that when one has very critical, negative, and pessimistic things to say (as I often did), it is essential to present them with humour and irreverence. Otherwise, you can easily lose an audience. I confess that much of my humour in those early days was sexist by today's standards, but I do not apologize for using humour per se.

The use of humour and plain language, however, led to another criticism by academic colleagues. They said that I was a popularizer, and they didn't mean it as a compliment. Again, I refuse to apologize for using ordinary language rather than professional jargon when speaking to non-academics. In fact, I believe that academics who criticize people like me for being popularizers are just plain jealous that they can't put their own thinking into language more easy to understand.

In more recent years, my colleagues seemed to give up their attempts to discredit me as a mere popularizer, but they have found a more insidious and effective way to rein me in. I am convinced (but cannot prove) that for years I was banned from participating in university activities, other than the classes I was teaching, because I was thought to be too politically incorrect. For example, I have seldom been allowed to contribute to the University of Toronto's Executive Development and Executive MBA programs.

More specifically, I got in trouble for strongly opposing affirmative action legislation. Some minority and women participants who attended my lecture took offence and informed university authorities. They naturally, but unfortunately, bowed to the complainants because the Executive Development and Executive MBA programs generate a lot of revenue for the business school. Heavens above, we certainly wouldn't want to risk that in the name of something as inconsequential as academic freedom.

I've also raised hackles and caused myself grief with my stance on political correctness In 1994, for example, because of my views I was *not* invited to a conference at the Centre for Industrial Relations at my own university, a conference I would like to have attended and to which I should have received the courtesy of an invitation since I was the founder of the Centre. At the time, I was outraged, and I wrote a memo I planned to distribute via the University of Toronto's *Bulletin*. Eventually, I decided that making the matter public would do too much harm to the Centre.

This is what I wrote on June 28, 1994, and then buried in my files: "We all are aware of the tremendous damage political correctness is doing in universities south of the border. Only occasionally do we see how much harm it can do closer to home.

"Perhaps the most tragic example of the cost we pay for not standing up to this menace was inflicted upon Jeanne Cannizzo, that young female assistant professor who organized an African exhibit at the Royal Ontario Museum. Despite the praise this exhibit received from renowned experts, she was hounded off this campus by dissidents who did not share her view of the African experience.

"My own recent victimization by those more politically correct than myself pales in comparison with hers, but naturally makes me more sensitive to this threat to our freedom. Petty as this little slight to me may be, it is still revealing.

"Recently, a conference on 'International Development in Workplace Innovation—Implications for Canadian Competitiveness' was held at this University, sponsored by our Centre for Industrial Relations and Centre for International Studies, as well as the Ottawa-based Public Policy Forum. This invitational conference was attended by leading industrial relations scholars from all over the world as well as my campus colleagues.

"I was not invited to this conference despite being the Founding Director of the Centre for Industrial Relations, teaching our leading graduate and undergraduate courses in the area, and considerable writing on subject matter germane to the conference. Given my background, I think I could have contributed something to the conference. Certainly, I would have learned a great deal.

"When I asked after the fact why I was not invited, I was told it was an oversight. Suspicious as I frankly was about this explanation, I was prepared to accept it until one of the participants at the conference informed me that he had been surprised by my absence and had inquired about my whereabouts.

"This individual was told by one of our esteemed colleagues who helped to organize the conference that my point of view would hardly be found acceptable among the kind of group that was attending this gathering. I find this attitude shocking to say the least.

"Having just spent three frustrating and futile years on the CBC Board of Directors trying to rid that organization of its political correctness so that every major viewpoint could be aired, I now find the same evil force at work in my own back yard.

"Suppressing alternative points of view is bad enough on a public broadcaster. It is the very antithesis of what a university is supposed to be all about.

"It sickens me to think about the depths to which some of my colleagues will sink to ensure that nothing contrary to their own points of view is aired, but I guess I shouldn't be surprised in these days of political correctness, right or wrong as it may be.

"The whole experience makes me realize why tenure is so important. While its abuses should be corrected, the basic principles it embodies must remain inviolate."

John hired me as the first Librarian for the Centre for Industrial Relations. I'd just taken a year off and got my degree, and I wanted a change. My background was business, and businesses rely on very current information, so a business library is much different from an academic library. John wanted the same thing, and he was looking for someone to set it up. I said, "Look, I'll give you three months to show you what I'm trying to do. Then you can decide whether you want to hire me." He said absolutely not and worked at getting me on the payroll of the University of Toronto Library over the objections of the Chief Librarian. I was told you could hear Professor Crispo shouting at him through the closed door of the Librarian's office. Also, it was a matter of the autonomy to set up and operate the collection.

Getting me on the payroll was the first step. Then, John had to get money from government, corporations, and unions for the collection itself. The early years were tumultuous, always a struggle to get funding. He fought very hard to maintain the library's autonomy and to get recognition for me. At least the University gave us half a house. I think it was the second floor.

We worked very well together. We had the same ideas and commitment. For me, the job was most important. Money didn't matter as much, and it was the same for him.

John is one of my favourite people. I didn't see his shenanigans, although I heard about them. He's so high strung, and he didn't completely fit into the academic mold. And yet he was a scholar. I don't think people realized how solid his scholarship was because he was so often performing. To meet him, of course, you were impressed by his personality. I also think he felt very comfortable in the business community, maybe even more comfortable there than in the academic community. That's probably why he did so well raising money for the Centre. Essentially, he's very conservative.

Jean Newman, Founding Librarian,
Centre for Industrial Relations, University of Toronto

I'LL TAKE THAT WITH RELISH

I have to admit there were times that I enjoyed my excesses. A couple of my appearances before the bloated and bureaucratic Canadian Radio-television and Telecommunications Commission (CRTC) were highly entertaining, although I'm not sure they served any useful purpose.

My first CRTC encounter was as a "CKO Survivor" trying to save CKO All News Radio. CKO was being taken over by the Quebec-based Cogeco Cable Inc. as part of a deal that would provide Cogeco with a lot of new cable capacity while allowing it to shut down the money-losing CKO. But CKO was the only national alternative to the CBC in terms of radio news and could have been saved if targeted at commuting drivers where its main audience was to be found.

The hearing was highly memorable. One reason was the phalanx of lawyers Cogeco brought. Each had one or two oversized legal briefcases. I suggested to the CRTC Commissioners that the briefcases were likely just for show and challenged the Commissioners to check. But the Commissioners were too busy thinking up ways to make Cogeco cough up concessions that addressed their individual pet projects and biases. The CRTC eventually extracted hundreds of thousands of dollars worth of concessions, money that could have gone a long way to saving CKO, but, of course, the CRTC didn't have any interest in that part of the dastardly Cogeco deal.

My second CRTC encounter was when I appeared before the august tribunal to urge that the CBC's license not be renewed on the grounds of bias and inefficiency. I was due to appear in the morning but was shifted to the evening so that my presentation wouldn't be covered live by C-PAC. Luckily, I had other things I could do in Ottawa that day, but I kept dropping in on the hearing to see how it was going. I was appalled by how boring and tedious it was.

By the time I appeared, I was angry and frustrated. I knew my cause was hopeless and I had nothing to lose. I began by asking the Commissioners what drug they were on that kept them looking as if they were awake when they couldn't possibly be. Then I asked what antidote individuals assigned to ask questions of different witnesses were on to keep them awake. I explained that both of these drugs would be equally useful for Faculty meetings, which I acknowledged were almost as boring and tedious as CRTC hearings.

At this point, the Chair told me I was on the verge of contempt of the Commission. Throwing caution and discretion utterly to the winds, I asked him how I could get beyond the verge since I could think of no greater honour to be carved on my tombstone than something like "He was held in contempt by the CRTC." The Chair warned me that I had almost exhausted my allotted 10 minutes for testimony and that I better get down to business. I replied that what I'd said so far didn't count and asked the secretary to roll the timer back to zero. To the consternation of his colleagues, the secretary did so. He must have had some sneaking sympathy for me.

Naturally, my testimony had no impact whatsoever on the CRTC and wouldn't have even if I had treated the Commissioners with the respect they so richly did not deserve. The CRTC always treats the CBC as a sacred trust. It puts the CBC through a few hoops but it never grills the CBC about fundamental flaws. This will never change as long as the Commissioners are selected from the ranks of political hacks and other unemployables.

John Crispo is extremely intelligent, has an innovative mind, and doesn't follow fashion or faction. I think he's an original. He's an interesting person. The sparks fly anywhere near him.

Mind you, the first time I met him, sometime between 1975 and 1980, he didn't make any particular impression. I was writing a cover story on labour for Maclean's, and John was one of about 20 people I interviewed.

He struck me as articulate, well-versed, and a good interview, but nothing jumped out.

It was a few years later that we locked horns. I was Managing Editor of CBC Radio News, and John was going on about the CBC's bias in covering the news. I was quoted as saying that the CBC's duty was to look at any piece of legislation critically. Of course, I meant analytically, but John took it negatively, hit the roof, and claimed it was typical of the CBC's left-wing bias. He went public, so I did, too. As a result, some bright-eyed producer set up a series of radio debates between the two of us. He'd say something attacking my position, and I'd respond. We'd argue publicly, but afterwards it was always friendly. He was very funny about me being a reckless revolutionary lunatic. In fact, I was quite delighted.

John's problem was that he went so far in his declamations that people inside the CBC didn't take him seriously. It's a pity because he had some good points. For example, there was a squishy, soft centre in journalism, but it was due to laziness, not left-wing bias. Still, I liked him and his fire and how he could see through a lot of the bullshit. I found myself defending him in meetings. "No, he's not a right wing nut."

Michael Enright, CBC Broadcaster and Writer

No Thanks for Being Me

Sometimes I got into trouble just for being in the wrong place at the wrong time or being associated with a group deemed to be up to no good.

One of the most amusing occasions was when I appeared on a panel for a Canadian Conference of the International Foundation of Employee Benefits. The Foundation is made up of labour and management trustees who serve on the boards of labour-management, health and welfare, and pension funds. While the Foundation's meetings are basically educational, they are usually held in appealing, if not always exotic, locales. Trustees are treated to lots of time for leisure activities as a kind of payoff for all the unpaid hours they donate to their duties.

The Canadian Conference that got me in trouble took place in Bermuda. (I also remember ones in Hawaii and on a cruise ship sailing from Vancouver to Anchorage and back.) As I recall, I was on a lively panel with M. Beauprés (I think his given name was Yves), the President of Domtar, who had just removed me as Chairman of the Domtar Joint Labour-Management Committee, and Marc Lalonde,

Trudeau's Executive Assistant, who had just told me I wouldn't be doing any more government work because of my strenuous opposition to wage and price controls. I remember kidding both of them about what an honour and privilege it was to share a platform with two powerful individuals who had just fired me, something they both vigorously denied.

I had a great time until I got home and found a message from my University's President asking me to explain how I was going to deal with *The Toronto Star*'s editorial attacking the Foundation for holding its convention in Bermuda, especially when the Canadian dollar was under pressure and Trudeau was urging Canadians to stay home to help preserve its value. Marc Lalonde really got it in the neck because he was Trudeau's sidekick, but *The Star*'s editors didn't spare me one little bit. They'd found out I had missed a couple of classes to attend the Bermuda gathering and demanded to know where my priorities and responsibilities lay. Never mind that I had arranged for excellent substitutes. In any event, I don't think I replied to *The Star* by letter—I vaguely recall the President advising against it—but I do know I used the incident in subsequent speeches to argue that someone neutral had to be at this labour-management meeting even if it was held offshore.

Sometime after the Bermuda incident, I joined the Board of the Foundation. Although I was soon in big trouble with its union members because of my strong stance in favour of free trade, I might still be on the Board if I hadn't turned up in the wrong place at the wrong time. I was in Banff to address a convention of what were known as union-free contractors, and I was warned in advance that if I appeared before this group I might lose my Foundation Board membership. Of course, that was like waving a red flag. I'd have risen from my death bed to address the group. More than a thousand unionized construction workers picketed the conference and that seemed to be the end of my career with the Foundation. I regretted the loss because the fringe benefits were fantastic. But I didn't regret standing up for freedom of speech and assembly.

Years later, in December 2000, I was delighted to be invited to address the Canadian Conference of the Foundation in San Francisco. My wide-ranging talk on the subject of "Whither Canada?" was so well-received that I thought it might be possible to get back into the Foundation's good graces. I'm hopeful because I was invited to address the Foundation's next major conference in November 2001 on Maui on the topic of the future of medicare.

Occasionally, I got into trouble without saying anything provocative. Once, many years ago during my left-of-centre days, it occurred at a dinner party. Cesar Chavez had organized the California grape boycott, and Canadians were picketing grocery stores for selling California grapes. During dinner the hostess went out of her way to tell me and the others present that the lovely centrepiece on her dining room table was full of California fruit, particularly grapes which she'd proudly gone through the picket line to purchase. I could only take so much. I got up from the table, picked up her centrepiece, walked to the front door, opened it, and hurled the whole offensive decoration out the door. This ended an otherwise pleasant evening and a budding friendship.

There are times when even the most careful observer would admit that I am utterly blameless. Recently, my wife and I were invited to the home of a banker friend for dinner on condition that I not talk about the proposed mega-bank mergers then being hotly debated. My wife accepted the invitation and warned me to stay away from that subject. I behaved myself until the hostess brought up the topic herself. She said something to the effect that she now felt she understood my opposition to the mergers, which she attributed to me not owning any shares in the banks. Well, that did it. The battle of words raged. Even my wife agreed that I had been unduly provoked and had every right to fight back, although she did feel I had reacted more strongly than warranted. Later, she learned that the hostess had goaded me deliberately. Apparently, she thought her dinner party need livening up.

ON BEHALF OF...

My career as a lecturer and speaker has been full of memorable moments. Some of my fondest memories are related to audience reaction.

During one of my early classes, a very disruptive, somewhat deranged, well-known radical student decided that loud whistling would wear me and the class down. It didn't work, but one commerce and finance student got so upset he marched over and punched out the whistler, actually drawing blood in the process. The puncher was horrified at what he'd done in a moment of anger. The whistler headed to the President's office, waving his tennis racket and singing "Onward Christian Soldiers, with the cross of Crispo going on before." The President's staff was so nonplussed that no one reacted quickly enough to stop him from entering the President's office. The President was there meeting with some members of the Student Administrative Counsel (SAC), who took the whistler under their wing. Later, I got a concerned call from the President. After I explained what had happened in class, the matter was closed.

Occasionally my public appearances also got pretty rowdy. One night in 1987 or 1988, at an anti-free trade rally in East Vancouver, things nearly got out of hand. I was debating with David Orchard, the left-wing nut from Saskatchewan much loved by the media for his near-violent opposition to the FTA. The media was so enamoured of Orchard that he eventually ran a surprisingly effective, though ultimately unsuccessful, campaign for the leadership of the national Progressive Conservative Party. How ironic.

Anyway, on the night we debated in East Vancouver, the crowd got pretty ugly. I didn't help by asserting that they weren't bothering me because I had a farm and they didn't seem any worse than the critters I had in my barnyard. At that point, the Chair, Jack Webster, that famous West Coast broadcaster on whose show I appeared regularly until some ill-informed reporter wrote that I was being groomed to replace him, whispered to me that if I said anything more to provoke the crowd, he was going to leave before the howling mob charged the platform. Fortunately for all concerned, Orchard's organizers of the confrontation began to act as marshals and settled the crowd down.

On occasion I have been thanked in unforgettable terms. Once in Toronto I had a speaking engagement on free trade to what I think was called the Canadian Magazine Publishers Association, an organization still opposed to free trade. The publishers gave me a cordial reception even though they didn't like what I had to say. At the end, the Chair got me as I was dashing to the door to catch a limousine waiting to get me to my next speaking engagement. She urged me to stop on my way out so I could at least see the large and beautiful coffee table book the publishers were giving me as a token of their appreciation. She held it high over her head and said something to the effect that I was lucky I wasn't still sitting beside her. Otherwise, she, like the rest of the audience, would be sorely tempted to bring it down hard on my head. She got a great laugh and even greater applause as I scuttled out as fast as I could.

The most memorable thank you gift I've ever received came from the Canadian Veterinary Medicine Association, which also didn't share my views on free trade. The Chair insisted I open the gift on the spot so he could explain its significance both to me and the audience. It was a glass replica of a Canadian goose in full flight mounted on a piece of granite. There were three reasons why it was a very appropriate gift, the Chair said. First, it was made of glass and therefore very transparent, just like me. Second, it was a Canada goose, the very epitome of free trade because it flies back and forth without stopping for customs, immigration, or anything else. And finally, as a goose it symbolized the royal goose everyone in the audience would like to give me. I'd be hard pressed to name another occasion when my speech has been so effectively upstaged by the words of thanks.

The sequel to this story is that I decided to give this lovely goose to Brian and Mila Mulroney as a thank you for one of the dinners my wife and I were so fortunate to attend at 24 Sussex Drive. I got the chance on December 12, 1988, but the problem was that I didn't have an opportunity to fully explain the significance of the goose to either Brian or Mila. It's probably languishing unexplained somewhere in the public archives. What a sad ending for a beautiful symbol of the free trade agreement for which Brian and I fought so hard.

 AND IN CONCLUSION

I started this chapter on an apologetic note. I am ending it less apologetically. I guess this reflects the fact that I will never change. I know I have gone too far too often, and I have some regrets. But I suppose I am unrepentant in the sense that I still believe that strong messages should be delivered strongly, even if the price of passion may be losing some potential converts in the process.

I've only seen John totally nonplussed once. It happened at Whistler a couple of years ago, but it actually started at Devil's Glen the year before. We were sharing a T-bar lift at Devil's Glen and, as we went up the hill, John kept pulling the bar to his side. I kept saying, "Don't do that," and I had to keep pulling the bar to my side to keep the balance. When we got to the top, I said, "I'm never going to ride a T-bar with you again."

At Whistler, a year later, we were skiing with another friend. We had to take a T-bar for the final bit, and I said, "No way. I'm going up with Dave." So John looked around and found another skier who was on his own and the two headed up the hill. Dave and I followed. Near the top, Dave and I saw a deep mark in the snow. Obviously, someone had fallen off the lift and skidded for some distance. We looked around and saw John standing in the trees, covered in snow, with a weird look on his face.

Later, we met at the bottom of the hill and we asked him what happened. John explained somewhat sheepishly. "When Doug said he wouldn't go up with me, I found someone else, a single skier, a big guy, about 6' 2", a beginner. As we were riding up, he said, 'This isn't working.' And I said, 'No, it isn't.' The next thing I knew he'd pulled the bar from under me!" The beginner had got the better of him, and John was as close to speechless as I've ever seen him.

Douglas B. Skelton, P.Eng., Retired Consulting Engineer and Long-time Friend

Chapter 8

Endgame

Before I leave this life, I have one final battle to fight, one more issue of public policy on which to speak out with passion. The cause is euthanasia. By this I mean the right of an individual with an incurable disease who is facing intolerable pain and suffering or is incapacitated to decide to terminate his or her life and to be given help in doing it. We are intelligent beings, and we should have a say in how and when we leave this life once we are, in effect, on the verge of leaving it.

My interest is deeply personal and of long standing.

When I retired from the University of Toronto, I'd already had one serious health warning, a bout with prostate cancer. The treatments appeared to have worked, and I looked forward to what I hoped would be many healthy, active years enjoying life with my wife and children, continuing to comment on public policy issues, and pursuing business opportunities.

Maybe I'll get my wish, and maybe I won't. The odds suddenly swung against me when the cancer returned. Fortunately for me, I have excellent medical care, the love and support of my family, a strong constitution, and a positive attitude. So I am hopeful that I will still get to enjoy many healthy, active years. I've already had more than I anticipated or expected.

The experience, however, pushed euthanasia to the front of my mind again.

Years ago, my mother died, not a terrible death, but a long death. The last five years she spent in bed, rarely saying anything but "Help, help." In fact, my oldest grandson, who was a toddler at the time, still refers to her as "Nanna Help Help" because those were the only two words he ever heard her utter.

Now I find myself facing the possibility that I may face something comparable, being ready to go but being forced to linger. I admit it: I'm a coward. I don't want to find myself ending my days in pain and suffering, or, worse still, physically helpless and dependent on others for care in dealing with every bodily function. I want the right to die with dignity at a time of my own choosing. I want the right *not* to be a burden: on myself, on my wife, on my family, on my friends, on society.

I'm certainly not alone in this view. There have been many courageous people who have already spoken loudly and clearly for this right, and ordinary Canadians by and large approve. In July 2001, for example, *The Globe and Mail* reported that 57 per cent of those polled said that if they were suffering an incurable, extremely painful illness, they would want help to die. What I found even more interesting was the response to a question about helping someone you love who asks for help in dying. An astonishing, and to me very encouraging, 76 per cent of those polled felt that someone who has helped end the life of a loved one suffering from an incurable illness should not be prosecuted. (See "Mercy killers should not face trial, pollsters told," by Michelle MacAfee, *The Globe and Mail*, July 2, 2001.)

I am ashamed and embarrassed to be living in a country where we treat animals more compassionately than we do human beings. In December 1999, when Big Ben was stricken with colic, *he* was euthanized to stop his suffering. (See "Big Ben jumped his way into hearts of Canadians: Decision made to end suffering after horse stricken with colic," by Beverley Smith, *The Globe and Mail*, December 13, 1999.) Every day, ordinary people find themselves having to make the same decision for their much-loved pets. They do what is right; they end the animals' suffering in the most humane and kind way possible. I've done it myself three times, twice with horses and once with a family dog.

There are no words to describe the anger I now feel, even more intensely, about our gutless and spineless legislators who will not even debate the issue. Why won't they? Are they afraid of going up against the Roman Catholic Church or other religious groups? Or do they think it's too controversial to risk any political capital?

Another critical aspect—other than humanism—is financial. There's a powerful economic and fiscal argument to be made in favour of permitting euthanasia.

Right now, 50 cents of every dollar spent on health care in Canada is used to treat people who are in the last six months of their lives. Should we be doing that? Well, sure, for those who want to hang on to the bitter end. But for those who say, "I have no more quality of life; I'm ready to sign off," we should be there to help. We'd be doing the compassionate and humane thing, and we'd be saving the health care system a pile of money. Just think of how many hundreds of dollars a day the average hospital bed costs, never mind the drugs and other supplies needed to keep them moderately comfortable. And for what? To ease our consciences? Think of how much more effectively those health care dollars could be used for treating victims of illness or injury who *want* to live.

Of course, we'd have to have safeguards to make sure that those who were opting for euthanasia are mentally competent and are doing it of their own free will and not because an heir to the estate is getting antsy.

A doctor I know suggested a way that might work. First, create panels of three people—a doctor, a lawyer, and a layperson—whose job would be to determine whether the individual is mentally competent and whether the individual is, in fact, terminally ill and going to be exposed to great pain and suffering or be incapacitated. Things should be kept simple and informal as possible, but the applicant—the person who wants to be euthanized—should meet with the panel.

Assuming the panel agrees that the individual is making a reasonable decision given his or her circumstances, the next step would be to have the person euthanized at the time and place of the individual's choice with the help of a specialist who is trained to help people move on painlessly. We could call them Doctors of Relief.

I'll admit it gets tricky when deciding exactly what safeguards to put in place, but others have managed to find a way, so why can't we? The Dutch, for example, have practised physician-assisted suicide, euthanasia by another name, for 25 years. Until recently, the Dutch courts tolerated the practice leniently if certain conditions were met: hopeless suffering, voluntary and persistent requests, and at least two medical opinions. Now, they've given it formal, legal status. (See "A great leap for humanity: The Dutch move to legally help those who believe 'enough is enough' has the advantage of openness and accountability. It's time for Canada to take the same step," by Arthur Schafer, Director of the Centre for Professional and Applied Ethics at the University of Manitoba," *The Globe and Mail,* January 2, 2001.)

Maturity, mental competence, and physical state are the three big question marks.

There's no magic way to test for maturity; the best we can do is decide on an age as a cut-off point. I'd be in favour of age 18, since we generally admit people who have reached that age to the ranks of adulthood for other purposes. For those under 18, we'd have to have more checks and balances, but they should have the option, too. After all, why should they be condemned to a life of pain and suffering or incapacity just because they haven't clocked enough years yet?

Mental competence can be equally difficult to assess, particularly if people are in excruciating pain. My guess is it's a lot harder for them to appear as sane and rational as they truly are under those circumstances. So, to make sure they are covered, everyone should name a person in advance as a precaution. This person's role would be to act as proxy if that circumstance arises.

Physical state—the actual medical facts—are likely to be more easily established, although, of course, there can still be question marks there. We'd have to look at the balance of probability and err on the side of the applicant's wish.

For me, the big test—the only one that really counts—is quality of life as defined by the individual. Speaking strictly for myself, being free of pain and mentally alert doesn't add up to quality of life. If I can't ski and golf and go horseback riding and talk and give speeches and walk around, if my life is lying in bed waiting for the end, that's not life. It's a living death, and I don't want any part of it.

The point is that every individual should have the right to spell out what quality of life means to him or her. It shouldn't be the family or friends or doctor or anyone else. They shouldn't have anything to say about it. It should be strictly the individual's judgement that rules for or against euthanasia.

So, that's my case. With luck, I'll be around for many more years helping to get euthanasia into the open where it belongs. Maybe I'll even live long enough to take advantage of it.

John and I met on a ski lift in the early 1980s. When we got on the same chair, I noticed his name badge. By coincidence, I had just read a long feature by him in that morning's *The Globe and Mail*. It had something to do with labour relations in Europe. I told him how much I enjoyed it, and we started talking. He seemed impressed that I'd read it.

My first vivid memory of John is chatting, talking with me and others. He's a real chat. He's a quick study with virtually a photographic memory. He seems to absorb everything he reads. He never has to go back to it. He doesn't do research in the conventional sense. He reads and talks to people.

How would I describe him? John is very compassionate and emotional. He's a great crier. I don't think he'd cry except in front of his family and when he's watching figure skating. He also gets very emotional about the military and marching bands.

John is an idealist, something of a cynic, but also realistic and practical. He's a people person, although sometimes he has to be reminded to see the people side of people and be a bit more diplomatic. There are times when I want to kick him under the table.

John brings me great pleasure because he's so totally active and alive. He lives each day to the fullest. He's enriched my life with his companionship and interest in the world and people.

Barbara Crispo, John Crispo's Wife

Was It Worth It?

Working on this memoir has been a fascinating experience that's helped me clear away the clutter and get to the core question I set out to answer. Have I made a positive and significant contribution to my academic field and to public policy in general? Have my mistakes and misjudgements outweighed the value I brought? Have I used my talents, time, and energy well? Has it been worth the effort?

To begin, I must confess that I'd forgotten a great deal about my professional career. While digging through files, I found articles I didn't remember writing, speeches I didn't remember delivering, and names of groups I didn't remember addressing. One that really struck me was finding a speech I drafted for Brian Mulroney along with correspondence about it. Writing a speech for one's Prime Minister could well be regarded as a highlight in anyone's career. I was astonished to discover it and even more astonished to realize I had forgotten it completely.

I also found a good many speaking notes, which reminded me of something else I'd forgotten: the experience that made me realize I cannot deliver a speech well from a fully written text. I learned my lesson many years ago when I was granted the great honour and privilege of delivering the Labour Day luncheon address at the Canadian National Exhibition on September 6, 1965. The luncheon always followed the Labour Day parade, and I was the first non-labour leader and non-politician asked to give this address. I wrote a humdinger, "Looking Back and Looking Forward: Can Organized Labour Stand the Test of Time?" but I delivered it so poorly I remember the humiliation this day. I made a vow then that I would never read a speech again. I kept my word.

FUNNY MONEY

If I were to answer the core question from a strictly financial point of view, I would probably have to say no, it wasn't worth it. I didn't see or couldn't accept the many possibilities available for harvest in tandem with an academic career.

If I'd gone along with the intellectual corruption at the heart of the arbitration process, I know I could have made a lot more money. Even if I had carried on with conciliation and mediation (much more honest and, therefore, less lucrative procedures) I likely could have done much better financially. Giving speeches was a lucrative sideline, but I never developed it fully, financially speaking. My primary goal was usually to carry a message, rarely just to earn a fee.

I also failed to take advantage of opportunities to sell myself to an institution as a consultant or spokesperson. To earn significant money that way one must pledge oneself to stand with the group through right and wrong, thick and thin. I could never bring myself to do that. I can support only that in which I truly believe. When I aligned myself with a group, it was temporary and in order to support a particular cause. But once the cause had run its course, I would be on my way to another issue.

Finally, I'm sure I could have pumped up my net worth if I'd been willing to sell my soul to the corporate world. Thinking about all those stock options, bonuses, and other benefits senior executives and Board members get just for breathing can make one dizzy. But the price is corruption, in the sense of having to set aside or compromise one's ideals and values. I've never been good at keeping my eyes, ears, and mouth shut, playing games, or back-stabbing, Nor do I see the generations coming up behind mine cleaning up corporate practices and attitudes. If I'd been able to bring myself to be just half as greedy as the typical dot-commer, I'd be a wealthy person today.

Now that I'm retired from my academic position, I am pursuing a variety of business interests, but only on my own terms. I'd would love to do well in business without compromising my principles and with people I can truly trust. It's possible that I may yet achieve the kind of business success that others take for granted. If I do, it will be a radically different kind of capstone to my career.

John Crispo always had a knack for being on the right side of the right issue at the right time and always made a contribution to the cause he favoured.

Wendy K. Dobson, Director, Institute for International Business

---

GROUP THINK

The fundamental problem with all groups and institutions, whether public or private, is that they cannot regulate themselves effectively. It doesn't matter who they are, what they do, or how worthy their cause. It just can't be done.

An example is the police, whose associations I have addressed several times. I'm a strong supporter of police forces in general. I believe that police play a critical role and do a very difficult job in any civilized society. But, like any group, the police are bound to have some bad actors. Any self-respecting profession should be willing to weed them out. Yet the police seem just as unwilling or incapable as doctors, lawyers, stock brokers, and, yes, university professors, of coming to grips with people whose inappropriate behaviours and attitudes tarnish the reputation of the whole profession and all of its practitioners. Instead, the instinct for solidarity and self-protection kick in, overwhelming every other consideration. Nobody cleans house.

This fundamental human weakness is one reason I've never been able to commit to any group on a long-term basis. Even if they were willing to weed out the unfit in their midst, I've always had another problem with groups—advanced rigidity of thinking.

All groups have a purpose, objectives, a doctrine. I have no problem with that. The problem comes with the dogmatic approach that binds everything and everyone together and the assumptions that go with it. Swallow it all or be called a traitor. No independent thinking allowed. For example, for a long time committed unionists were also expected to support the NDP. Everyone in management was deemed to support the

Progressive Conservatives. Supporting the Liberals would be daring and uttering social democratic notions would be suicidal in career terms. Only the most courageous would dare to dissent, and only those already firmly established as leaders were likely to survive their departure from the narrow, well-defined groove of acceptable thought.

I often found myself drawn to a group regardless of its shortcomings, especially in its early stages, but I could never stick around for long and certainly never long enough to be indoctrinated permanently. I'm not sure when my need for freedom of expression and thought became overriding, but it never stopped developing. Once I was granted tenure, any fears I may have had about challenging the existing order and status quo dissipated completely. When I saw something I believed to be wrong in society at large, or in any specific group, I never hesitated to speak out against it. And the more I did so, the more compelled and driven I felt to continue on this course.

Very few individuals enjoy complete freedom of expression and thought in our society. Those few who do don't always take advantage of it. Wherever one works—even in universities, which are thought to be bastions of free thought and freedom of expression—there are pressures to toe the institutional line. Over the years, many individuals have approached me after a class, a media presentation, a speech, or seeing a newspaper article and expressed envy at my freedom to express my feelings and viewpoints without fear of retribution.

I don't know how to set a value on this luxury, but I do regard it as precious. Intellectually, I began to think for myself early on and never gave up the habit. Mentally, I know I am healthier for the freedom I have enjoyed. And psychologically, I have seldom allowed anything to stay bottled up inside me. I've been extremely fortunate to be in the position of being allowed to withstand the storms of debate and controversy because I knew myself to be placed in a position as secure and independent as it is possible to be in any society.

The first time I saw John teach, he said, "They pay me to lean against a blackboard for three hours a week and read for the other 37 hours."

The first time I met John it was in his office one-on-one. I was considering doing a Ph.D. and wanted his advice. He said, "All you have to remember is those who can, do. Those who can't, teach. Those who can't teach, go into politics."
He's been my mentor unknowingly ever since.

Richard Leblanc, C.M.C., B.Sc., M.B.A., LLB, J.D., LLM, Ph.D. (Candidate),
Corporate Governance Program, Schulich School of Business, York University, Toronto

THE FRUITS OF FREEDOM

So, what have I accomplished, professionally speaking?

As an academic, I've written many worthy academic articles and books, some of which I think may have been the best on their topics to that time and several of which still stand the test of quality today. I'm particularly proud of *International Unionism: A Study in Canadian American Relations* (Toronto: McGraw-Hill, 1967), *Industrial Democracy in Western Europe: A North American Perspective* (Toronto: McGraw-Hill Ryerson, 1978), and *Free Trade: The Real Story* (Toronto: Gage Educational Publishing, 1988).

I founded the University of Toronto's Centre for Industrial Relations. The Directors who succeeded me have developed it into one of the leading centres of its kind in Canada. It attracts and graduates very good students with Masters and Doctorates who are now teaching and working throughout North America and in other parts of the world. My only regret is that the Centre isn't currently complementing and supplementing its excellent academic programs with more interaction with both the labour and management communities through public policy conferences.

I was the first Dean of the University of Toronto's Faculty of Management Studies. (It's now called The Joseph L. Rotman School of Management.) Its continuing challenge is a faculty culture that emphasizes individuality to such an extent that teamwork seems to disappear. I admit to being guilty of this fault myself for years although I saw the need for more faculty commitment to the institution as such in my later years, when I served as Chairman of its Executive Committee and then Speaker of the Faculty Council. Somehow, the Dean of this Faculty (or

School or whatever it is called next) must persuade more faculty members to combine their individual interests with those of the School. Otherwise, it will never achieve its full potential or be ranked with the best national and international institutions.

An aggravating circumstance has been the School's inability to recruit and retain the best of faculty members. During the 1990s, the School lost some of its finest colleagues to leading business schools in Great Britain and the United States. The reasons go far beyond the obvious economic payoffs—huge salary increases, summer supplements, reduced teaching loads, and so on. But they must be identified and addressed just the same or the University of Toronto's School of Management will inevitably slide down the merit scale.

I've taught tens of thousands of students over the years. One of the most rewarding things about teaching is meeting them years later in so many settings. I've run into former student on airplanes, in audiences, on golf courses, on the ski slopes, and, yes, even on panels where we're both invited guests. Perhaps the memorable encounter is meeting a former student at a café in Paris. He was sitting near me and my wife, Barbara. I must have given him a very good grade because when he spotted my wallet falling out of my back pocket, he retrieved and returned it quickly.

I admit to some jealousy when I see so many of my former students doing so much better financially than I ever did. Sometimes I think faculty should be paid a small fraction of their former students' earning. Needless to say, I have not yet found a former student who agrees with this proposition.

There's another amazing aspect to teaching and that's seeing how students seem to age much more quickly than the teacher. When my older students approach me, I often tell them they must have mistaken me for my father, who was really their teacher. I actually fool a few of them, at least for a moment or two.

As a commentator on public policy, I've delivered thousands of speeches to business, management, labour, educational, and political groups. I believe from the feedback I've received that I have had an influence, if only by stirring up people's thinking.

It's more difficult to assess the impact I may have had through the media. I've written hundreds of magazine articles and op-ed pieces for newspapers. I've been a commentator on radio and television countless times on countless topics. For years, for example, I voiced my views three times a week on CKO All News Radio with Robert Holiday, and I still run into people who remember that daily commentary and joust. It never ceases to amaze me how many readers and listeners pick up on and remember something. I also continue to be amazed at how many want to dispute my point of view.

There have been a few times, however, when I've felt I've really made a difference in terms of public opinion or public policy. I know, for example, that I changed the course of labour law in several jurisdictions in Canada. A very specific example is allowing contractors' associations to be accredited, giving them the equivalent of union certification, as a way of countervailing the power of unions in the construction industry. My friend, Harry Arthurs, who went on to become President of York University, and I developed this concept in the 1960s, and it was incorporated subsequently into almost every provincial labour relations act in the country.

I am just as confident that I had some effect on changes to other labour laws. One was the fight for the right of civil servants to join unions, engage in collective bargaining, and even strike as long as there were appropriate mechanisms in place to protect the public interest. Another was Trudeau's wage and price controls, against which I spoke and wrote all over the country. At about the same time I was just as vehemently and vociferously opposed to Trudeau's musings about the democratic corporate state and his equally dangerous and foolish notion of an industrial strategy for Canada. I like to think that my strong and vocal opposition played a part in ensuring that neither of these ridiculous and risky ideas went anywhere.

Although it's difficult for me to assess the effect I had on the great free trade debate, I'm convinced I made a big difference there, too. I worked long and hard on it, campaigned and debated across the country, and saw how I moved many audiences. I've also been told by many powerful and not-so-powerful individuals that I had a major impact. I hope so, because this was truly the greatest single cause of my professional life.

I am much less clear about the effect I had on the CBC. I know that, as a Board Member, I was instrumental in stopping the Board from undercutting the CBC Ombudsman over *The Valour and the Horror*. I also think the CBC is now a little more balanced and fair in its coverage on contentious current affairs. Certainly, the CBC is managing to deliver programming with a whole lot less money (about 30 per cent less, I think), proving that it really was as inefficient and overstaffed as critics like me claimed. But how much of the credit do I deserve? I really can't say.

I'm also not at all clear about what effect I had, if any, on the 1998 rejection of the mega-bank mergers, and I regret that the reason for my opposition was misinterpreted in some quarters.

At times, I know I had no effect—or, at least, ended up on the losing side. One of those occasions was at the University of Toronto. I lost out in my very public battle both against our so-called unicameral governing council system and against the granting of voluntary arbitration to the Faculty Association. Outside the University, I'm sure I was on the losing side of many other battles. One of the worst was my long-standing fight against deficit financing by one federal government after another. Many economists joined me, and none of us take comfort in saying "I told you so."

One dimension of John is an extension of his personality. He has a great sense of humour. He can spark responses; you can't stay neutral. He loves engaging people.

John also has a sense of mission. He has a very high profile in terms of strong views and public positions. He takes unpopular positions, rightly or wrongly.

The other dimension is John as the researcher. He did some excellent research, especially in the 1960s. He made an astounding contribution in Industrial Relations. His book on international unions is very important. Later, he became a social commentator and critic and moved away from research. I think the field is poorer for it.

My vivid and lasting memory of John is chairing those early conferences at the Centre for Industrial Relations. You could see the early roots of John the social commentator. It was very exciting and very public.

John was a good friend to me. Without John there wouldn't have been a Centre. I have great respect and admiration for John. It was a pleasure to work with him.

The Late Noah Meltz, Ph.D., Professor Emeritus, Department of Economics,
University of Toronto, and then Professor of Economics,
School of Business Administration, Netanya Academic College, Jerusalem

AWARDS & HONOURS

When you're a loner, you can't expect many honours, and my expectation has been very largely fulfilled. To my astonishment, however, I did receive one shortly after I taught my last class, and I still don't know how to react to it. Toronto's *Now* magazine announced I'd been voted best post-secondary school teacher in Toronto for the 1998 academic year. I wasn't quite sure how to react, especially when I found a list of discounted advertising rates attached to the letter giving me the news and a suggestion that I take advantage of these rates to take out an ad thanking all those who voted for me. I declined the generous offer, but I wish to take *this* opportunity to thank all of those who made the *Now* award possible....

I'd also like to take this opportunity to thank Thomas J. Kierans, Former President & C.E.O. of the C.D. Howe Institute, for arranging an honour that means a great deal to me. Thanks to Tom, I was made a lifetime member of the Institute. I was amazed and thrilled. I have so much respect for the Institute's work. It has no peer as a think tank in this country. I also have a long history with the Institute, beginning with its share of the sponsorship of the Canadian-American Committee, which paid for my research on international unionism. Over the years, I have enjoyed many stimulating C.D. Howe seminars. I think I was made a lifetime member of the Institute because of the often noisy and provocative interventions I have contributed to these sessions.

SUMMING UP

So, to answer the core question, my answer is, on balance, "yes." Overall, I believe I've made the most of the opportunities that came my way. I also believe that the opportunities I've missed and the mistakes I've made haven't been so dramatic or dreadful as to cancel out my accomplishments. But I also recognize I've been very, very lucky. I've had the great good fortune to live and work in the best of times. I was given the opportunity to be myself. I believe it's an opportunity that comes less and less frequently these days. Would I do as well if I were starting today? Impossible to say. But I can say with confidence that I would still do my best to storm the barricades and shake up the power elite.

John Crispo is not everyone's cup of tea, but, as gadflies go, he's my gadfly. In my 10 years at the C.D. Howe Institute, John did more to provoke informed and constructive discussion at our regular Roundtables than any of his colleagues—combined.

Thomas J. Kierans, Former President & C.E.O., C.D. Howe Institute, Toronto

Postscript

The tragic events of September 11, 2001, took place after this manuscript was completed. I was so greatly moved by this appalling act of terrorism, however, I think it is appropriate to add this postscript with my reflections on these dreadful acts.

Soon after the extent of the destruction became apparent, I started recording my reactions, as emotional as they were. I did this because I knew I would have to address myself to the horror of it all in several forthcoming speeches.

I first heard about the tragedy from a Muslim business associate and friend, who called me right after the first World Trade Center tower was hit. I will never forget his admonition that I might not want to talk to him by the end of the day.

I turned on the T.V. shortly before the second tower was hit and simply couldn't believe what I was seeing. I remember thinking how surreal it was and how good filmmakers had become at special effects.

I am sure I did not capture in my notes all of the emotions I experienced that day, but I think they were a mixture of anger, disbelief, frustration, and shock. At that point, however, the desire for retaliation wasn't one of them.

Over the next few days, I was mesmerized by the events and their aftermath, and I know I wasn't totally myself. Nonetheless, I remember attending a meeting about two weeks later at which I met some Americans. By then, I felt pretty strongly about a number of concerns which had been emerging in my mind.

I recall telling the group how ashamed and embarrassed I felt at the time about being a Canadian. But I also expressed my chagrin and surprise about the state of the U.S. in some of the same areas that were disturbing me about Canada, and I briefly compared the status of the two countries in five respects: leadership, immigration, intelligence, internal security, and military preparedness. Since then, I have had time to think further about the differences I noted at that time.

In terms of leadership, the comparison has been pathetic. I've always favoured George Bush over Al Gore because I felt Bush was bright enough to realize he would need a lot of help. It frightens me to think of Gore in Bush's place without the likes of Cheney, Powell, Rice, and Rumsfeld surrounding him.

While Bush was more than rising to the occasion, "The Chret," as I have resorted to terming Canada's hapless and hopeless leader, was proving once again that he can't put two worthwhile words together in either official language. The contrast with Britain's prime minister, Tony Blair, was so stark as to be sickening.

In the next three categories both countries have demonstrated distressing shortcomings, but they matter much more in the U.S. than in Canada. U.S. immigration policies and practices were apparently as leaky and porous as ours. In Canada, you just have to holler "refugee" and you're in with what at times appear to be more prerogatives and rights than Canadian citizens have but with few, if any, corresponding obligations and responsibilities.

As an aside, I remember when my younger daughter married a Bermudian and moved to Bermuda, only to discover that she wouldn't be entitled to full citizenship for 10 years and then only if she had not broken any laws. She wanted me to come to get their law changed. While this demonstrated amazing faith in me, I declined and suggested instead that she come back to Canada and tell Canadians that she had come across a country that really valued its citizenship, unlike Canada, where we do not recognize that our citizenship is the most valuable in the world.

When it comes to intelligence and internal security, Canada is virtually bereft in the former category but perhaps no worse off than the U.S. in the latter. In both categories, it was extremely disillusioning and troubling to find that the U.S., by far the most powerful country in the world, was almost totally wanting.

I still find it hard to fathom that the U.S. had no inkling of what was coming and that a relatively small group of terrorists could commandeer four fuel-laden commercial aircraft from three different airports at precisely the same time and wreak the terrible havoc they did.

The after-the-fact offsetting positive for the U.S. has been the might and skill of its military, which is now, as I write this, well on its way to settling accounts with al-Qaeda and its closest allies. In contrast is the shameful state of our military. It is nothing less than a travesty compared with our disproportionately large and valiant contribution to the winning of World War II.

Where we, and I guess this means the U.S. and to a lesser extent Britain, go from here in terms of dealing with suicidal terrorists and those who support them remains to be seen. It is inconceivable that we will be able to eliminate all the risks involved, but we may be able to dramatically decrease the incidence of state backing of such activities.

In the meantime, let me acknowledge how wrong I may have been about the potentially most serious aspect of the whole retaliation exercise. From the outset, I feared that it could degenerate into a terrible confrontation between what would ultimately boil down to the Christian and Islamic worlds.

This fear led me to read a terrific book, *The Clash of Civilizations and the Remaking of the World Order,* by Samuel Phillips Huntingdon, who is the Albert J. Weatherhead III University Professor at Harvard University. It had a profound impact upon my thinking about everything from the situation in the Balkans to the current crisis. Although perhaps too much of a pessimist about the fate of Western civilization, Huntingdon really made me think about where the world could end up in terms of the civilizations he identified.

In my own stumbling way, I believe I was working my way to something similar in these memoirs when I expressed grave misgivings about the prospects of moving towards ever more free trade and total globalization, at least in the forms we have known them.

I suspect I'm too old to rethink everything I have so strongly believed in and championed—especially in terms of the viability of what I have always termed fundamental Western values in the rest of the world—but those who share my views may well have to do so.

John Crispo, December 2001

In Other Words

Many people contributed delightful anecdotes and insightful observations about me for my memoirs. Those that couldn't be accommodated in the main part of the memoir are offered here for your interest and amusement. They are arranged in alphabetical order by the surname of the contributor.

Martin G. Evans, Professor of Organizational Behaviour,
The Joseph L. Rotman School of Management, University of Toronto
I first met John in Spring 1966 when I came to U of T (from New Haven, Connecticut) for a job interview. He'd just set up the Centre for Industrial Relations and was a rising star. He'd launched the Centre a year before with a big conference. All I remember was that there was no snow and I thought, "This is Canada, there should be snow."

When I arrived (in Fall 1966) to take up the job, the culture of the school was changing from old businessmen delivering the benefit of their wisdom to an academic approach. The Dean was a Ph.D. academic, but in style he was a good budget manager, not a visionary.

There were periodic revolts among the faculty in attempts to get rid of this Dean. I remember one faculty meeting where one faculty member who shall remain nameless was being particularly obnoxious. He was on our side of the revolt. I remember John saying to the Dean, "Some of us are embarrassed by the company we are forced to keep."

I was away from U of T in England from 1971 to 1973. My next significant contact with John must have been at the period of my promotion to Full Professor in 1974. John was Dean, and this story indicates how the system has changed.

At that time, the Dean received recommendations and advice of a Committee, but the Dean was the one who made the decision. Around the time of the Committee meeting, John told me he wasn't going to recommend me for promotion. He had some concerns about the quality of my teaching, especially at the M.B.A. level. The next day I took my daughter to the Santa Claus Parade. I was pretty depressed, but what could I do? Life has to go on.

When I got home, my wife had a telephone message for me from John. He'd been to a cocktail party the night before and discussed me with four colleagues. All four recommended me for promotion, so he had changed his mind. It says something about John's flexibility as well as how the system has changed.

John went to a cocktail party in Rosedale during the grape and lettuce boycott and when he saw the huge centrepiece crowned with grapes, he said, "Ah, California grapes," and threw the whole thing out the front door and into the snow. How did I get the story? It was common knowledge. He probably told it himself in the faculty lunch room.

George Fleischmann, President and C.E.O.,
Food and Consumer Products Manufacturers of Canada
John Crispo is one of Canada's last remaining iconoclasts, and in taking on the CBC and the University of Toronto he has shown us the influence that a determined individual can still have on the huge bureaucratic organizations.

John Gilfillan, Q.C., Long-time Friend
My first memory of John is sitting on a ski lift in Vail, Colorado, in 1972. He was reading out of his ratty little notebook and talking to himself. He would get coaching from everybody and write their pointers in the notebook and carry it with him. When he was skiing or golfing, I'd hear him saying things like "John, do this" or "John, do that" or "Slow down, you baboon, slow down." At first, I thought he was talking to me. Then I realized he was talking to himself.

One trip we signed up for a day of powder skiing, cat skiing, I think it was called, in Aspen. It was snowing very heavily and the guide told us to buddy up. The guide also said to stay on his left.

John and I agreed to be buddies. There wasn't room for everyone in the snowcat, so we sat on the roof. When we stopped, it took me some time to straighten up and get ready because my back was giving me trouble. But John took off like a rocket, on the right, and I lost sight of him. Sometime later, I heard him calling for help. He'd gone right over a hill and into a creek. He was stuck up to his neck in snow and slush. I helped him out, and he took off again. So much for buddying up.

At the end of the day, we had to ski off a steep lip of snow. When I got to it, I heard John calling for help again. This time he'd lifted his poles and got them caught in the branches of the trees lining the lip. The guide and other skiers couldn't see him from below. We laughed a lot about that one.

John has three passions: his wife and family; his farm; and Devil's Glen. He gets obsessed. At the farm he built his own cedar fence all the way down to the highway. Once his wife had a huge party at the farm and he was nowhere to be seen. "Oh," his wife said, "He's taken his lunch to the barn." He worked on the roof all day while we partied. I was afraid to go to the farm for fear he'd put me to work.

John's very sharp and very quick off the mark. For example, my wife was taking a woodworking course and when someone asked how we'd met. John joked that I'd got her out of an ad in Popular Mechanics.

A few years ago, John and his wife bought a condominium beside a golf course. He described it as one of Canada's few gated communities and invited me and my wife for a visit. We arrived to find a guardhouse and a woman in uniform. I asked for an inmate by the name of Crispo and said I was his parole officer from Corrections Canada. She called through and the next thing, she's laughing so hard she's rolling on the floor of the guardhouse. John said I wasn't his parole officer, I was his sex therapist, and asked if I was with a man or a woman because I'd be in a better mood if it was a woman.

The thing with John is you have to be quick, too. You can't give him a chance to retaliate. A couple of years ago we were golfing, and he said, "Oh, I forgot to tell you, I've retired." I said, "How can you tell? It's a distinction without a difference."

When he golfs with his wife, he's sickening. He's always saying things like, "Great shot, hon." Once I said to her, "This guy's annoying. Does he always bother you like this?"

Jim Gillies, Ph.D., Professor of Policy,
Schulich School of Business, York University, Toronto

I met John in 1965 when I returned to Canada from UCLA to be Dean of the School of Business at York. It was very rare for us to work together, but we got to know each other socially. As time went on, John and his wife started coming to our island in Georgian Bay for week-ends in the summer.

Once my son Ted and his best friend, who were about seven or eight at the time, hid under John's and Barbara's bed. John and Barbara came to bed later, got in, settled down, and then heard sounds under the bed. John got out of bed and looked under it. When he saw the boys, he feigned a heart attack and scared them to death. They thought they'd killed him. The next morning early, John crept into the cabin where the boys were staying and threw two buckets of water over them. He really got even. He was always good for some horseplay.

John is a wonderful athlete in individual sports, like water skiing, snow skiing, wind surfing, sailing. One winter the four of us went sailing in Antigua, with a crew, of course. At times, we were afraid he was going to windsurf all the way to the Azores.

John likes being on the edge. The times he likes best are when the waves are the roughest. He loved to take our power boats out, and if the waves were high, John was happy.

John met Barbara when skiing. He saw this very pretty girl and he hung around trying to find out if she was single. When he heard that she was, he says he knocked down about 10 people to get the seat next to her in the ski lift.

John was at Ditchley Hall, an old, English country home, very posh, filled with Lords and Sirs. Everyone is Lord This and Sir That. Well, John got tired of calling everyone "Lord" or "Sir," so he started calling the Chair, who was "Sir John something," "Jack." When leaving, John said he'd had a really good time and looked forward to coming back, whereupon the butler replied, "Don't count on it."

John is a very complex person. He thrives on being outrageous, and he's clever and does it well. I say his writings are crisp and his ideas are outrageous, but the fact is he's commenting from a secure position on the inside. He's a child of the

Establishment. His role is to be a gadfly and to attack the community of which he was a part and has never really left.

Because he's Establishment himself, John is always thought of as fascinating, but no one has ever felt threatened. Well, that's not quite true. John has loads of friends, but in a sense he has been cast out by the Establishment. He was never invited on to the Boards of major Canadian corporations, which is the thing one would expect for someone in his position. He was a little too much across the line for them.

The Honourable Mike Harcourt, Former Premier of British Columbia
John Crispo is the only right wing ideological warrior that us left wingers will allow to insult us in debate, then insult and wittily engage in post debate dinner and drinks. If only Conrad Black and Michael Walker could learn from Crispo.

Buzz Hargrove, President, Canadian Auto Workers Union
Once, John and I were scheduled to debate at the Schulich School of Business. John was supposed to speak first, but he was late and the professor was getting nervous, so we decided to start without him. I told the students I was going to give John's speech because it was always the same and I knew it by heart. When John arrived, the students started cackling. He was at a loss. He couldn't figure out what was going on.

John Crispo, an unabashed right-winger, understands the importance of hearing different points of view. Although we disagree on most key public policy issues, encouraging debate is one of his strong points.

Senator Edward Lawson
My favourite Crispo story involves flowers. I was in Toronto and John suggested the two of us send a bouquet of flowers to a mutual friend who had just opened a business. John ordered the flowers, and then we arranged to have lunch. We met at the friend's business because we wanted to make sure the bouquet had arrived. What we found instead was a funeral wreath with a big R.I.P. banner across it.

John went roaring back to the florist. "How could you do this? Aren't you ashamed of yourself? How could this happen?" The florist said, "You haven't heard the worst." Our bouquet was last seen on a hearse. Our greeting was prominently displayed. It read: "Good luck in your new location."

Sharon Lines, John Crispo's Daughter
My earliest memories of my father are of him sitting in his den at the back of the house clipping newspapers and putting the clippings in files. He kept everything. He's very thorough. I must have been three or four at the time because I recall being old enough to sit at the dining-room table.

I also remember summers at Eastbourne on Lake Simcoe at my grandmother's cottage. We'd swim to the rock pile in the middle of the lake and back.

John's very athletic. He taught me to swim, ski, and ride horses. We did lots of sports together.

As an adult, John has become more sensitive and involved than he's ever been. He's learned a lot as he's aged. I think having grandchildren has changed him, too. He has three now. Two of them are my sons. Nicholas is two-and-a-half and Benjamin is about three months' old.

If I had to describe John's character to a stranger, kind isn't the first word that would spring to mind. But he can be kind. Last summer (2000), he brought Geoffrey, his other grandson who was 10 at the time, to Bermuda for a visit. They did everything together and at the end of very day they would spend at least an hour writing up a diary about what they'd done. It was really sweet.

The Honourable Peter Lougheed, Former Premier of Alberta
I've never forgotten John winding up a 1988 pro-free trade rally after three of us had spoken strongly in support of the FTA but with some restraint. He got up and started by saying, after all that bafflegab, "Let me tell you what this deal is really about and why it's absolutely vital to Canada." That's vintage Crispo!

Randal Palach, C.E.O., eBox Inc., Toronto, Ontario
John is a new friend. We first met in 1999, but I already knew him as a personality from his radio show. What I liked at first was his eyes—they have a lot of sincerity. We exchanged hors d'oeuvres, small talk, and finally business cards. It's easy to confide in him because he's such a careful listener.

We went one step at a time. When I introduced him to our founder and chairman, it turned out both used to be professors at U of T and they had a lot to talk about. I was shut out the whole lunch. It's typical, you know. Every time we go out, we meet somebody who knows John. He's phenomenally well-known and well-liked.

Every business needs a John Crispo. He's a good coach, and he's very honest. He asks the tough questions, and he stirs up the pot. He has incredible passion. Passion is part of his personality and it's very infectious. He knows how to listen and he listens caringly. He's very disarming. You can open up very easily because he's such a good communicator.

I consider John a great new friend, and I'm proud to know him. I'm looking forward to the years to come. I would trust him with my business.

The Honourable Bob Rae, Former Premier of Ontario and now Partner, Goodmans LLP
John Crispo has taught me, worked with me, enraged me, enlightened me, and made me laugh. I can think of few people with whom I have disagreed more often, and whose bantering company I have enjoyed more. He is a loveable iconoclast, and the nimblest dinosaur on the neo-conservative dance floor.

Peter Russell, O.C., Professor Emeritus, Department of Political Science, University of Toronto
I was a colleague when John was Dean. At the time I was Principal of Innis College, U

of T had a practice of pulling together the Principals, Deans, and Directors (PDDs) with the President to discuss university affairs. I would go and say my piece, but John was most vigorous in his interventions, especially when he wanted to challenge a policy or plan. He was not cowed by his company and spoke clearly and well.

I always thought of John as a bit of a bulldog. He wanted the University to promote on merit and become more efficient. I remember once we were at a critical time of cutbacks and one big issue was how to deal with them: across-the-board cuts, regardless of efficiency, or selective cuts based on rates of enrolment. John always was an opponent of across-the-board cuts. He said the University wasn't rewarding successful programs and research. John's critique of some of the plans had an influence. Some would argue that every part of the university is important. Others would say that the university had to move with the times.

John and I didn't work together much. One time we did was when John organized a book on free trade. I provided a chapter on the constitutional dimensions because one of my fields is constitutional politics. I admired John's leadership and I enjoyed our collaboration.

David Soberman, Ph.D., Assistant Professor, Marketing, INSEAD, Fontainebleau, France

I first met John in 1991 when I started my doctoral studies at the University of Toronto. I worked as his Teaching Assistant for five years. After one year as a grader, I became Head T.A. I hired and managed several T.A.s, attended all of his classes to make notes for the exams, and wrote a manual on how to manage his Introduction to Business Class. He was a dream boss. He'd stand up if there was a problem. If enrolment and hours weren't right, he'd do his best to sort it out.

It was obvious that John was very well connected. He invited these amazing guest speakers—Buzz Hargrove, Bob Rae, Maude Barlow, Maureen Kempson Darke, the Treasurer of Ontario, Heather Reisman, June Rowlands, Tom Kierans, Diane Francis. He'd bring in diametrically opposed guests and be the moderator. He would provoke both in a polite way but really put them on the spot. It was like a very entertaining T.V. show. He made his students see things they wouldn't have otherwise seen and make them think about things.

John is a special person who has real compassion and cares for people. He's an excellent discussant and provoker. He knows how to get to the root of problems. He asks the questions others don't ask or don't think to ask. I recall another professor saying, "I'm not sure if he's the academic of gadflies or the gadfly of academics." John will always find the flaw in an argument or presentation. He'll ask the really justified question.

Douglas B. Skelton, P.Eng., Retired Consulting Engineer and Long-time Friend

John and I lost contact with each other in the early 1960s as our careers took different paths. John went into academics, and I went into business. In 1966, coincidence brought us together. John and his family joined the Devil's Glen Country Club near Collingwood where my family and I were already members. We were delighted to meet again.

My wife and I had just bought a country property near Collingwood, and I invited John and his family. John walked in and said, "I gotta get one of these," and very shortly afterwards asked me to look at a place up in the Escarpment. It was a beautiful, old, Upper Canada, two-storey stone building that needed a lot of work like ours did. I said, "If you don't buy it, I will," and he said, "That's good enough for me."

Ever since then, we've shared many common interests including our families, downhill skiing, Devil's Glen, farms, renovations, and horses. But we are still very different people, and we've often expressed those differences. For example, we have different points of view regarding the policies and direction of Devil's Glen. But we agree on the fundamentals of ethics, motives, standards, expectations, and approach to business.

I believe that our differences have strengthened our relationship. I also believe that this strengthening is due to John's ability to express a difference of opinion without expressing any lack of respect for the other person. He doesn't demean the other person. Similarly, John will receive a different point of view without being hurt or angry or rankled.

However, while John will receive a different of opinion without rancour or offence, in fact, he will even encourage people to disagree, he reacts most, most powerfully to personal criticism. He is a strong, expressive person who says and stands by what he believes.

Mel Watkins, Professor Emeritus,
Economics and Political Science, University of Toronto

My first clear memory of John is meeting him at M.I.T. in 1956. We were both graduate students, but I was a year ahead of him. He made a vivid impression with his boyish enthusiasm and charm.

John is a good-hearted person. He walked into a classroom right after John F. Kennedy was assassinated. A student asked, "How do you think this will affect the stock market?" John's answer was, "It's terrible to ask a question like that at a time like this. I won't even consider dealing with it." This may be the answer most people would give in the circumstances, but not necessarily a professor in a business school. I think it is the mark of a good person.

We're both political animals and initially we were very close in our views. The great divide came in the 1960s when we were both on faculty at the University of Toronto over issues such as the Vietnam War and Canadian nationalism. We split politically but not personally. It was a very divisive time and emotions ran high.

John sees himself as someone who is his own person, holds to his own views, and is a dissenter. I don't see him that way. I think he tweaks the nose of the giant but never actually challenges. He always ends up on the safe side. He's a populist, but he doesn't rail against the system itself. For example, he criticizes bank presidents for being paid too much, but he doesn't question whether big corporations should exist.

I have to give John some small credit for the fact that we're still speaking to each other. We've both made efforts to maintain our friendship. We debated often and with good humour. I'd be asked, "Why are you so nice to Crispo?" My answer would be, "Because we're good friends and plan to remain so." I admire him. There's a real honesty about him.

Patrick Watson, Broadcaster, Author, & Former Chair,
Board of Directors, Canadian Broadcasting Corporation
John Crispo's being a professor certainly redefines the word "academic." From my close encounters of the hard kind, during his tenancy of a seat on the CBC Board of Directors when I was Chairman, I came to the conclusion that he was the only sexagenarian I ever met who was a truly arrested adolescent. Maybe the "arrested" part was wishful thinking. I don't think we ever agreed on anything during a Board meeting except the time for adjournment.

But much as we disagreed, I am unable to find any rancour in it, even after I had to once give him an official Corporate blast for speaking publicly on something that should have stayed in the boardroom.

And outside the boardroom we found a mutual interest in jazz, about which (despite his academic credentials or lack of same) he was both knowledgeable and hugely enthusiastic. So curious bystanders were occasionally treated to the unlikely prospect of the two gladiators sitting down amiably over a beer or something, in a smoky club, listening to some genuinely smoky music. That's Crispo.

Mining Crispo

John Herbert Gillespie Crispo was born on May 5, 1933, in Toronto into very comfortable circumstances. His father Herbert was a successful manufacturer's agent. His mother Elizabeth ran the household with the help of a maid. His younger brother Martin, born in 1935, completed the family.

After finishing Grade 5 at Allenby Public School, John went to Upper Canada College as a day boy. Summers were spent at the family's cottage on Lake Simcoe where, as a teenager, he played up to 48 holes a day at the nearby nine-hole golf course. By his 20s, he'd reduced his handicap to zero.

John's rebellious streak showed up early and was probably at least part of the reason for what was apparently a sometimes difficult relationship with his father. One of his first public rebellions was at Upper Canada College where he complained to the principal about the unfairness of a practice that allowed a student who had failed and, thus, attended the College for an extra year to qualify for the coveted ceremonial positions of Head Boy and Head of Battalion. John's position was this practice gave students who failed a much better chance to qualify than students who passed every year and thus attended the College for the standard number of years. John wanted the principal to bar students who had failed a year from taking these positions, but the principal refused. "A lot of those failures were from very wealthy families, and all they (the school officials) cared about was money, money, money," explained John. "And my father wasn't in that league. There was no way he could buy me a failed year."

Despite what he dismissed as an indifferent academic education at Upper Canada, John went on to an illustrious career that included many scholarships, fellowships, research grants, publications, and appointments and a prominent role in the public policy issues of the day.

Many years later, likely in the 1970s, John returned to Upper Canada as guest speaker for a weekly assembly in the guise of an illustrious graduate who was now a respected professor. Instead of giving the expected uplifting and motivational address, he talked about Upper Canada College's place in what he then saw as a sick society. "I told them how rotten their parents were. I told them their parents were businessmen and professionals and rip-off artists of all kinds and that's what they were training their children to be, and I said the students were going to turn into blood-sucking leeches like their parents and this school wasn't doing anything good for society, and so on and so on." He got a standing ovation from the student body, but no thanks from the principal who was so horrified he left the platform, his entourage trailing obediently behind him. On the way past John, according to John's account, the principal said, "I think I'll be able to save my (grade) twelves and thirteens, but what about my nines and tens and elevens?"

John immediately returned to the podium and held up a hand to quiet the assembly. He said, "Your principal is very disturbed by the address I've just given you and thinks it's unfair to the school and your parents. I want to tell him I'm free for the rest of the morning and I'm more than willing to stay here and listen to his criticisms of me and answer your questions." Naturally, the students went wild and the principal refused to respond to John's challenge.

John eventually left the stage and went to the principal's office to retrieve his coat. The principal's secretary came in with a beautiful silver tea service, expecting to offer refreshments as planned. The principal, says John, went berserk. "Get that tea out of here! I'm not serving tea to this (inappropriate epithet)!" is the way John told me the story.

John not only didn't get tea; he also didn't receive another invitation from the school for many years. He was invited back eventually to discuss the free trade issue. On that occasion all went smoothly until some students told him he was the second best speaker they had ever had. The best? Stephen Lewis. John argues that Stephen is more eloquent but he (John) is more articulate.

All of this was utterly new to me. I knew very little about John when we first met on November 28, 2000, in his office at the University of Toronto. The purpose was to discuss this memoir. John had written a draft that was so dense with excerpts from previously published articles, it was virtually unreadable. Certainly, John Crispo the person was lost to view. The question was whether John and I would take to each other, and, frankly, I doubted it.

I became aware of John during the free trade debate (I was on the opposite side). I wasn't aware of him during The Valour and the Horror controversy (but I was on the opposite side of that one, too). Having read his own attempt to tell his story, my impression was that he was far too right-wing, bombastic, overbearing, and pedantic for my taste. He never met a detail he didn't adore, unless it was a date, in which case he generally drew a blank. But he did have some funny stories to tell and I thought it might be possible to extract and polish the gold.

What I found when we met that November afternoon was a friendly, intelligent, likeable, unpretentious, witty, charming, generous man with a puppy-like eagerness to please. He was ready and willing to discuss everything openly. I found myself warming to the idea of the book. After an hour of talking around the project, we agreed on terms and set an appointment for our first in-depth interview.

It was also during this initial meeting that I flummoxed John for the first and only time during our dealings. When I gave John my business card, he dithered about where to file it, under my first name, my last name, my business name.... He had evolved an eccentric system all his own. "Just put it under 'G' for Genius," I said. He was struck speechless, something I soon discovered was an exceedingly rare circumstance.

I told John that even though *Rebel Without a Pause* was the memoir of a professional life, we needed to provide a picture of John the person. So during our first interview, on December 13, 2000, I dug into his family background and early years. But when I tried to pin him down on dates and specifics, I kept striking out. John would say, "I just don't remember." I was convinced, however, that if I asked the same question often enough and in enough different ways, eventually I would unlock the gate and hit the mother lode.

Finally, it sank in. John is a performer. Life is a stage, and he is the star. He is an accomplished raconteur who never allows anything inconvenient to get in the way of the story. He will remember the bizarre and absurd and tell wild and wonderful tales, often making ruthless fun of himself, but he simply doesn't register the mundane, like dates or names or times of year.

It was around this time I also came to understand it would be impossible to convey a sense of John the whole human being without outside help, and so I hatched the plan to talk to people who'd worked with, associated with, or crossed swords with John over the years. John was amenable and helpful. He gave me names and contact numbers, and in many cases he paved the way. He also agreed without demur that he would have nothing to say about what stories were told and how they would be used. That for me confirmed his intrinsic modesty and solid sense of self. It also added a dimension to the project that suddenly made it exciting and interesting as well as useful for my portfolio.

John and I worked closely over a span of several months. He continued to impress me with his openness and trust. When I told him I was considering writing an afterword about what it was like to work with him, his reply was simply, "Whatever you think is best for the book." Few people can give over that degree of control, especially when their own lives are being laid open for examination and comment.

The result is, I believe, an interesting book about an interesting man who lived and worked in a particularly interesting time in Canada's history. I hope everyone who reads *Rebel Without a Pause: Memoirs of a Canadian Maverick* enjoys it as much as I enjoyed the experience of helping John bring it to life.

Marion E. Raycheba, Fall 2001

The Crispo Papers

I have published extensively in many forms and forums. My list of credits includes countless scholarly books and papers, reports and analyses, op-ed articles, newspaper columns, and letters to the editor. What follows is a short list of books I wrote or edited and chapters I contributed to books. The books are listed in alphabetical order by title. The chapters in books are listed in alphabetical order by chapter title.

BOOKS

Canadian Industrial Relations: The Report of the Prime Minister's Task Force on Labour Relations. With A.W.R. Carrothers et al. Ottawa: Queen's Printer, 1969.

The Canadian Industrial Relations System. Toronto: McGraw-Hill Ryerson, 1978.

Can Canada Compete? Toronto: Hemlock Press, 1990.

Collective Bargaining and the Professional Employee. Toronto: Centre for Industrial Relations, University of Toronto, 1966.

Construction Labour Relations. With H. Carl Goldenberg. Ottawa: Canadian Construction Association, 1969.

Fee-Setting by Independent Practitioners. Ottawa: Prices and Incomes Commission, Information Canada, 1972.

Free Trade: The Real Story. Toronto: Gage Educational Publishing, 1988.

Industrial Democracy in Western Europe: A North American Perspective. Toronto: McGraw-Hill Ryerson, 1978.

International Unionism: A Study in Canadian American Relations. Toronto: McGraw-Hill, 1967.

Industrial Relations: Challenges & Responses. Toronto: University of Toronto Press, 1966.

Making Canada Work: Competing in the Global Economy. Toronto: Random House of Canada Ltd., 1992.

Mandate for Canada. Toronto: General Publishing, 1979.

National Consultation: Problems and Prospects. Toronto: C.H. Howe Institute, 1984.

The Public Right to Know. Toronto: McGraw-Hill Ryerson, 1975.

The Role of International Unionism. Ottawa, Canada, and Washington, D.C., U.S.A.: National Planning Association, 1967.

CHAPTERS IN BOOKS

"The Case for Free Trade," *The Free Trade Papers,* Duncan Cameron (Ed.). Ottawa: University of Ottawa Press, 1987.

"Collective Bargaining: Lessons from Abroad," *Collective Bargaining in Canada,* A.S. Sethi (Ed.). Toronto: Nelson Canada, 1989.

"Competing in the Global Village," *Meeting the Global Challenge: Competitive Position and Strategic Response,* Strategic Briefings for Canadian Enterprise Series, Jerry Dermer (Ed.). Toronto: Captus Press, 1994.

"If I Were Prime Minister," *If I Were Prime Minister,* Mel Hurtig (Ed.). Edmonton: Hurtig Publishers, 1987.

"Organized Labour and National Planning," *The Prospect of Change,* A. Rotstein (Ed.). Toronto: McGraw-HIll Ryerson, 1965.

"Responding to Canada's Competitive Challenge," *Meeting the Global Challenge: Competitive Position and Strategic Response,* Jerry Dermer (Ed.). Toronto: Captus Press, 1992.

Crispo Unleashed

This Appendix was a must for me because my op-ed and op-ed-like articles highlighted the widening of my interests over the length of my professional career. This sample of articles also reveals my many positions on different issues in their least academic and most readable form. It also tends to reflect what was getting the best reception in my never-ending speeches. They are listed by date of publication from the earliest to the most recent. For information about my more academic publications, please see Appendix C.

University Students Deserve Change (*The Toronto Star,* September16, 1969)
In my last column, I took The Star to task for its frontal attack on tenure, in any form, and its more-than-implied suggestion that the government's panel on future directions for post-secondary education recommend it be done away with.

Having acknowledged, in that column, that our present system of tenure is in need of radical reform, I would like to devote this one to two other fundamental changes this panel should explore, if it really wants to make a difference to higher education.

The first one is relatively simple and straightforward, but, doubtless, would be the cause of great consternation in some quarters. Based on my 35 years of teaching at the University of Toronto, I have come to the conclusion that we are making a tremendous mistake when we take in students directly out of high school.

While some secondary school graduates may be ready for college or university, the majority are neither mature enough nor motivated enough to benefit as much as they could if they were not allowed to enter until at least a year later.

Many first-year university students strike me as lost souls not knowing quite why they are there or, more important, why they are enrolled in the courses in which they find themselves. In all too many cases, they appear to be coming to university because their parents think they should, either because they went there themselves and thought it beneficial, or did not, and think they would be better off if they had gone.

Some potentially good students would be lost under this proposal. But I am convinced this loss would be minimal, compared to the gains to be garnered by having a student body that chose to come to university after trying something—anything—else, for a year. As for the transitional problems involved, much of these could be solved by linking this new approach to the eventual termination of Grade 13.

My second proposal: Turn colleges and universities into private institutions by removing all direct government funding, except for research grants.

Instead of the government funding colleges and universities based on some enrolment formula, it should provide income-based vouchers to the most qualified students. These vouchers should be income-based in order to move us closer to the equality of educational opportunity we purport to believe in.

Admittedly, there would be some serious administrative problems with this approach. The value of the voucher, for example, would clearly have to vary in accordance with the differing costs of various types of higher education. This would probably prove a more manageable challenge than allowing for living costs when students choose to leave home to attend university.

I do not pretend to know how best to deal with these problems, but I am confident the beneficial effects of this approach would be so great it would be worth the effort to find appropriate solutions.

So what are the advantages of an income-based voucher system, other than equalizing opportunity?

One would be that students would be placed more in the driver's seat when it comes to the pursuit of a higher education. This benefit would be maximized if my first and second proposals are coupled. Prospective college and university students, who are mature and motivated, would doubtless make more effective and intelligent use of their vouchers.

But by far the greatest benefit of this second proposal would flow from turning colleges and universities into private enterprises, with bottom lines, and the very real potential of going out of business.

In the first place, this would undoubtedly drive them to operate more efficiently, creatively and productively—that is, competitively.

At the same time, they would also have to be much more conscious of their potential and current students as clients and customers deserving of the best of service.

Too many professors now view students—especially at the undergraduate level—as necessary evils and nuisances that must be suffered in order to generate the money and time required to do their own research. After all, publish or perish still reigns supreme in the universities.

These two proposals could have many positive effects on our system of higher education. Not the least of these would be enough competition to drive marginal institutions out of business, provided the government would allow this to happen.

This province has far too many universities—I cannot speak to the college side of this issue—and the best way to reduce that number is to let the marketplace sort out which ones survive. A few could thrive by specializing as first-rate undergraduate liberal arts teaching institutions, but more should simply go under.

To come full circle from my previous column, if these two changes were introduced, institutions of higher learning might well reform their present tenure system on their own.

As private enterprises that could go out of business, they could no longer afford the luxury of professors who were not performing effectively.

The Whipsaw *(The Globe Magazine,* November 29, 1969)
To conclude, then, there is inherent in the present ferment on our campuses a tremendous potential for both creative and constructive progress and negative and destructive reaction. The challenge confronting the universities is to ensure an environment that brings out the former and inhibits the latter.

In the first place, universities should anticipate or at least be responsive to the legitimate concerns of the student body and react to them as quickly as resources permit. Where they cannot do so the reasons for their shortcomings must be fully documented and explained.

At the same time, universities must not adopt an overly permissive attitude in which freedom becomes licence. This can best be done by dealing with each issue on its merits rather than on its ideological colorings. In the final analysis, however, where a firm 'no' is in order, it should he justified and adhered to. Where at all possible, of course, such a 'no' should only be given after a thorough airing of the issue and a promise of a continuing dialogue if that is desired. Assuming reasonably effective leadership at the top, the greatest opportunity for effective and creative action lies in the faculty. It must lay aside its vested interest in the status quo and actively. promote legitimate reforms if it wishes to retain its present pre-eminence. At the same time, when confronted by a crisis the faculty must not preclude an effective university response by falling back on its all-too-prevalent mentality of soft-headed liberalism. Otherwise in its sincere desire to avoid the use of force, even where force is deliberately employed against the university, the faculty may in fact invite the repeated use of such force.

This suggests that the faculty holds the key to the challenges confronting the university. Until it makes up its mind that the time has come to introduce some marked changes and draw some lines there is no hope of any solution emerging. The unfortunate thing is that the nature of the academic is such that he may rise to the challenge too late and thereby forfeit control of the university to forces either within or without its hallowed halls that are inimical to its survival in any worthwhile form.

Wake-Up Call for Ontario on Western Alienation (*The Globe and Mail,* November 21, 1980)

Canada is difficult to govern in the best of times because of the many competing and conflicting regional interests. Currently the importance of understanding Canada's inter-regional differences cannot be exaggerated. It is especially critical for Ontario to appreciate the position of the other regions because of its pivotal position.

What disturbs me most in this context is Ontario's failure to comprehend how badly it is perceived in the West. The West has always felt bitter and suspicious about Ontario's role in Confederation, but these negative feelings have been rising at a disturbingly high rate recently.

Historically, the West has from the outset had a number of reasons for misgivings about Ontario. Ever since they entered Confederation, the western provinces have been convinced the country was run by an Ottawa-Ontario or Queen's Park axis They have long pointed in particular to the original 'national policy" as a strategy designed primarily to benefit Ontario's "golden horseshoe" at the expense of the rest of the country. Reinforcing this so-called infant industry protectionist policy was a freight-rate policy which to this day discriminates in favor of manufacturers in Central Canada.

Most westerners will admit there have been offsetting policies favoring the West, but deny the policies begin to provide anything like an equivalent counterbalance. Examples of such pro western policies include subsidized freight rates for grain shipments and the higher-than-world prices for western petroleum products until they became competitive.

The West is still convinced the Ottawa-Ontario or Queen's Park axis decides major policy issues in the country. One only has to allude to the Constitutional and energy crises to sense why this view persists. Prime Minister Pierre Trudeau's major ally in the constitutional battle is the Premier of Ontario, William Davis. So eager was Mr. Davis to back Mr. Trudeau's constitutional proposals that he went out of his way to undermine his own federal leader's position.

As for the domestic price of oil and gas, two questions come to mind when westerners think about Ontario's views First, they ask themselves what Ontario has ever sold the West at less than world prices plus tariff. Yet Ontario has been insisting the West provide its oil and gas at less than half world prices. Westerners also wonder what the price would be if Ontario were the major producer of oil and gas. Rightly or wrongly, they are persuaded it would be much closer to the World level.

What really bothers the West about Ontario is its seeming reluctance to yield its once preeminent economic position. For a century Ontario was the leading province by virtually every economic standard. Now it seems to be acting as if that is its inalienable right. At the least, Ontario appears to want to deny the West its newfound place in the sun. To this end Ontario is backing Ottawa in what to the West amounts to basic changes in the rules of the game.

Traditionally, the federal Government has financed the bulk of its activities under an across-the-board tax system which extracted proportionally more revenue from the wealthier provinces. Now it has decided to add to this system—which will in itself yield more from the West—a series of oil and gas taxes which hit the West harder than any other region.

Given all these developments, it will be surprising if significant separatist forces do not emerge in the West. Yet Mr. Trudeau has the audacity—or whatever it is—to assert that the chances of separation in the West are "absolutely nil". At best, this represents ignorance of what is happening in the West. At worst, it represents irresponsible provocation. It had to be taken at its worst when the Prime minister goes on to accuse westerners of "hysteria"" and "paranoia" in relation to their reaction to his plans for them.

But my point is that Ontario will have as much to answer for as Mr. Trudeau if a serious separatist movement emerges in the West. This is because the West does not believe it has friends in Ontario.

In the first place, it blames the Ontario electorate for returning Mr. Trudeau to power on an anti-western platform aimed dishonestly at the fumbled Clark-Crosbie attempt to force Canadians to face the facts of life on energy prices. For the sake of a phony made-in-Canada-energy-price promise, Ontario did in fact re-elect Mr. Trudeau.

As for Ontario political leaders, the West could not be more disillusioned. Mr. Davis lectures the other premiers for pursuing regional interests while doing the same thing himself at the expense of the West. Meanwhile, Ontario Liberal leader Stuart Smith in effect accuses Alberta Premier Peter Lougheed of being Canada's blue-eyed sheik, while Ontario NDP leader Michael Cassidy insists Ontario industry must be subsidized by low western oil and gas prices.

Despite short term political risks involved, Ontario's party leaders must begin to demonstrate more statesmanship. Otherwise, they risk jeopardizing their own province's future as well as that of the country. Ontario's relative position in Canada is bound to slip. The danger is that an absolute position could deteriorate as well.

But that does not have to happen as long as Ontarians realize they can benefit from the boom that will sweep the West if Canadians come to grips with a realistic energy policy. After all, Ontario is Canada's industrial heartland and has the capacity to supply the bulk of goods and services required in the West.

Yet none of this may come to pass if Ontarians continue to alienate the West and to turn whatever good will remains there into bad will. Unlike Quebec, the West could separate and prosper for years even if only as a modern day version of what is disdainfully termed hewers of wood and drawers of water.

It is time Ontario woke up to the fact that it is shortsighted to persist in lending its support to Ottawa's repeated assaults on the West's legitimate aspirations, concerns and interest. At least, Ontario should press Ottawa to take a closer look at Alberta's last energy offer to the federal Government before the latter decides to proceed unilaterally on its own. If I understand that proposal correctly, it would have almost doubled the federal share of oil and gas revenue increases from 10 to 20 per cent.

In return, the West would have to be willing to participate in meaningful revision of Canada's corporate tax system and equalization payments system. On the corporate tax side, such a revision would require that the oil and gas industry be treated in a manner more comparable to that of other industries. On the equalization payments side, there is the need to ensure such payments more accurately channel funds from the truly have to truly have-not provinces. Most notably this would require that the equalization payments formula take into consideration resource incomes, which it does not now entirely do.

The Market-Based Approach, A Way to Avoid Wage Controls
(*The Globe and Mail,* October 12, 1981)
Within a year or so Canadians could again find themselves operating under a regime of wage and price controls. Although the new regime will doubtless bear some other label, it is almost certain to take the form of some kind of state imposed income policy.

Before we are saddled with such a policy it is useful to try to understand three things: first, why such policies have so much appeal; second, why, despite that appeal, they never solve the underlying problem; and third, the least damaging form such policies might take.

It is not difficult to understand why incomes policies have so much appeal. As inflation becomes more rampant people become increasingly concerned. They demand remedial action beyond ameliorative measures such as indexing. Becoming desperate in the face of this concern, and not knowing what else to do, the politicians eventually respond by resorting to something like controls.

Canada is in the midst of just this kind of process. Inflation has been rising and shows no signs of letting up. Public pressure on politicians to do something is growing. At the same time the politicians are receiving conflicting advice from the economics fraternity. Straightforward monetarists and traditional Keynesians now must vie with the new supply-side school for attention. If only because of its seeming simplicity, those advocating some sort of income policy command more and more attention.

As the pressure on the politicians mounts, even those who have strong misgivings and reservations about incomes policies begin to waver. They realize they must appear to be dealing with the problem even if they are not. Controls of some kind become almost irresistible in order to satisfy the public outcry for any kind of action.

The problem is that controls never work in the long run and seldom have much effect in the short run. Moreover, where they do have some short-term impact, this can and often is more than offset by the upsurge which follows their elimination. This reflects the fact that controls by their very nature only deal with the symptoms of the problems they are supposed to address.

Aside from their psychological and shock effects, the main rational for controls is to come to grips with alleged abuses by labor and management and other producer groups in the economy. Thus, upper limits are placed on the amounts each of these groups is allowed to extract from the system. But this is precisely the sense in which controls deal with symptoms and not problems.

If all manner of producer groups do in fact wield so much power in our economic system that they can extract excessive increases, it's no use simply placing temporary limits on those increases. If we really want to do something meaningful about such excessive increases we have to get at the power of the groups which lie behind them. Otherwise we will not have accomplished anything on a continuing basis.

Something like a costs and incomes review board to monitor all cost and income movements in the country could zero in on increases which are flagrantly and persistently above average. Where it could find no economic justification for such rises, it would determine what measures could be taken to prevent the offending groups from extracting such increases in the future.

The fundamental flaw in such an approach is that it would depend upon the politicians following up the board's advice. Since this would require politicians to move on an even-handed basis against any number of vested economic interest groups, it is not surprising that politicians have taken so little interest. They would prefer to deal with the symptoms of the problem rather than with the problems themselves.

That being the case it is important to figure out the most constructive or least damaging form a controls or incomes policy might take. There is actually a wide range of options to choose from, although I will deal with only two. The first, known as a tax-based incomes policy, is receiving a lot of attention but should be rejected almost out of hand.

The second, so little known that it bears no name, might appropriately be termed a market-based incomes policy.

Turning first to the notion of a taxed-based incomes policy, it is based on the idea that the tax system should be used to limit individual income increases. Thus, in the extreme, a 100 percent income tax surcharge might be placed on any increases above a specified level. The rigidity such an approach would impose upon our need to change income differentials in order to realign our labour force should be enough in itself to warrant dismissal of this approach.

As an alternative, it has been suggested that corporations could be used to impose a limit on their workers' incomes by allowing them to deduct only a given percentage of wage and salary increases as a business expense. This would move away from the undue rigidity involved in the previous approach but would have no impact on the public sector, which periodically is responsible for as much if not more inflationary costs and incomes pressures as the private sector.

If politicians feel driven to impose some form of controls or incomes policy upon us they should consider a market-based policy. In its most extreme form, this might entail a freeze on all costs and incomes except where there is demonstrable shortage. Thus, no cost or price increases would be permitted except for a type of labor, good or service which was in short supply relative to the demand for it.

Such a policy obviously would impose serious administrative problems, but these should be examined before they are deemed unsolvable. Even if this policy proved more expensive to implement, it might be worth the added expense in order to make the state of the market an over-riding consideration in any short-run controls or incomes policies program. Such an approach would have the added advantage of moving us in the direction the aforementioned costs and incomes review board.

Market-based approaches are required in both the short and long run to strengthen the interacting role of supply and demand in our economic system. By concentrating on abuses of economic power, such approaches offer the only real hope in the long run if we want to retain anything like a competitive economic system, let alone a non-inflationary one.

Work-Sharing: Cure or Curse? (*The Globe and Mail,* April 24, 1984)
Some leaders of the labor movement are again mistakenly championing the cause of work-sharing as an answer to this country's serious unemployment problem. This purported cure perennially comes to the fore when the labor movement feels especially desperate and frustrated about society's failure to come to grips with massive unemployment. As understandable as this concern is, it is misplaced and could do more harm than good.

Essentially, work-sharing entails spreading the work available among more workers. At best the effect is to reduce the amount of outright unemployment by converting it into underemployment for a lot more workers. Where this process ends depends on how far one pushes it. That could be pretty far if one followed the advice of Samuel Gompers, the founding president of the old American Federation of Labor, who once argued that "as long as one worker is unemployed, the hours of labor are too long."

This is not to quarrel with the long term trend toward a reduction in working time which has taken many forms, including longer vacations and shorter working days. Historically, this trend has entailed what is known as the income-leisure choice involving a tradeoff between more money and more time off. As productivity has improved, workers have chosen to allocate some of their share in the proceeds to reduced hours of work rather than to further increases in their incomes.

Beyond this long-term income-leisure choice, a case can be made for work-sharing on a temporary basis to avoid layoffs due to a recession, technological change or some other short-term disruption. This is why it has made sense for the federal Government to encourage the use of unemployment insurance funds to facilitate work-sharing schemes. Instead of paying unemployment insurance to those laid off, it can be used to supplement the reduced income of those who participate in work-sharing in order to avoid layoffs. All concerned can benefit from such an approach for a short period of time.

The case against work-sharing arises only when it is held up as a longer-term solution to continuing unemployment. At best, as already indicated, work-sharing only converts unemployment for a relatively small number of workers into underemployment for a much larger number of workers. It can only have this effect, moreover, if workers accept a proportionate reduction in their pay when their hours are cut. All other things being equal, employers then should be willing to employ additional workers to make up for the time lost by the reduction in working time of their otherwise remaining work force.

However, unemployment is not even converted into underemployment if employees involved in work-sharing insist on maintaining their take-home pay while working fewer hours. This is because the employer's labor costs then rise, thus compelling an increase in prices, and thereby inducing a contraction in demand. Unless one makes some totally unrealistic assumptions about productivity increases, profit margin decreases and\or demand shifts, the net result is bound to be a reduction in the total hours of employment.

The basic flaw in work-sharing stems from the fact that it is based on the lump-of-labor fallacy. This fallacy holds that only a fixed and immutable amount of work is available at any given point in time. Carried to its logical extreme, this implies that the fairest thing to do is divide this amount by the number of people willing to work and decree the hours of work for everyone to be that quotient or result.

Of course, the amount of work demanded is not a fixed and immutable amount. It is influenced by a host of variable, some external, as with the state of the US and world economies, and some internal, as with the fiscal and monetary policies of the Federal Government. Perhaps more important that anything in the long run is the competitive position of the Canadian industry.

Unless this country becomes and remains more competitive, especially in relation to its major trading partner, the United States, there is no way that it can generate a meaningful and sustained higher level of employment. All sorts of proposals can be thought up to throw money at the unemployment problem but that will not solve it.

As for work-sharing, it could have a perverse effect upon those it is supposed to benefit, that is, workers, In the first place they may be persuaded to go along with it in the forlorn hope of assisting their unemployed brothers and sisters even though they themselves would prefer more income than leisure. Worse, by increasing their employer's labor costs and making them less competitive, they could jeopardize their own jobs, as well as those already threatened with layoffs."

White Driving a Risky Route for Workers (*The Globe and Mail,* December 10, 1984)

One hesitates to take on Bob White, the Canadian director of the United Automobile Workers, because he is the articulate, bright and charismatic darling of the media, who can seemingly do no wrong. Yet someone must take him on because, far from proving the folk hero of the labor movement as he is so regularly portrayed, he could be doing immense harm to his own members' long-run well-being, as well as to that of the Canadian auto industry and the country as a whole.

Until recently, it was easy for someone like me to share what appeared to be Mr. White's convictions about the UAW as an international union. Working for the UAW as a graduate student when Walter Reuther was still president, it was natural for me to come to view this union as a logical link between Canada and the United States. After all, it seemed only natural to have the UAW as an international union on the labor side to offset the power of the big three multinational corporations on the management side. This logical and natural link was if anything strengthened by the emergence of the Auto Pact between the two countries and the more integrated production facilities to which it gave rise.

As logical and natural as the UAW was and remains, there were always bound to be tensions between its Canadian section and the United States headquarters. Apparently these tensions became especially serious during the recent GM negotiations in Canada. Mr. White has more than implied that the U.S. headquarters of the union put pressure on him to settle for the U.S. pattern which he was determined to vary if not exceed.

Actually, the U.S. side of the union should have favored a higher settlement in Canada to narrow the $7.50 per hour labor cost advantage enjoyed by the Canadian plants relative to their U.S. counterparts.

Apparently this adverse competitive situation was more than out-weighed by UAW headquarters' concern that it would look bad if the Canadian section appeared to negotiate a better deal than had been secured in the United States.

However great the tensions became during this period, one has to question the way in which Mr. White has chosen to go about resolving, or should one say exploiting, them. Instead of engaging in anything resembling quiet diplomacy with his U.S. colleagues, Mr. White chose to mount a frontal media assault on them. To the surprise of some members of his own staff, he decided to use a meeting of the Canadian Council of the UAW as a launching pad for well orchestrated campaign for more autonomy of the Canadian section of the union.

He is to argue for full autonomy for the Canadian UAW at a meeting of the International Executive Board in Detroit today.

Given the way he has been proceeding, one can only surmise that Mr. White has been looking for an excuse to break away from the international union. If nothing else, this should serve to clarify his own immediate personal plans, about which there has been much speculation. Apparently it is not be politics or the presidency of the Canadian Labor Congress. Rather, it is to be the beginning of what he would like to build into a European style metalworkers union a la the IG Metal in West Germany. With a severed Canadian UAW as his nucleus, he would then try to woo the Canadian machinists, steelworkers and others away from their international unions, a demanding but not impossible challenge.

This course of action is fraught with peril for his present auto industry members, the industry and the country as a whole. This is because it could jeopardize further investment in the auto industry under the Auto Pact, if not eventually the Auto Pact itself—and all this despite the $7.50 competitive labor cost advantage enjoyed by Canadian plants.

There have already been private and public rumblings among the senior United States executive of at least two of the big three producers about the wisdom of further investment in Canada while they have to deal with what to them is a maverick union leader. If that maverick union now chooses to break away from the UAW, these rumblings will certainly grow and may be translated into action. Not even $7.50 an hour may be enough to warrant having to buckle under to a Canadian union leader who can use the leverage of integrated production arrangements between the two countries to extract differentiated, if not incremental settlements in this country.

In the longer run, there is the question of the Auto Pact itself. When it was launched it was very important to have the United States side of the UAW support it. If that support should dissipate because of a split in the union, the Auto Pact might not survive, especially if the U.S. side of the industry grows increasingly disenchanted with Mr. White. It is in this ultimate sense that Mr. White could be risking many of his members' jobs by undermining an industry which probably could not sustain itself on anything like its present scale without the Auto Pact.

It is unfortunate that Mr. White has chosen to use his unmatched combination of negotiating and public relations skills for more constructive purposes. Instead of trying to provoke a split within the UAW, he should be trying to strengthen the international union link between Canada and the United States. That link may well prove vital to the continuation of the Auto Pact and could prove equally critical in many other industries if the present mood of the two countries' federal administrations leads to even closer economic ties.

Critiquing the Critics (*The Globe and Mail,* May 18, 1991)
The immediate media outcry to my appointment to the CBC board of directors was far more negative than I had anticipated—and I had anticipated a lot. It came from a fairly well know cabal of largely Toronto based media types who collectively consider themselves "the Canadian media." Fortunately for me, it was followed by a more balanced and fair commentary, including some articles that could even be considered positive.

I don't deny that my style sometimes gets me in trouble. I speak forcefully and sometimes with perhaps a little exaggeration and overstatement. When I appeared before the CRTC on the CBC, I spoke forcefully because I felt strongly. Undoubtedly, I did go too far when I said the CBC was " a lousy left wing, Liberal—NDP pinko network."

My critics have repeated this hyperbole ad nauseum. But most of them have ignored the fact that I also said that I believe in the CBC despite my misgivings about its performance in news and current affairs. I also made it clear that none of my criticisms had anything to do with its drama, music, sports and other presentations.

What most of my critics have chosen to downplay or ignore is my basic message about the media in general and the CBC in particular— to put it bluntly that they are potentially the most dangerous and evil force in our society. They are the single most influential force, yet are accountable to virtually no one.

Just before I joined the board, I learned that the CBC does have an appeal mechanism to deal with claims of lack of balance and fairness. I have been criticized for not knowing such a mechanism existed, but I'm not alone in this. Virtually none of the groups and individuals who have complaints about the CBC's lack of balance have heard of it either.

One of the first things I want to do as a CBC director is to see that the existence of this ombudsman is well publicized. I also want to ensure that he or she is as impartial, independent and objective as possible and has adequate power to provide remedies to victims of biased commentary and reporting.

How successful I will be remains to be seen. It doesn't encourage me when my views on balance and fairness are so distorted by CBC insiders.

Take Dan Oldfield, president of the Canadian Wire Service Guild, who claims to represent "the corporations 500 or so editors and reporters." This is what he had to say about me in an open letter.

"But fairness to Crispo has nothing to do with reporting accurately on the events that affect Canadians. No, fairness to Crispo is a Tass-like organization that will carry forward the pro-free trade, pro-Meech Lake, pro-GST and pro-war message of the government."

Nothing could be further from the truth. If this is what the president of some 500 CBC editors and reporters thinks is a fair statement about me then I can only express the hope that he is not representative of his membership.

Or consider the media coverage of my appointment. Michael Valpy got so worked up that he returned to the subject over the course of several columns. At least he tried to call me before he cut loose, which none of my other critics felt moved to do. Mr. Valpy seems to believe that no one who is strongly critical of the CBC should serve on its board. Building on this theme he made the more sensible suggestion that all such appointments be subjected to more parliamentary scrutiny than they are. Mr. Valpy was first off the mark, leading the way for many of his more lazy colleagues to simply crib his ideas. The worst was his colleague Jeffrey Simpson who followed Mr. Valpy's first assault. One of his silliest analogies raised the question " Would General Motors invite Ralph Nader on to the Board?" To compare the CBC to GM is ridiculous. The CBC is a public corporation; its board should reflect a range of public opinion.

In the Toronto Star, Gerald Caplan and Dalton Camp attacked me in one edition. Mr. Caplan declared that I was irrelevant and trite, then implied that my appointment could mark the end of the CBC. The sleaziest attack came from Mr. Camp who speculated that I might have known of my appointment to the CBC board before I appeared before the CRTC and that the appointment might have depended on my doing a job on the CBC at those hearings.

Later on the Star more or less made up for this tirade with an editorial cartoon of me interviewing myself on the topic of "intellectual faggots in the media."

Allan Fotheringham, having nothing better to say, made up a story about my trying to take over Jack Webster's talk show in Vancouver while I was on a sabbatical leave at Simon Fraser University.

The most mean spirited outburst came from Diane Francis, who accused me of ranting and raving and made the specious argument that because she and other right wingers sometimes appear on the CBC that proves there is balance.

On the other side of the media ledger were Doug Fisher and Peter Worthington, among others. The first was Andrew Coyne, who had this as his opener: "Anyone who attracts the scorn of Jeffrey Simpson, Allan Fotheringham, Dalton Camp, Michael Valpy and Gerry Caplan, all in the space of four days, can't be all good. Surely John Crispo has some faults worth mentioning?"

He then went on to compare my plight with that of Susan Eng, a controversial gadfly somewhat to my left, whose appointment to the chair of the Metropolitan Toronto Police Services Board was also greeted with consternation. Mr. Coyne concluded: "Eng can count on well placed admirers to fill the papers with sympathetic prose in her defense. Crispo just has me—and I don't even like him that much."

Doug Fisher recalled that he had written a column just the week before my case blew up, saying that anyone who dared to criticize the CBC's "work in news" would be "ridiculed" by the likes of critics who "see the CBC as their kind of organization."

Mr. Worthington reinforced the cabal thesis: "What is instructive in the case is not that some people are upset with the appointment—that's inevitable with anyone who has strong clear opinions backed by evidence—but the speed and intensity of the reaction.

Last by hardly least was Barbara Amiel. After reviewing her own experience with the CBC bias, she adds: "Knowing John Crispo as I do, I believe that he will try simply to get the CBC to pull itself together and understand that it should not become a propaganda machine for any organized group."

The CBC's on air reaction to my appointment was mixed. The fairest in its coverage was Midday, which had a feisty debate between host Valerie Pringle and myself. I gather they ran our heated exchange unedited, which is as fair as you can get.

Contrast that with my treatment by The House, with host Judy Morrison. It ran an item featuring members of all three parties attacking me with varying degrees of intensity. That was followed by what I felt was an unfairly edited version of an interview with me. During the interview. Ms. Morrison challenged me to point out a recent example of lack of balance and fairness on the CBC. I cited Peter Gzowski's show with his "triplets"—Dalton Camp, Stephen Lewis and Eric Kierans— in which all four had a great time going over me. This part of the interview was edited out, just as I predicted it would be.

On editorial pages I have fared much better. The Halifax Chronicle-Herald said: "As a steward of so much public money the CBC has an obligation to listen to the views of its critics. What better way to ensure this happens than to put one of them in its boardroom?"

The Ottawa Sun opined: "Clearly, Crispo's three year term won't be easy... but anyone who comes along demanding 'balance. Fairness and efficiency' from CBC News and Information will have our support."

At the other end of the spectrum was the Montreal Gazette: "The last thing that Canada needs is the presence of a cultural Luddite on the CBC board, lashing out to smash what he does not like."

The Edmonton Journal put me on notice; "The government, in its wisdom, has appointed Prof. John Crispo, a long time critic who now declares a commitment to the CBC that few would have surmised. Let's seem him demonstrate that commitment."

The politicians also enjoyed something of a feeding frenzy. The NDP termed my appointment part of a scorched earth policy directed by the government against the CBC.

Sheila Finestone did most of the speaking for the Liberals and resorted to misquoting me about the Prime Minister's motives in appointing me. She said on the aforementioned House show that I had said that the Prime Minister was putting me on the CBC board to do a number on the corporation.

On the same show, one of the Tories, in the person of Felix Holtmann, said he felt the CBC had been quite fair to him and his party, and that despite the fact that no matter who is in power the CBC regularly features three party panels with two against the one representing the government.

What have I learned from the experience? That you can get into a pack of trouble if you speak your mind in this country. On the other hand, no one was paying attention to my concerns about the CBC until I did so.

I've also learned that nothing Brian Mulroney does these days is going to be judged on its merits. It's almost as if he should advocate the reverse of what he wants in order to get it accepted. That's not healthy.

Finally, I've learned that there is indeed a media cabal who believe they know what is best for this country. They tolerate criticism by one another but woe betide anyone who attacks the collectivity, this time in the form of their beloved CBC.

If I had it to do over again, I'd probably tone down some of my overstated rhetoric, but not at the expense of making my basic point in a telling fashion.

I know I won't be the most welcome addition to the CBC board. My fellow board members are bound to have misgivings and reservations. Then, too, many CBCers have a distaste for me which is quite disturbing.

I did not accept this appointment to try to destroy the CBC. I think its news and current affairs programming could be more balanced, and that there should be an effective procedure to ensure equal time for all views. I also suspect that the CBC could make more efficient use of taxpayers money.

Meanwhile I will probably be appearing even less on CBC than I have in the recent past. Some of my few remaining friends there have told me nobody dares to use me for fear of being seen as kowtowing to me.

This is why I will continue to do commentaries in the private media, even though some will doubtless suggest that this represents a conflict of interest with my membership on the board. If this is ever ruled to be the case I will resign, since nothing—not even the opportunity to help improve the CBC—is worth giving up my freedom to speak out on all manner of public affairs issues.

The Valour, the Horror, the Travesty (*The Toronto Star,* March 9, 1993)
The Gemini award for best documentary series to those who produced The Valour and the Horror is a disgrace and travesty. This award was made less in honor than in spite and ignorance, and should stand as an embarrassment to those who voted for it.

The Valour and The Horror received this award in spite of the CBC ombudsman's well-researched finding that parts of it were inaccurate, distorted and pure invention; in spite of a critical, well-reasoned report from a Senate sub-committee; in spite of the military historians who detailed the various falsehoods the series contained; and in spite of the injustice the series has done to Canadian veterans.

This award is the last straw for me. For too long now I have remained silent on the media frenzy over The Valour and The Horror. I kept quiet out of deference and respect for my colleagues on the CBC board of directors, whom I can only hope will understand why I feel I must speak out now.

To begin, I should acknowledge my own biases. As soon as I saw the series, I concluded that The Valour and The Horror represented one of the most flagrant forms of revisionist history I was ever likely to view, especially in the case of the Bomber Command episode. This conclusion has been reinforced by just about everything I have read since then.

Why people like the supporters of this series feel they have to denigrate Canada's great and valiant contribution to the Allied cause during World War II in such an unfair way is beyond me. Perhaps what bothers me most about these programs—aside from the unwarranted hurt they have inflicted upon our veterans and their families—is that they exacerbate the traditional tendency among Canadians to diminish rather than celebrate their real national achievements.

As strongly critical as I personally felt about the series, I recognized that there was no choice but to trust the CBC's ombudsman system to determine whether the series violated our media accountability standards. I counseled every veterans' group which approached me to do likewise.

In the end, my faith in this system was rewarded, a matter of great satisfaction to which I will return. First, however, I want to deal with the media's—or perhaps I should say certain sections of the national media's—irresponsible reaction, both to the ombudsman's report and the decisions by the CBC's board of directors that followed.

Most of the national media reaction to both the ombudsman's report and our handling of it was ill-informed and inaccurate at best and dishonest, malicious and vicious at worst. Our president, board and ombudsman were subjected to a wide array of lies, slanders and smears in a most deceitful misinformation campaign.

Much to my chagrin, our few replies to this diatribe of untruths were meek, mild and muted. Trying to behave like decent, fair minded people while those supporting the series did just the opposite meant that the board's position, though it was absolutely the right one, was overwhelmed by the one-sided media campaign against it.

Perhaps the most outrageous charged leveled us by those who sought to distract attention from what was wrong with the programs was the absurd claim that we were just doing the bidding of the government, the Senate Sub-Committee on Veterans' Affairs or this country's veterans. These charges were totally without foundation.

As for the government, I was not even aware that it had a position on this subject. As far as I know it still does not. In the case of the Senate subcommittee, our board's chairman, whether rightly or wrongly, protested its hearings from the very outset. Members of CBC management, wisely or unwisely, urged the sub-committee to discontinue its hearings and declined repeated requests that they appear as witnesses. Ironically, those who made the series themselves chose to give support to he sub-committee by appearing before it while CBC executives were refusing to do so. Turning to the veterans, they simply exercised their right of free speech by registering their complaints and concerns about the series.

What a dispassionate study of broadcasting and newspaper coverage during the days and weeks following release of the ombudsman's report and the CBC board's decision to uphold it will demonstrate to future students of the issue is a manufactured crisis. This crisis was created by the supporters of the series and their friends at the CBC and elsewhere who, in a few cases knowingly, but in most cases trustingly and in ignorance, helped those supporters to turn their petulance at the series being criticized into a phony issue of free speech.

CTV news, the major private alternative to the CBC, dealt briefly with the matter on the first day and as far as I know never returned to it. At CBC, almost every radio and TV information program had to get into the act, some of them several times, while various employees parroted their evident bias, much of it based on lack of knowledge in solidarity with The Valour and The Horror and those who supported it. Editors and writers at some of the country's major newspapers did likewise and the result was a mockery of the ideals of balanced and fair, let alone thorough, journalism.

Though major parts of the national media falsely accused the CBC board and management of censorship, what has always been most at stake in this case has been not media chill but accountability chill.

By maligning the CBC's ombudsman, the supporters of the series were clearly hoping to silence not only him but any future independent authority who might point out and criticize irresponsible use of the airwaves. Regrettably, as I have said, massive numbers of our own producers and journalists joined in this cabal or conspiracy.

Instead of condemning the CBC for upholding and acting upon its ombudsman's report on The Valour and The Horror, members of the media should have been praising the corporation for having the courage to be critical of itself. Had they engaged in anything like the thorough investigation undertaken by the ombudsman—or even taken the time to read his report and his comments on the Galafilm response—they might have been better informed and a little fairer in their work, even despite the obvious agenda which some of them were following.

Instead, they revealed why much of the media increasingly commands so little credibility in this country The desperate segment of the national media which ran amok with this issue—blithely signing petitions in support of one side of a story to which it was supposed to be giving impartial coverage—clearly believes it should not be questioned for anything it or its friends do.

The CBC ombudsman's report represented a triumph for the concept of media accountability, for the integrity of the CBC as a public broadcaster and for professional journalism in general. It upheld the important principle that while journalists should be controversial and provocative, they must get their facts straight and not proceed on the basis of some preconceived notion or distort and make up evidence when they can't find what they are looking for.

I feel very strongly about this principle and believe we should all be grateful to the CBC ombudsman for so profoundly underscoring it. It took guts to stand up against a vindictive national media clique in the name of integrity and principle.

The courage and honesty the ombudsman has shown deserves the support not only of the CBC board but of the public whose trustees the CBC's board of directors are. In the end, our handling of this trying case will decide the future of media accountability at the CBC and whether the corporation is run just for the benefit of its staff and their friends or truly in the public interest.

I believe that the CBC, its producers and its on air news and public affairs personalities can and must be both free and responsible. If this mutually compatible and essential combination is not rigorously maintained throughout the organization then the CBC ultimately will not survive.

The CBC is a public trust, largely funded by public money, and none of us—producers, journalists, management or board members—should ever let ourselves forget it.

Crispo's Cure: A Vocal Critic Pleads for Fairness at the CBC
(Maclean's, September 26, 1994)
Why Prime Minister Brian Mulroney appointed me to the CBC board of directors remains a mystery to me. It certainly was not because I was a Tory since I have never belonged to any political party. Certainly I had been very critical of the CBC's apparent campaign against the Canada-U.S. Free Trade Agreement. I was also so upset by CBC Radio's coverage of the Desert Storm war that I suggested we should change its name to Radio Iraq. While these stands may have appealed to the Prime Minister, I doubt that he would have favored my equally strong criticism of the CBC for its inappropriate and pathetic support for the Meech Lake accord during its dying days, even though I personally supported the accord itself.

In any event, once I was named, most of what I call "the national media Mafia"—a description I still think they richly deserve—went wild. The predominant left-wing faction had a feeding frenzy at my expense. Many claimed that I had been appointed to the CBC as a pay-off for my support of the FTA. But if appointing me to the CBC board is the sort of thing the Mulroney government was doing for its friends, I hate to think what it was doing to its enemies.

I look back upon my service as a member of the CBC board of directors with mixed, though largely negative, feelings. Despite the very high price I paid, both personally and professionally, I now do believe in the principle of the CBC more strongly than when I was named to the board. Especially with the world's new satellite technology, it is important that there be at least one significant national Canadian presence in the coming galaxy of choices.

My continuing support of the existing CBC is strongly qualified, however, by two fundamental concerns. As far as its news and public affairs is concerned, it must strive for much more accuracy, balance and fairness than it is now achieving. At the same time, and in general, it must learn to operate as efficiently, innovatively and productively as any other broadcaster-private or public-in the world, a challenge that the CBC cannot meet until it overcomes its excessive layers of management, its obsolete work rules, its general overstaffing and the intransigence even today of its unions.

When I was left of centre and a regular fixture on the CBC from the late 1960s until the early 1980s, I did not think much about its leftwing perspective, presumably because I felt very comfortable with it or simply was not conscious of this institutional bias. As I slowly moved to the right of centre and gradually faded from its radio waves and screens, I became very conscious of it—some would even say biased.

What do I mean by accuracy, balance and fairness and media accountability? At the time I was appointed to the CBC board, my legion of media critics deliberately and falsely claimed that I wanted to turn the CBC into a right-wing propaganda agency. Nothing could be further from the truth.

Anyone who knows me knows that I thrive on the cut and thrust of a good debate. Aside from factual reporting in CBC news, what I expect of its public affairs shows is a thorough airing of every controversial issue. This means having equally articulate and bright protagonists on the major sides of such issues and letting them go at it, preferably live and unedited. Then, listeners and viewers can judge for themselves where they stand, safe from any editing or filtering, i.e. distorting and twisting, by CBC producers.

Strangely enough, if only on paper, the CBC has actually become a world model for media accountability. The corporation does have sound journalistic policies and accountability statements, and it also has two full-time ombudsmen to deal with complaints about inaccuracies and lack of balance and fairness. The problem is that despite hundreds of on-air announcements about their existence, very few people have ever heard of them. And the public won't know how to benefit fully from the presence of these ombudsmen until they appear regularly on the CBC's news and public affairs shows, citing complaints they are currently handling about these very shows to explain their role.

When one of the CBC's ombudsmen does find major fault with a program, the producers and their cronies react with noisy fury, afraid that if fault is found with the work of one of their number it will lead to closer scrutiny of their own work, too. This became all to apparent during the furor over The Valour and the Horror, which so inaccurately denigrated Canada's magnificent contribution to the Allied cause during the Second World War that it represented one of the worst propaganda pieces ever aired here or anywhere else under the guise of a so called documentary.

After the CBC ombudsman completed his consultations with several leading military historians and found the series flawed, and the board upheld that finding, a number of the media jackals in Canada went berserk. They aligned themselves with the self-serving producers who, in order to draw attention away from the errors and faults in their programs, libeled and slandered the board, the corporation and its president and the ombudsman, falsely accusing all concerned of everything from censorship to bucking under to some illusory "political pressure."

A large section of the media in Canada followed The Globe & Mail's totally misleading attack on the CBC for its handling of the issue. Despite what the Globe alleged, we did not buckle under to any government pressure, we did not even appear before the Senate committee looking into the matter, and we had nothing to do with the veterans legitimate pursuit of their concerns about the series.

Perhaps worst of all was the charge that anyone who found fault with The Valour and the Horror was creating media chill. In fact, the real issue was accountability chill. As long as journalists in the CBC continue to take the position that legitimate and honest criticism of their work compromises freedom of the press, it will remain difficult, if not impossible, to hold them appropriately responsible for their product and for the public to trust them.

In my view, media accountability is still little more than a paper tiger in the CBC. This is because news and public affairs is a force unto itself in the corporation. It is loaded with untouchables like the Peters, Mansbridge and Gzowski—who are still not subject to any real checks and balances. As Knowlton Nash, one of the deans of the CBC's untouchables, said recently on the air: "My role of the journalist is to establish the national agenda." He, and his equally arrogant friends, truly believe this to be their God-like role, and there is no real challenge to that dangerous, subversive point of view in the CBC.

In any event, the CBC should not take its future for granted and should carefully consider what its priorities ought to be in whatever future it has. On the financial side, it cannot anticipate anything like its present billion-dollar public subsidy, especially as governments are cutting back on other such sensitive spending as that for medicare. It is particularly vulnerable in this respect as, like virtually every other network in the world, it is losing audience share in a splintering TV and radio market.

The CBC's English broadcasting arm should concentrate its energies on its radio and Newsworld networks. It already has a well-established radio network-albeit in need of some new formats and new voices-and Newsworld is growing, although it would have to have more resources of its own since it now draws quite heavily on material from the main network. Canadians will always want to know what is happening within their own country and the CBC should provide Canadians with their most reliable and up-to-date source of news about themselves.

However, given the fiscal plight of the country, I do not believe that the CBC can much longer afford or justify local radio and TV news production all over the country. Among other things, the CBC must learn to draw on respected private local stations to provide it with regional material of national interest for national services.

I realize that anything I say about the CBC will be suspect if only because of my past harsh criticisms. In addition, I have no doubt it will be said that I am both bitter and paranoid because of my experience at the hands of the CBC, or at least its news and public affairs staff. I would plead guilty to considerable bitterness but to very little paranoia.

I am bitter because of the price I have paid personally and professionally for fighting for what I believe to be right on the media in general and the CBC in particular. I never experienced more personal strain and stress than during The Valour and the Horror debacle. I knew that what the producers were getting away with was totally wrong, but the board and the senior management of the CBC, though almost all of them agreed with me generally, kept pressuring me to remain silent. I did so for too long and hope and trust I will never let that happen to me again. One should never hold back, even out of courtesy to colleagues, from flatly telling the truth about a situation, especially when one is a public trustee as I think you are when you serve on the board of a public corporation like the CBC.

Professionally, I have suffered because my career has always depended on media exposure. But the real reason why I have been virtually banished not only by the news and current affairs folks in the CBC but also by their colleagues in CTV and elsewhere is because I have been such an outspoken critic of them all. They are quick enough to condemn and criticize everyone and everything else, especially anyone of whom they choose to disapprove, but they cannot take any heat in their own kitchen and readily use their control over access for revenge and to silence voices they do not approve of or agree with.

It is actually quite frightening if you think about it. They are a self-selecting media establishment elite who can and do blackball anyone who reveals their faults or who has the intestinal fortitude to stand up to them. I tried and failed and do not really recommend it to anyone else. They probably cannot be beaten but I will not give up, as many have suggested I should, and toe their line in the hope that they might then allow me to rejoin the debate on the future of this great country.

My future vision for the CBC is of an organization much diminished from its present role, and consequently it will be rejected out of hand by CBCers and their lobbyists. But if the corporation is to survive as in any worthwhile forum, it has no choice but to decide on a few essential priorities and to fully concentrate on them.

Even then, I would continue to challenge its existence until it determined to offer more accurate, balanced and fair news and public affairs programming and to manage itself overall more efficiently, innovatively and productively. Canadians should demand and insist on no less. After all, the CBC was established and funded by Canadians to be their public broadcaster, not just an expensive propaganda agency for its self-satisfied and self-serving news and current affairs staff.

Crispo Replies (*The Globe and Mail,* April 6, 1995)
A recent article in the Globe and Mail reveals how far a big lie can travel and grow once it gets started. I wish to clarify the record on this lie.
I refer to Ray Conlogue's Globe and Mail article entitled Media Howl Gives Impression of Culturally Intolerant Quebec (Feb. 18), in which he claims that "Crispo then abused his authority by making intimidating telephone calls to producers, journalists and even the CBC Ombudsman."

As his source for this outrageous lie, Mr. Conlogue cites Knowlton Nash, apparently from his recent book The Microphone Wars: A History of Triumph and Betrayal in the CBC. In that volume, Mr. Nash claims that I repeatedly tried to influence the ombudsman while he was preparing his report on the Valour and the Horror.

There is absolutely no truth to that or any of these other allegations, as I hope and trust all those who served with me on the CBC Board will know. I fought hard for my belief in accuracy, balance and fairness while I was on the board, but I never stooped to the kind of behaviour imputed to me in the unsubstantiated public charges of Mr. Conlogue and Mr. Nash.

New Labour Law Needs to be Fair, Not Extreme (*The Toronto Star,* September 28, 1995)
In yesterday's Throne Speech, Premier Mike Harris reiterated his promise to rescind Bill 40, a pro-union piece of legislation passed by Bob Rae's New Democrats.

In earlier attacks on Bill 40, Harris appeared to place most of his emphasis on the harm which Bill 40 purportedly was doing to investment, and consequently jobs, in the province. An even stronger case can be made against Bill 40—indeed I did so at the time before the appropriate legislative committee—because it simply was bad legislation.

Our labor relations legislation should be as balanced and fair as possible to both employees—organized or otherwise—and employers. With this objective in mind, the Harris government should not go too far in the other direction in order to avoid a B.C. type pendulum approach to labor law every time the government changes.

It is appropriate to start with preamble to the Ontario Labour Relations Act, which was unduly complicated by Bill 40. This purpose clause should be kept brief and simple. First of all, it should state that one of the primary objectives of the act is to facilitate organization among groups of workers who want to form a union. In this respect—in a rough analogy—the labour relations act protects the right of workers to unionize just as incorporation acts provide investors with the privilege of limited liability if they choose to invest in corporations.

The second purpose of the law should be to spell out the reciprocal rights and responsibilities of all the parties involved. Usually, this is done by indication practices in which the parties cannot engage. These proscriptions are known as unfair labour practices whether they are directed against employers or unions.

A third purpose of the act is to provide for various dispute-settling mechanisms. These can range from fact-finding, through conciliation or mediation, to binding arbitration.

A fourth purpose should be to lend assistance to labour and management in order to meet the competitive challenge that confronts them both. In practice, this may only require more creative use of traditional dispute-settling mechanisms.

Finally, of course, on critical purpose of the labour relations act must be to protect the public interests in collective bargaining. Basically, these interests are threefold: in the preservation of collective bargaining as part and parcel of a free society; in approaches designed to ensure that strikes and lockouts do not jeopardize the public's health, safety or well-being; and in policies and practices available to avoid unduly inflationary wage settlements.

Canada and Quebec: A Worst Case Scenario (*The Globe and Mail,* October 20, 1995)
As the Quebec referendum on separation approaches, I find myself ever more fearful of a worst-case scenario that would follow from a win, even a narrow win, for the Yes side.

First, let me make it clear where I stand on Quebec's position in Canada. For as long as I can remember, I have favoured a constitutional provision recognizing Quebec's different, special and unique status in this great country of ours. Although resisted by all the other provinces, such a status reflects both history and reality.

Even with no change in the status quo, however, I believe Quebec is much better off in Canada than on its own; for, even with all its faults, the rest of Canada has been the major factor standing in the way of Quebec's total assimilation into the North American English community.

Now to the scenario. A Yes vote would undercut both Quebec's and Canada's credibility beyond our borders. Foreigners would dump our federal and provincial bonds, put immense pressure on our dollar and drive our interest rates up substantially. Canadians with means would add to this carnage by transferring as much of their capital overseas as they could.

As if this weren't enough, the resulting instability and uncertainty would jeopardize what has been booming domestic and foreign investment in Canada. The result for both Quebec and the rest of Canada would be less employment, lower growth and a decline in our standards of living.

The devastating consequences of the decision to separate would hit Quebec fastest and hardest. This could provoke a tremendous backlash against those who had so misled Quebeckers about the price of leaving Canada. There might even be enough public reaction to force the separatists to further water down their already dishonest position to try to hold some facsimile of the federation together.

If that happened, I think English Canadians would be so angry and bitter over a Yes vote that most would be ready to write off Quebec for good. They have been remarkably respectful, tolerant and understanding while Quebeckers have been deciding our mutual fate. Let Quebeckers opt for separation or whatever the separatists euphemistically call it, and the attitude of English Canadians could reverse overnight.

So even if Quebeckers quickly realized how badly they had been deceived and forced their devious and messianic leaders to try to put Confederation back together again, English Canada might turn its back on them once and for all. That would be disastrous for all of us.

What happens to the rest of Canada if Quebec chooses separation and there is no reconciliation because of the inevitable ill will and tension that would follow? First, the rest of Canada would become a kind of East and West Pakistan divided by what could become a very unfriendly Quebec.

That basic problem aside, Canada without Quebec becomes a country with most of its voters living in Ontario. I have no idea what it would take to get the East and the West to live with such a situation, but it would be difficult to work out a reasonable compromise.

In the meantime, Western separation could become a real force. I have long felt that if Quebec separates, British Columbia should do likewise. It is probably the one province that could go it alone and prosper, since it sends only 8 per cent of its exports to the rest of the country. It might ask Alberta to join it for its oil and gas, but probably wouldn't reach farther east.

If the rest of Canada started to disintegrate, I suspect the Atlantic Provinces and the poorer Western provinces would fall into the United States after Ontario does. Ontario would have no other choice in order to protect its auto industry, which accounts for 50 per cent of its critical exports to the U.S.

Before any of this happened, there would be the matter of the divorce settlement between Canada and Quebec, which would present staggering problems, beginning with vexing question of who represents the rest of Canada in any such talks.

Foremost is the issue of the future of the Crees, who occupy the northern two-thirds of Quebec and want to stay in Canada. They have a strong case to do so, since the land they dominate was not originally part of Quebec but was added to its territory only as part of Canada.

What if the Crees refused to go along with Quebec's separation and appealed for Canadian and international help? Would the rest of Canada support their remaining in Canada? How far would it go?

And what about the division of the national debt that many separatists are so cavalier about? They seem to forget that, just as one form of retaliation, Canada could veto their entry into the North American free-trade agreement, if the U.S. Congress were not disposed to do so for its own protectionist reasons in the face of Quebec's many heavily subsidized industries.

In the end, if Quebec does choose to try to separate, the sad irony could be that Quebec would also end up tin the U.S. I would like to be there when Quebec goes to talk bilingualism in Washington. The kindest thing it would likely be told is to speak Spanish.

Sympathetic though I have always been to Quebec's warranted aspirations within Canada, I too will be somewhat unforgiving if they are shortsighted enough to reject their already secure place in the world's finest country. But this would not be the first time emotion and irrationality triumphed over logic and reason, mainly because of a few articulate ideologues who couldn't care less about the average citizen because of their desire to be bigger fish in a smaller pond.

To ascertain the true wishes of Quebeckers, the federal government might follow a Yes vote in Quebec with a clearer referendum question of its own. If asked a straight question like, "Do you think Quebec should separate from Canada and form an independent country on its own?", Quebeckers would doubtless vote No.

But the ensuing conflict and damage could do irreparable harm to what was left of the country's fabric. Quebec authorities could, for example, alienate the rest of Canada by placing every conceivable obstacle in the way of such a referendum.

Nobody in Quebec, or the rest of Canada, should underestimate what is at risk in the Oct. 30 referendum. If Quebeckers allow themselves to be misled into voting Yes, they could set the stage for the disintegration not only of the rest of Canada, but of their own society.

Public Sector Collective Bargaining Has Failed (*The Toronto Star,* February 21, 1996)
As a long-time defender of free collective bargaining in all of our public services, I find myself in an increasingly uncomfortable quandary. Well before 1965, when Quebec started the trend toward adapting the private sector model of collective bargaining to the public service, I had strongly endorsed such a move. I also have tended to oppose selective programs that the federal and provincial levels of government have introduced to try to control wages and salaries in the public and quasi-public sectors under their respective jurisdictions.

I must confess, however, that my resistance to such measures gradually weakened as I witnessed private sector workers taking much bigger hits than their public sector counterparts as the country experienced what, at times, appeared to be a never-ending recession.

This disparity between private and public sector workers was, until recently, reflected in both bigger pay cuts and larger layoffs among the former. There were some modest exceptions to this rule but, in general, collective bargaining proved a much better protector of the existing and even improved terms of employment for public union members than their brothers and sisters in the private sector.

My position shifted most dramatically when Bob Rae introduced his famous "social contract." Instead of forcing all public and quasi-public, institutions in the province to impose differing numbers of payless "Rae Days" as his chosen means of fiscal restraint, I argued that he should have legislated an across-the-board wage and salary rollback.

Now I find myself wanting Mike Harris to do the same thing, directly rather than indirectly, as I think will be the net effect of his sizeable cutbacks in transfer payments to the so-called MUSH sector (municipalities, universities and colleges, schools and hospitals).

I have no quarrel with the general thrust of these cutbacks; we are confronted by a fiscal challenge, which, if not yet a crisis, will surely become one if we do not call a halt to the runaway spending habits of the Peterson and Rae governments.

My problem is that I do not believe that collective bargaining, as it is now practised in most of the MUSH sector, can cope with the wage and salary cuts required to match these cutbacks in provincial transfer payments without a great deal of acrimony and bitterness. This is because these are institutions that devote the vast majority of their budgets to labour costs that, consequently, will have to bear the brunt of the cutbacks.

Besides this, two major factors lie at the root of the extreme difficulty the MUSH sector likely is to have trying to cope with the new economic facts of life.

The first of these factors relates primarily to the fact that the MUSH sector simply does not operate on a bottomline basis and , therefore, never has had to worry about going out of business. This primary problem has been aggravated by the corresponding loose way in which much of this sector has conducted its collective bargaining, assuming, at least until recently, that no matter what it gave away in wages, benefits or inefficient work rules would be covered by somebody else.

Gravely aggravating this generally deleterious situation has been the availability or imposition of arbitration in some of these sectors, If arbitration of wage and salary disputes was ever an honourable process, it long ago lost that claim as arbitrators and their legal sidekicks turned it into a make-work project that not only is more and more expensive and time consuming but, more seriously, less objective than it is political. Most arbitrators worry more about the ABC's of their record—that is their acceptability, batting average and credibility—than they do about the merits of the disputes they purport to judge.

Ontario has now instructed arbitrators to pay more attention to the ability to pay and fiscal capacity of public and quasi-public employers, than in the past, but that is unlikely to do much good. Alberta ordered arbitrators in that province to pay more heed to the ability to pay, of similar employers, and to the state of the labour market for the workers in question—i.e., whether their employers had any recruitment or retention problems—but it appears to have had little or no effect. Arbitrators there, as elsewhere, continue to worry more about the possibility of being vetoed by unions as future arbitrators than they do about anything else.

So what should the Harris government do in the face of this combination of potential fiscal bankruptcy, and a largely broken-down and lopsided collective bargaining system, in much of the public sector? I would suggest an immediate, short-term strategy which would short-circuit the system temporarily and a longer-term rescue strategy designed to restore it to some form of workability.

For the time being, I think the government has no choice but to suspend collective bargaining, in the entire public service, in the name of what I would argue is a fiscal emergency. During this period, the government should order whatever across-the board wage and salary decreases are required to balance the books. I suspect this will amount to around 10 percent over the next two or three years.

To prepare for a return to something resembling free collective bargaining in the entire public service, two or three years down the line, the government should announce that there will be no more compulsory arbitration of disputes in this sector. Instead, it should permit strikes subject to a partial operation of essential service provision to be administered by the Ontario Labour Relations Board or, better still, by a part-time Public Interests Disputes Commission which reports to the Legislature.

Much of what I have written here contradicts much of my earlier teaching and writing. It reflects my profound concern that we are up against an incompatible set of fiscal and negotiating circumstances that compel us to think in terms of new and even heretical terms. My fear is that if we do not reconcile the seemingly impossible now, I may become impossible to do so later on without far more draconian measures than I am advocating at this stage.

Tenure Vital to Academic Freedom (*The Toronto Star,* Sept. 16, 1996)
In a recent editorial ("Questioning tenure," Aug. 19), the Star urged Ontario's recently appointed panel on future directions for post-secondary education to examine, very critically, the issue of tenure.

The editorial referred to tenure as "really nothing more than a glorified system of featherbedding."

While I have been critical of tenure in its current form throughout virtually my entire career as a professor, I think this editorial was guilty of gross exaggeration in order to make a half-valid point. The editorial further states that "a majority of professors defend tenure on the grounds that it protects their academic freedom. This is self-serving rhetoric. All kinds of systems are already in place to protect those freedoms."

As one who has benefited from and depended upon tenure, I must confess to my ignorance about these other systems. Tenure has been absolutely vital to the free wheeling approach I have taken as an academic.

Beyond the university I have, at one time or another, aggravated almost every major interest group in the country. I would not have felt anything like as free to alienate and annoy these groups had I not had tenured status.

In some ways, that status proved even more important to my position within the university. Again, at different times, I have publicly gone after everything from the university administration to our faculty association.

This brings me to the heart of the matter, in terms of what is legitimate and what is illegitimate about tenure. To begin with, tenure should be seen as a very special privilege and not an absolute right.

I still believe that tenure is indispensable to ensure academic freedom for university faculty members. Too many vested interests outside and inside the university would like to silence those with dissenting or unpopular points of view.

A university that is worthy of the name should have on its faculty individuals who reflect a range of opinions on the major issues confronting our society. Particularly when it comes to a liberal arts education, students should be stimulated by varying points of view so that they can intelligently make up their own minds where they stand on contentious subjects.

What is illegitimate about tenure is that it has become so pervasive and powerful a force that it is hard to remove a tenured faculty member from a university staff for any reason.

Tenure is necessary for academic freedom but should only prevail as long as one is performing effectively in an appropriate combination of research, scholarship, teaching and related activities. If faculty members are not carrying out their responsibilities effectively, tenure should not protect them.

Many, if not most, of my colleagues would argue that this is already the case, but university dismissal rates for incompetence are so low as to make their position indefensible. If academics want to preserve tenure as a legitimate means for protecting their academic freedom, they must not allow it to continue to be used quite illegitimately as a means to protect incompetence.

If the government's panel on future directions for post-secondary education chooses to take on the issue of tenure—which I think it should—I hope and trust that it will recognize this vital difference. If it does so, it might come up with a sensible set of recommendations on tenure rather than an ill-informed and sweeping denunciation of the concept.

The Teachers' Strike about Control and Power (*The Toronto Star,*
November 7, 1997)
Before I review why I am so disturbed about the current, illegal, teachers' union strike, let me explain my general sympathy for teachers as distinct from their unions and leaders. There are several reasons why I tend to empathize so much with teachers.

The worst thing about being a teacher is having to deal with the results of poor parenting. Many parents today are failing to instill much discipline, manners or respect into their children, let alone a desire to learn.

Then there is society's tendency to dump all of its social problems on the education system. Whether the issue is crime, drugs or sex, there is a very real tendency for everyone else to throw up their hands in frustration and leave it to our schools and teachers to try to solve the problem. And meanwhile they are also supposed to provide students with a traditional education in the sense of the three "Rs," while at the same time preparing them for the cyber world which lies ahead.

Teachers also must stand up in front of a classroom and try to compete for students' attention, with all the instant forms of electronic gratification which is increasingly available to them outside school. How can any teacher hope to compete with channel and web-surfing which offer students many choices to keep them amused?

The teachers' union, and their leaders, are quite another matter, however. Their goal is quite simply more control and power, no matter how they attempt to dress up this quest in other guises, such as quality of education and parent, student and teacher well-being. There are three manifestations of this drive for control and power which really bother me.

The first is the illegal strike which they have called. Although they prefer to call it a political protest this only compounds the error of their ways. Assuming the issue is political—and that's what control and power is ultimately all about—then the proper recourse was to try to defeat the government in the next election.

Most of what is in Bill 160 is precisely what the government promised to do in its election campaign. Moreover, none of it is irreparable or irreversible. Since the government only has about two years left to run in its mandate, the unions and their leaders should have marshaled the considerable political forces which teachers can mobilize to replace the government with one which would do their bidding.

The second thing which bothers me, about these unions and their leaders is all the noise they make about control over education. The reason why they favour local school board control is because very few, if any, of our school boards are any match for the unions and their leaders, either in contract negotiations or administration. On the contract administration side, where this imbalance is particularly egregious, the unions and their leaders can throw millions of dollars into grievance procedures and arbitration cases, while most boards have so little money they have to be very selective about the few cases they can fight.

Finally, there is the mailer of having principals and vice-principals In the bargaining units.

Somebody has to represent management in our schools and that can only be the principals and vice-principals. In the name of collegiality, the unions and their leaders object to this principle because it would lessen their control and power over those who are now finding themselves trying to answer to two masters, school boards and unions and their leaders.

Having placed so much emphasis on the underlying issue of control and power, which is so critical to these unions and their leaders, let me not deny that the government is fighting the same battle. The difference is that the government is elected, and can be removed, by the people if it abuses its control and power, whereas the unions and their leaders are not and cannot.

Also, if more local community and parental influence—if not control and power—is the basic issue, then it is far more likely to be realized by the government's proposed school councils than it is by anything like our present or proposed structure of school boards.

I admire teachers and hate to see them so misled by their unions and leaders whose agenda is anything but what they purport it to be. If control and power was not the overriding issue that it is for them, they would not have led teachers down a law-defying garden path which can hardly enable them to command more respect from their students and their parents.

If this government is so wrong-headed about its educational policies the proper course is to defeat it democratically through the ballot box, not defy it illegally on picket lines.

It was good to see three of the teachers' unions decide to end their walk-out yesterday. Hopefully, the leaders of the remaining two unions will soon also come to their senses.

For Charest to Win, Other Jean Must Go (*The Toronto Sun,* March 10, 1998)
Like many other Canadians, I have been urging Jean Charest to fill the critical void left by Daniel Johnson's resignation as the Liberal party leader in Quebec. From the outset, however, I have qualified my call for such a dramatic move by Charest by an equally critical caveat.

I would urge him not to take this vital step unless Jean Chretien agrees to resign at least six months prior to the next Quebec referendum. Otherwise, the risks are too great that Charest will not be successful either in defeating Lucien Bouchard in the next election or in winning the next referendum.

It is my belief that no one can convince Quebec to remain in Canada as long as Chretien is prime minister. I say this despite the major part he played in saving the country during the first referendum campaign, playing a role then very similar to Charest's during the second campaign.

Since then, be has become an albatross around all our necks when it comes to national unity. First came his joint efforts with Pierre Trudeau in sabotaging all of Brian Mulroney's repeated efforts to bring the country together, highlighted by his very public embrace of Clyde Wells at the national Liberal leadership convention which he captured.

Then came his appalling performance during the last referendum campaign which we clearly would have lost had it not been for Jean Charest's valiant efforts.

This man has told us from the beginning that he is "the little man from Shawinigan.— Most of us took this as a joke when he was really being very honest with us. The problem is that neither he nor we ever realized just how little he really is.

Contrast this with Daniel Johnson who laboured long and hard to preserve this country but was decent and honourable enough to resign when he came to the conclusion that he could not defeat Bouchard. Think of how hard that decision must have been after all the slings and arrows he had to bear from his federal liberal counterparts and a very unfair media which could only talk and write about his so-called lack of charisma.

Chretien is simply too small to make a similar sacrifice for this country. And probably no one or group in the federal Liberal party is big enough to force him out because the party does have a majority and there is no effective opposition at the national level. This gives him almost dictatorial powers which he obviously relishes, especially when warning his potential successors to cool their heels.

Some will say I am naïve to call for the prime minister's resignation under these circumstances. But I have left him an out, small as that may turn out to be. While I would prefer that he resign right now, I think we could settle for an assurance that he will not be around for the next referendum.

With Chretien out of the way, I am confident that Charest could win the forthcoming provincial election in Quebec which Bouchard may couple with a third referendum on separation. I do not think he would take that chance if he is going to be up against Charest.

Even if Bouchard won such an election, and subsequently called a referendum ballot, he would be in serious difficulty with Charest as the opposition leader and Paul Martin as Chretien's successor. Together, Charest and Martin would be a formidable combination in such a confrontation over the future of Canada.

My one concern about Charest arises from his unwillingness to support Chretien's reference to the Supreme Court with respect to Quebec's right to resort to a unilateral declaration of independence if there is a yes vote in a separation referendum. Chretien has been pushing for a fair question, campaign and vote, if there is another referendum, and for the maintenance of the rule of law regardless of the outcome. Charest should have backed Chretien in these efforts, because they are not intended to deny Quebec the right to separate but only ensure that due constitutional and legal processes are followed.

The fundamental question is really whether Chretien is capable of being as big as Daniel Johnson has just proven himself when it comes to preserving the unity of this country.

I am sure he is not and that is why Charest is probably right in his current assessment. As I read him, he is saying, or rather implying, that he can better fight for our national unity as leader of a relatively weak national Tory party than as the leader of a revitalized Quebec Liberal party that could once again all too easily be jeopardized and even sabotaged by a jealous and vain and very small prime minister.

What a sad but true state of affairs in such a blessed and wonderful land.

Why We Must Say No to the Bank Mergers (*The Globe and Mail,* October 1, 1998)
(*Note: The underscoring in the text indicates what was edited out when published.*)
Intuitively, procedurally and substantively, I had serious reservations about Canada's two proposed mega-bank mergers, as soon as they were

announced. After reviewing these reservations-which, I believe, have become more valid over time-I will look at the alternatives with which we are not confronted.

Arriving at this position has not been easy for me as a long-time champion of capitalism, free trade and globalization, not to mention deregulation and privatization. Yet, in the end, I have come to the conclusion that the position I take in this article is quite consistent with the stands I have assumed in the past because they all eventually depend on effective competition.

Instinctively, I quickly came to the realization that these mergers were both executive driven by a small group of men who stood to gain immensely both in terms of money and power. Already grossly overpaid, these executives will doubtless at least double their incomes within 2 or 3 years of these mergers being consummated, if they are allowed to proceed. Collectively, their options alone will be worth tens if not hundreds of millions of dollars, more if they have their way. The rationale for these excesses, of course, will be the added responsibilities and risks they will supposedly be assuming.

They had no difficulty persuading their boards of directors to go along with their personal designs because their members as well as their shareholders also stand to benefit though not nearly as much as those at the top of the banks' managerial hierarchies. Given the speed with which these decisions were made by the boards, you know that little or no thought was given to the customer and/or the public interest involved. And, why should it have been otherwise since the boards of directors' only real mandate is to maximize the shareholders' returns on their investment?

Quite frankly, I would have had more respect for these executives, and their boards, had they just announced that they had found a way to make a lot more money for themselves, and their shareholders, and that in doing so they probably wouldn't be doing that much harm to their customers, and the public, and might even do them some good. What really galls me is to have them try to wrap up their own selfish interests in terms of their customers' and the publics' interests.

Procedurally, I am equally upset with their strategy and tactics. It was the banks that persuaded Paul Martin to set up a task force, in 1996, to examine the future of our financial institutions. Yet they could not wait until that task force reported, just a few months later, to announce their proposed mergers almost as a kind of fait accompli, not unlike putting a gun to the government's head. I described what they were doing, at the time, as a form or blackmail and I see no reason to withdraw that charge.

Some of the things bankers and the backers have said since then bear out this contention. Among other things they have said is that there would be a shareholders rebellion if the mergers were not allowed, that Canada would be viewed as a "Neanderthal" if the mergers were not approved and that the government better not lay down too stringent conditions for the mergers or they wouldn't go forward.

Substantively, there is more and more reason to doubt the case for these mergers. In the first place, it will result in a higher degree of bank concentration than in any other significant free enterprise country in the world. Secondly, there is considerable evidence, especially in the U.S., that bank mergers result in fewer and more expensive services, exactly the reverse of what our merger partners are promising.

Perhaps most damaging of all is a key quote from the McKay Task Force Report on the purported economies of scale that are supposed to result from such mergers. "The evidence we have reviewed does not sustain a case that, for most purposes, size is a strategically important variable or that all, or even most, mergers tend to bring about gains in efficiency."

One wonders what it is that the merged banks think they can do both domestically and internationally that they could not do on a cooperative or joint venture basis as separate entities. Jointly and severally, they already work closely together on things like chequing processing and technological change. Moreover, few international financings are handled by anything less than a consortium of banks and other financial institutions often including our existing Canadian banks. Even now, by the way, the two smallest banks in Canada, the Bank of Nova Scotia and the Toronto Dominion Bank, are doing more overseas business than their largest competitors.

My biggest worry is that the government will let the mergers proceed subject to certain conditions. Those conditions could be quite meaningless and serve as little more than protective political cover for the government, or, worse still, they might involve much more stringent regulation of banks and other financial institutions than we now have in place.

Although it might appear more safe and secure to regulate our banks in more detail, I think we have to go beyond our present regulatory standards, if we do not permit such large banks that we literally could not allow them to fail. If we go in that direction, we could be risking massive bailouts in event of even one bank failure, while at the same time making it more difficult for new banks to enter the business because of the higher regulatory costs involved.

Finally, in the context of possible bank failures, one has to ask whether such mergers should be permitted in this trying time of international economic and financial turmoil. One thing we are learning during this period is that the old adage, "the bigger you are the harder you fall," is especially true of large financial institutions with tremendous consequent pressures to bail them out.

I would simply bar these mergers at least until after we attract new entrants who can compete effectively with our branch banking systems. Otherwise, we cannot be assured of enough competition to keep these proposed mega banks treating us efficiently and fairly.

The only caveat I would add concerns the long run. If globalization and technological change continue to unfold the way they have been, we may well some day have truly world-wide banking for the full range of bank services. If, as and when that happens, we will have nothing to fear from unlimited bank mergers in Canada and probably much to gain. But let us not put the cart before the horse and gamble on something with too many risks for bank customers and the public at large.

My fear is that the banks involved in these mergers are already so powerful that our government will capitulate to them regardless of the merit or demerits of the case. These banks are lobbying furiously and there is little effective or organized opposition, except from the Bank of

Nova Scotia and the Canadian Federation of Independent Business. What is really scary is the number of business people-some of considerable significance-who have major concerns about these mergers but won't speak out against them publicly out of fear of retaliation. One can only hope and trust that our governments will not let this massive corporate power play take place because it too is afraid to say no.

I remain highly dubious and skeptical of the real motives behind these bank mergers, I detest the way they went about trying to pull them off, and I don't think they've begun to prove the benefits would outweigh the costs, except for their executives and shareholders. For all these reasons I urge the government not to approve these mergers under any circumstances at this time.

Bank Mergers? Not Without Much Greater Competition (*The Globe and Mail,* November 24, 1998)
In an article on this page on Oct. 1, I expressed grave reservations about the proposed Canadian bank mergers, but space limitations prevented me from noting the conditions under which they might be acceptable. Since then, the Royal Bank and the Bank of Montreal have launched a major public-relations campaign with the theme "Two Banks, One Pledge"—a campaign that addresses only one of the three reasons I gave for my reservations, and that one only partially. It seems a good time to revisit the issues.

Not surprisingly, the banks; campaign says nothing about the fact that by far the major beneficiaries of these mergers, if they succeed, will be a few top officers of the banks themselves. I still believe we are witnessing an attempt to establish a new mega-millionaires club as much as we are two mega-banks.

And I still resent the banks jumping the gun on the September report of the MacKay task force on the future of financial institutions, a report the banks had requested. They were deliberately putting a gun to the government's head and, worse still, may have led the MacKay group to call for more regulations than it would have had the mergers not been announced.

The "Two Banks, One Pledge" brochure has some reassuring things to say about staffed banking outlets (not branches as we know them), jobs and service charges—assurances that could be construed as a form of last-minute bribery to entice us into going along with the corporate machinations. Substantively, however, the banks have not yet proved their case.

One of the real issues is whether they will actually realize major economies of scale as a result of these mergers. The MacKay report's skepticism on this point is mild compared with what The Economist had to say on Oct. 31: "Huge, broadly diversified banks are not, on average, any more profitable than less far-flung ones. Economies of scale often taper off quickly with size ... Nor does a ubiquitous branch network seem to improve profitability. Most troubling of all, the economies of scope that are meant to come from bringing a variety of financial institutions together have proved elusive."

The Economist argued that if merging banks are to achieve significant economies of scale, they must be extremely adept at specializing, strategizing and targeting. These are not qualities for which our banks are renowned, and we must take it on faith that they can adroitly and astutely change their ways.

In the meantime, if these mergers are approved, some means will have to be found to protect Canadians from a much more concentrated banking industry. My fear is that the government will resort to increased regulation to achieve that objective.

In some ways, this is the direction in which the MacKay report would appear to have us move. The call for such things as countervailing consumer-watchdog groups (a pipe dream, given the ineffectual history of consumer-advocacy groups in this country) and annual reports by bankers to Parliament (a dreadful idea, because of the precedent it would set for undue political interference in business in general) are examples of just the thing that should not be required.

The only effective way to protect consumers and the public, if these mergers are consummated, is to open the doors wide to foreign competition. Yet this too poses a dilemma if Canadians want to continue to impose a limit of 10 per cent on the ownership of any of our major banks by any one company, individual or group.

The preference should be for more competition, domestic and foreign, rather than more regulation, since the latter is likely to lead to more red tape and therefore fewer new entrants. But unless we are assured of this increased competition before we accept the mergers, we will be putting the cart before the horse and leaving Canadians too vulnerable to oligopolistic abuse by these mega-banks.

My worst fear is that the government will come up with stringent-looking conditions that don't really mean much but that make the government look good. The bankers will then squeal like stuck pigs, but will eventually go along because they'll figure out how to work around the proposed conditions.

I am not as doctrinally and dogmatically opposed to these mega-mergers as my piece here last month may have made me appear—those space limits again—but I remain very dubious about the banks' original claims and the pledges they've made since. Unless the banks are first confronted by every conceivable form of competition, Canadians should not tolerate the mergers. They will leave us too vulnerable to the workings of the most powerful collection of business, economy and financial interests in this country.

Citizenship Is a Gift We Give Too Freely (*The Toronto Sun,* February 13, 1999)
Two important points to begin with. First Canadian citizenship is the greatest honour and privilege that can be bestowed on anyone. For that reason it should not be granted easily or lightly.

Secondly, immigration has played a critical role in Canada's development and should be allowed to continue to do so. If that is to be the case, however, our emphasis should no longer be placed on the masses—if I can call them that—but on those with skills which are in short supply in Canada.

My fear is that we've lost a great deal of control over our immigration policies because there are so many vested interests promoting their own particular causes. For example, there are many new Canadians who naturally want their dependents—sometimes in the form of quite extended families—allowed in, regardless of what they have to contribute to the well-being of this country.

The very fact that abandoned dependents now cost Canada hundreds of millions a year in welfare, and the like, bears out this contention. I simply cannot fathom why those who sponsor such dependents are not required to pay these costs, failing which, I would have little or no hesitation in sending such dependents back t the countries from which they came. And I'd be tempted to send back the delinquent sponsors as well.

There are also a variety of do-gooders who want us to take in all manner of refugees—economic, political and otherwise. Their politically correct posturing is designed to make the rest of us feel guilty if we don't fully agree with them.

Most disturbing are the host of immigration consultants and lawyers feeding on the system. The latter rely on public funding to appeal every case they can get their hands on as far as they can.

As more than an aside, I have to add that I have never understood why someone who enters this country illegally should be provided with both legal aid and living expenses until he or he exhausts every possible avenue of appeal. This often means these people are provided with a much higher standard of legal service and support than Canadians who cannot afford such help on their own.

Other things which grate on me include the fuss which is made when a federal commission dares to recommend that prospective immigrants should have to have a command of English or French before they come here. This would not only benefit the country they want to adopt but their own prospects once they arrive. The only time I would relax such a language requirement is when we require specialized, skilled workers and cannot find them with facility in either English or French.

When it comes to entrepreneurs who are allowed to buy their way into this country, on the other hand, I would not only adhere to the language requirement but add a very stringent residency requirement—

subject to legitimate travel abroad for business purposes—to ensure they are not just purchasing Canadian citizenship as an insurance policy against anything going wrong in their home countries.

I could probably live with many of my concerns about our loose-knit immigration policies if we would introduce just one major change which was bought to my attention when my daughter married a Bermudian and moved to that delightful island. She found, to her chagrin, that even though she had a husband who was born there she would only gain limited citizenship rights after five years and full rights after ten.

Furthermore, she could lose those rights if she ran afoul of the law or moved away for more than a two-year period.

When my daughter learned all this, she was quite taken aback and asked me to come down and help her change the law—as if I could have done anything for her. Instead, I suggested she think about it, a bit, and then come back and tell Canadians what it was like to move to a country that really valued its citizenship.

I think if we held our citizenship in the same high regard that Bermudians do, we would impose the same high standards on proposed new Canadians. In effect, we would be saying you're welcome to join us as Canadians if you prove, over an extended period of time, you're worthy of doing so.

When I mention this approach to other Canadians, most of them relate to it very positively but some ask what I would do if some countries refused to take back those who turnout to be undesirable candidates for Canadian citizenship. My answer is quite straightforward: I would simply tell any country that so refused that if they do not take them back we will not welcome any more prospective immigrants until they do.

Since I see little or no hope of removing some of the loopholes in our present immigration policies, I think the only answer lies in a more stringent test for Canadian citizenship once proposed new Canadians get her.

But I'm not holding my breath for such a requirement because there are too few politically incorrect Canadians who would be brave and courageous enough to back such a sane and sensible prerequisite for the most wonderful right anyone can hope to qualify for on this earth.

Devilishly Charming Couple (*The Toronto Sun,* February 27, 1999)
I have to admit to being enough of a political junkie to have followed the Clinton-Lewinsky affair right through to its inevitable unwarranted conclusion. One of the reasons I couldn't resist doing so was because of the way in which Clinton and his allies—with a lot of media complicity—managed to portray their Republican opponents as the only real partisans in the whole process.

In an earlier article, I acknowledged that Clinton and his soulmate, Hillary, are both very articulate, bright and charming when they want to be. But I also believe that they are a pair of the most Machiavellian devils ever to occupy the White House.

To be fair, I do not deny that the far right has been out to get the Clintons almost from the day they strode onto the national stage. But the Clintons' so-called right wing conspiracy could never have gotten anywhere in the absence of their unending pattern of illegal and unethical behaviour.

What bothers and even scares me, is my belief that both the Clintons, and many of those around them, are nothing less than inveterate liars and continuing obstructers of justice. While Ken Starr has become the scapegoat for all the Washington machinations over the past year, he was a victim of so much delaying, evasion and stonewalling tactics by the White House that this blame is almost totally misplaced. From Whitewater, through Travelgate and Filegate to Lewinsky, the Clintons, and their friends, did everything possible to suborn justice.

They did this while successfully condemning the Republicans for lacking the bi-partisanship that would have lifted the President off the hook sooner rather than later. This is such a distortion of the facts it boggles the mind.

Politically it never paid the Republicans to pursue the President for his crimes and misdemeanors even if they weren't high. This is because the US economy was doing so well that the American people simply didn't care whether the President had illicit sex with a young subordinate, in the White House, and did everything possible to cover it up afterwards.

And, let us be clear that it wasn't the sex that mattered the most, even if it would have been grounds for dismissal in the military and in much of the private sector. It was the bald-faced falsehoods about it and the sustained efforts to derail and sidetrack the ensuing pursuit of justice.

When the House of Representatives dealt with the eventual impeachment charges it did become a very partisan issue. But, the Democrats were just as partisan in their opposition to impeachment as the Republicans were in their pursuit of it.

Then, when it got to the Senate trial, the only real non-partisanship was demonstrated by the Republicans, enough of whom voted against the two charges of perjury and obstruction of justice, that neither was able to capture a majority vote let alone the two-thirds required for a guilty verdict.

Two things trouble me about the Democrats during this whole sorry episode. The first was their constant but seemingly feigned condemnation of the President's conduct. Their favourite word for his lying was "misleading": but they had harsher things to say about his overall conduct.

Their fallback position was a censure motion that would have been extra constitutional at best and of no immediate consequence to the Clintons who know no morality in this or perhaps any other area. Clinton and his congressional allies also knew that censure was not on, so they could safely talk about it without any fear it would ever come to pass. So he gets off virtually scot-free, in the short run, even if history should eventually catch up with him.

Meanwhile, the Republicans have become the fall guys who may bear the biggest political price of all. The American public has wanted this issue to go away for so long now that they may decide to punish the Republicans in the 2000 election.

Perhaps with a new face, like George Bush Jr., or even Elizabeth Dole, combined with a really appealing tax reduction campaign, the Republicans can turn the situation around. Otherwise, their only consolation will be that they did the right thing, which I believe, history will indeed bear out as more and more is unearthed about the underlying Clinton deceit and dishonesty.

The Corruption of Arbitration (*The Saturday Sun,* May 8, 1999)
With such a spate of public service strikes, it's not surprising that the public is so prone to ask why more of these disputes are not referred to arbitration. By arbitration, I don't mean conciliation or mediation but rather a process whose findings are binding on both parties.

The answer, unfortunately, is very simple. There has always been a case against resorting to compulsory arbitration in interest disputes because of the corrosive effect it has upon collective bargaining. But now the arbitration process has become so corrupted that governments are literally afraid to resort to it.

The reason for this corruption is clear. Because arbitration has become such a lucrative practice many, if not most, arbitrators no longer rule on the merits of the case. Rather they concern themselves more about their ABC's—that is, their Acceptability, their Batting average and their Credibility.

If arbitrators want to continue to do well they constantly have to worry about what labour and management are thinking about them since both sides keep scorecards on their records. Invariably, this means arbitrators must look more carefully over their left than their right shoulders.

Labour leaders are much more likely to react publicly and vociferously when arbitrators rule against them. In contrast, management leaders are more likely to drown their sorrows over a few rounds of drinks.

To see how risky arbitration has become, from a management perspective, let me review the history of the criteria which arbitrators are supposed to rely on when rendering their judgments. Way back , when I practised arbitration—before I became thoroughly disillusioned with the dishonesty of it all—there was a standard set of criteria relied upon. Largely, these were changes in the cost of living or inflation, productivity improvements, both on a micro and macro level, and internal and external comparisons with relevant groups of workers.

Many years ago, when Alberta found arbitrators in that province rendering ridiculously high awards in fire and police disputes, it ordered them to specifically address two other relevant factors. These were the ability to pay off the agency or employer in question, and the state of the labour market it was dealing with—that is whether or not there was a recruitment or retention problem for them.

Unfortunately, arbitrators in Alberta continued to play their petty little ABC games for the same reasons their colleagues do elsewhere. Arbitration has obviously become too enriching a practice for its participants not to put their reputations first and foremost regardless of how they have to bend the rules to maintain them.

There is no easy solution to this frustrating problem. One possibility, which I have long favoured, is to order partial operation of services deemed too vital to be totally shut down. One time in Montreal, for example, the transit workers were ordered to keep the subways running during the rush hours while being allowed to stop all the off-hour subway and bus services.

Another possibility is Final Offer Selection, a form of arbitration which forces each side to present its final and most reasonable position, in writing, with the arbitrator having to choose between one or the other. The process in itself tends to draw the parties closer together, thereby limiting the damage which the arbitrator can do.

Strikes can do a lot of harm and cause a great deal of inconvenience. But there is one thing which is often worse than strikes—especially in terms of its consequences over time—and that is compulsory arbitration.

This is why I'm proud of politicians who resist sending labour disputes to arbitration except as a last resort, when all else fails, and there is a very real threat to the public health, safety or general well-being.

Hey Students, What's the Hurry? (*The Saturday Sun,* May 22, 1999)
As Ontario phases out Grade 13 from its secondary school program, it is creating an unbelievable opportunity—which is unfortunately being

APPENDIX D 327

viewed as a problem. That potential problem, of course, is how to handle what will amount to a double cohort of students seeking to enter our community colleges and universities in 2004.

Instead of looking at this as a problem, it should be viewed as an opportunity that I have favoured for many years. That is, to insist that students not be allowed to proceed to any form of formal , post-secondary education until at least a year after they graduate from high school.

As a university professor for over 30 years, I gradually came to the firm conclusion that most first-year students are neither mature nor motivated enough to begin to take full advantage of a university education.

I suspect the same thing applies to first year students at the community college level.

Many, if not most, students go on to post-secondary education largely because of parental pressure that often includes telling them what course to take.

Whether or not they are community college or university graduates, parents are convinced their offspring will do better in life if they receive some form of higher education.

I can't quarrel with this notion. How could I, given my background and history? I just question its timing, especially in an age when we realize that life-long learning may well be a prerequisite to a successful career.

To illustrate the importance of some real life and work experience before going on to any form of post-secondary education, let me cite an analogy that's not fully appropriate but nonetheless insightful.

Most MBA programs in Canada now require at least two years work experience after a student completes his or her undergraduate education.

Last year at the University of Toronto, our average entering MBA student had over four years work experience, some of it quite advanced.

This make a tremendous difference in terms of their learning experience as MBA students. Besides placing greater demands on the faculty to be more relevant and up-to-date, it sets the stage for the students to learn a significant amount from each other.

These students are so much more mature and motivated if they decide to come back for an MBA when they're in their mid to late 20's that there is no comparison between their previous peers who have had little or no experience.

It makes a world of difference.

Obviously it would not make as much difference to insist high school graduates take a year off before going on to college or university, but I believe it would have something of the same effect. Whatever they did in the interim, they would be more mature and they surely would be more motivated if they simply did not go straight on to post-secondary school but actually decided to come back for more education later on.

To a large extent I wouldn't care that much about what they did during that one or more year interval. I would prefer they worked— even flipping hamburgers—because that would probably give them even more incentive to pursue a higher education. But even if they just backpacked around the work, I think it would provide them with a tremendous exposure to life and reality.

In concert with this general approach I'd like to see all levels of government introduce various types of youth work corps programs to deal with societal problems—particularly on the environmental front— which otherwise are likely to be neglected.

I'd pay the students a modest living allowance or stipend together with a voucher covering the cost of their first year's post-secondary education.

I know what I'm advocating here would make an immense difference in the lives of our young people and to the meaningfulness of their post-secondary education.

But I'm doubtful that even the double cohort problem we face will lead us to be imaginative enough to turn it into a wonderful opportunity instead of a serious problem.

Canada and Quebec Need Each Other (*The Saturday Sun,* Oct. 23, 1999)
Today I want to write about the central conclusion of a book I have no intention of reading. The book is entitled *Time to Say Goodbye,* and is, unfortunately, the product of one Reed Scowen, a disillusioned anglophone Quebecer whose credentials include having once been a well-known federalist.

Somewhat like an earlier book by David Bercuson and Barry Cooper, *Deconfederation,* Scowen's volume takes the position that it's futile to try to work out an enduring deal with Quebec and we might just as well break up the country right now. Given Bercuson and Cooper's Western roots, their work didn't surprise me nearly as much as Scowen's.

While I can understand the frustration with Quebec's aspirations, which I find all over the rest of Canada I think it helps to realize that what we are dealing with in Quebec is the same type of tribalism we find all over the world. In many, if not most countries—with the notable exception of the United States with its melting pot—minority groups of various kinds are insisting that their special characteristics be acknowledged, enshrined and protected, or they will try to go their own way, if that is at all practical.

What really aggravates me about those who want Canada to sever its links with Quebec is that they do not seem to realize that Canada is less likely to survive as an entity without Quebec. Partly of course, because most of our region's north-south ties with various parts of the U.S. are rapidly strengthening while our traditional internal east-west ties are dramatically weakening.

Then there is the critical question of whether we could sustain a kind of East and West Pakistan, even if we retained free access to direct routes between Ontario and the Maritimes. If anybody thinks this would be easy, I would suggest they reconsider and study this prospect very deeply.

The biggest obstacle to continuing Canada without Quebec would be that Ontarians would then have the majority of the votes in a federal election. No amount of tinkering with some version of a Triple-E Senate would be likely to pacify the concerns this would give rise to in the West.

I have long held that if Quebec leaves Canada, on any basis, it is likely to lead to the total disintegration of the country and its eventual absorption, piece by piece, by the U.S. I used to think B.C. could go it alone, especially if combined with Alberta, but given the hapless and hopeless voting habits of British Columbians I'm not so sure about this any more. But maybe, in a common vote with Alberta, they could come up with a credible and effective government that could spearhead a new separate state.

On the other side of the country, the Atlantic Provinces could be driven to join the U.S. out of desperation. Not an insignificant number of Newfoundlanders still wonder whether they should have joined the U.S. in the first place instead of Canada.

As for Ontario, it might feel compelled to become a part of the U.S. simply to protect its auto industry if the rest of the country started to break up. This backbone of Ontario industry is now protected by NAFTA, but no one can predict what happens to Canada's role in that trading arrangement if this country should start to fragment.

Lest anyone think the U.S. might not accept parts of Canada, piece by piece, they should ask themselves whether America's old Manifest Destiny is really dead or just dormant. Certainly the U.S. would rather pickup our pieces than run the unlikely risk some other country should get involved.

The most ironic thing about this whole hypothesis is what would eventually happen to Quebec, which has never appreciate how Canada has protected its language and culture form the U.S.'s homogeneous influences. When Quebec also had no other choice, it too would have to join the U.S. but would receive no respect for its Quebecois language, let alone things like its bilingual labeling and linguistic sign police.

Those who want to break up this great country—whether they are separatists in Quebec or others who are simply fed up with the whole debate—should think much more profoundly about the outcome of such a split. Quebec is much better off in Canada and Canada is a better country because of the diversity that Quebec offers. Both would probably disappear as direct entities if they ever split up.

To Keep Quebec, Chretien Must Go (*The Toronto Sun,* Nov. 12, 1999)
When is enough enough, when it comes to Jean Chretien? He has gone from being the man who once saved this country in the first Quebec ref-

erendum to the man who may destroy it in the forthcoming election and referendum in that same province.

His shortsighted, stupid and untimely intervention in the Quebec election campaign is completely unforgivable. It matters not whether what he said was taken out of context or distorted. Given the separatist tendencies of the francophone Quebec media, this was bound to happen. Chretien should not have said anything—nothing at all. He should not even have granted an interview.

Nor does it matter whether he did it unwittingly or wittingly, although it is interesting to speculate.

He may have done it unwittingly because he has been saying such strange things about the APEC demonstration debacle that one is compelled to question if he is in full command of his faculties.

He could have done it wittingly to sabotage Jean Charest because he is almost pathologically jealous of the man. Just recall the night of the last near fatal referendum when he pre-empted Charest's time on national television even though, and especially because, it was Charest and not him who saved the country's bacon that time.

Ironically, it was Chretien who played that critical role during the first referendum campaign when he barnstormed the province defending Canada. People tend to think it was a couple of speeches by Pierre Trudeau which saved the country in that 1980 referendum, but the real credit still belongs to Chretien.

But time long ago passed Chretien by in Quebec. He is worse than yesterday's man and has been for some time. That's why I warned, on the air and in print that Charest should not accept the Quebec Liberal party leadership without a public commitment from Chretien to resign before the next referendum. I should have added "and before the next election."

Now look at what Chretien has done. I think he's made it very difficult for Charest to win the election. Charest was already facing an uphill battle given the way the National Assembly seats are distributed in Quebec. Now it will almost require a superhuman effort for him to recover.

Worse still, Chretien has set the stage for Premier Lucien Bouchard to call a quick referendum, if, as I now expect, he wins re-election. He stands a much better chance of winning such a referendum with Chretien as prime minister than with someone like Paul Martin.

The challenge for the Liberal party is to get rid of Chretien fast for the sake of the country. Yet where is the Dalton Camp of that party? Dalton was the Red Tory (he still is) who led the campaign to rid the PCs of John Diefenbaker after it became clear to almost everyone that he was doing far more harm than good to his party and, more importantly, to the country.

Everyone in the Liberal party is afraid to challenge Chretien because he is a virtual dictator, given his commanding position as leader of a strong majority party with no effective opposition. No one who wants to be leader dares take him on because that would probably be the kiss of death in the forthcoming leadership campaign.

The only faint hope is that Chretien is not as little as he has repeatedly told us he is. Quite to the contrary, I feel he is petty and vindictive, as well as little, and that is a lethal combination for us all. Someone or some group very powerful in the back rooms of the Liberal party must somehow force him to move along quickly before it is too late.

I have no idea who that someone or group is, let alone whether he, she or they could pull it off.

If the Liberal party does not do so it will forfeit any right to its arrogant but all-too-accurate claim of being Canada's natural governing party. Worse still, it will quite possibly end its history with a hapless and hopeless leader presiding over the break-up of the greatest country the world has ever known.

Make no mistake about it. We are on the verge of a potential tragedy which only the immediate resignation of Jean Chretien is likely to forestall. And he is clearly not big enough to make that sacrifice for the sake of this country.

So the question is whether the Liberal party cares enough to force him out. I doubt it, and that is why I am in a state of despair.

Index